CULTURAL PLURALISM ON CAMPUS

by

Harold E. Cheatham and Associates

an ACPA Media Board Publication

American College Personnel Association

American Association for Counseling and Development
5999 Stevenson Avenue
Alexandria, VA 22304

Cover Design by Sarah Jane Valdez

Library of Congress Cataloging-in-Publication Data

Cultural pluralism on campus / by Harold E. Cheatham, and associates.
p. cm.
Includes bibliographical references.
ISBN 1-55620-086-2
1. Intercultural education—United States. 2. Minorities—Education (Higher)—United States. 3. Pluralism (Social sciences)—United States. 4. College student development programs—United States. 5. Educational equalization—United States. 6. Minority college students—United States—Crimes against. I. Cheatham, Harold E.
LC1099.3.C83 1991
370.19'342—dc20
91-12709
CIP

Printed in the United States of America

To

V. Arlene Tabb Cheatham

TABLE OF CONTENTS

Foreword   vii
Anne S. Pruitt

Introduction   1
Harold E. Cheatham

PART I: RESOLVING INEQUALITY

CHAPTER 1: Affirming Affirmative Action   9
Harold E. Cheatham

CHAPTER 2: Identity Development in a Pluralistic Society   23
Harold E. Cheatham

PART II: DEVELOPMENTAL NEEDS

CHAPTER 3: The Minority Cultural Center on a Predominantly   41
White Campus
Lawrence W. Young, Jr.

CHAPTER 4: Organizational and Administrative Implications   55
for Serving College Students With Disabilities
James S. Fairweather and Judith J. Albert

CHAPTER 5: The Role of Developmental Education in   73
Promoting Pluralism
Jeanne L. Higbee

CHAPTER 6: Integrating Diversity Into Traditional Resident   89
Assistant Courses
Lissa J. VanBebber

CHAPTER 7: Planning Programs for Cultural Pluralism: 117
A Primer
*Leila V. Moore, H. Jane Fried, and
Arthur A. Costantino*

CHAPTER 8: NCAA Policies and the African American   137
Student Athlete
Mitchell F. Rice

CHAPTER 9: Racial Violence on Campus   149
Camille A. Clay and Jan-Mitchell Sherrill

Part III: Funding and Evaluating Cultural Pluralism Programming

Chapter 10: Planning for Cultural Diversity: A Case Study   161
    James B. Stewart

Chapter 11: Evaluating University Programming for   183
    Ethnic Minority Students
    Shanette M. Harris

Epilogue   203
    Harold E. Cheatham

FOREWORD

The role of student affairs in institutions of higher education is undergoing significant changes in concepts and practice, particularly in response to racial and social diversity. The need to be sensitive to the distinctive cultures that our students represent is clearly apparent. Traditional patterns exemplified by the "melting pot" are not adequate to address their needs.

The American College Personnel Association (ACPA) has a penchant for being proactive and, thus, sets forth this publication to help achieve this goal. *Cultural Pluralism on Campus* offers practical responses to everyday situations that confront all who are involved in moving our higher education system toward the concept of cultural pluralism. It explores issues like affirmative action, racism, funding, teaching, evaluation, and athletics—some of the difficult problems that we seldom discuss frankly. It might be said that these are issues that are broader than student affairs, and that we cannot be held responsible for the way an institution responds. Yet any effective approach to cultural pluralism must be institution-wide. Hence, student affairs bears a major responsibility to debate these matters and to be informed.

The growing influence of the "politically correct" issue in academia—which turns on whether opinions about race and gender should identify proper attitudes toward intellectual and other problems—serves to constrain the willingness of academicians—and that includes student affairs—to speak out on issues such as the ones on which this book is centered. We ought to rejoice that ACPA has taken the initiative to address these timely topics.

Our professional association commends Harold Cheatham and his associates for undertaking this responsibility. We are fortunate to have within our midst professionals to whom we can turn for such powerful insights.

Anne S. Pruitt
January 14, 1991
The Ohio State University
ACPA President 1976–1977

ABOUT THE AUTHORS

Harold E. Cheatham is professor of education in the Department of Counselor Education, Counseling Psychology, and Rehabilitation Services Education, Pennsylvania State University. Dr. Cheatham's professional affiliations include membership on the ACPA Media Board, ACPA Theory and Research Board, editorial board of the *Journal of College Student Development* (1978–1984), the *Career Development Quarterly*, and the ACPA/NASPA Task Force on Professional Preparation Programs. A 1990–1991 Fulbright scholar to India, Cheatham has previously taught and studied cross-cultural counseling and related topics in India, China, and the Soviet Union. His writing and research currently is focused on psychosocial development of African Americans—particularly identity development. He is editor of the 1987 special issue of the *Journal of College Student Personnel,* "Blacks in U.S. Higher Education," and coeditor (with James B. Stewart) of *Black Families: Interdisciplinary Perspectives.*

Judith J. Albert is presently working for the United States government in Bonn, Germany, to provide educational counseling and services. Previously she was a research assistant for the Center for the Study of Higher Education at Pennsylvania State University. In 1985, she served as a project assistant with SRI International. She received her doctorate in education from Pennsylvania State University in 1989. Her study focused on the adequacy of postsecondary service structures for serving students with disabilities. Dr. Albert has received two master's degrees, the most recent in guidance and counseling from the University of Nebraska at Omaha and the other in perceptual motor development from Purdue University. Her undergraduate degree was in physical education from the University of Nebraska. Dr. Albert has experience in many areas of education: She has worked as a counselor for minority students and for high school and Equal Opportunity Program students, as an educational therapist, as a coach, and as a teacher. She has earned several awards and honors, the most recent being the Graduate Student Alumni and Research Award from the College of Education at Pennsylvania State University in 1988.

Camille A. Clay is assistant vice president for minority affairs at Towson State University. Previously she was a senior counselor at the Towson State University Counseling Center. Before entering the field of higher education,

Dr. Clay held several positions in the field of community mental health. She earned her doctorate at George Washington University in counseling and human development after completing courses of study at Hampton Institute, University of the District of Columbia, and Psychiatric Institute Center for Group Studies. Dr. Clay is very active in the Washington, DC, chapter of the American Mental Health Counselors Association: Last year she served as president, and currently she chairs the licensure committee. Dr. Clay also maintains a part-time counseling practice.

Arthur A. Costantino is currently serving as the interim vice president for student affairs at the University of Toledo. Previously he was associate vice president for student affairs at the University of Toledo, director of the Center for Student Involvement and Leadership at Pennsylvania State University, dean of students at Behrend College of Pennsylvania State University, and director of residence halls at Pennsylvania State University. Dr. Costantino is founding partner of Human Relations Associates, a company that provides training and consultation in race relations; sexual harassment, recruitment, and retention of underrepresented groups; and cross-cultural communication. Dr. Costantino has a PhD in sociology from Pennsylvania State University and an MA and BS in sociology from Michigan State University.

James S. Fairweather is associate professor and senior research associate at the Center for the Study of Higher Education at Pennsylvania State University. He received his doctorate from Stanford University and his undergraduate degree from Michigan State University. He has 13 years of research, teaching, and project management experience, with research interests in undergraduate education, faculty issues, quality of academic programs, and postsecondary access for handicapped and other disadvantaged youth. He is currently senior investigator for the National Survey of Postsecondary Faculty, sponsored by the National Center for Education Statistics; consultant to the Pennsylvania Legislature for the Study of Postsecondary Financial Assistance Programs for Economically Disadvantaged and Minority Youth; and senior investigator for the National Science Foundation Study of Curricular Change in Undergraduate Engineering Programs and Its Impact on Retention of Women and Minorities. He is author of over 40 journal articles, technical reports, or book chapters, and has made more than 20 conference presentations. His research has been funded by the U.S. Departments of Education and Agriculture, TIAA-CREF, the National Science Foundation, the Exxon Education Foundation, IBM, the Dutch National Government, and the National Institute of Education. He has served as consultant to several companies, government agencies, associations, and institutions of higher education, including IBM, the New Jersey Department of Higher Education, and the Commonwealth of Pennsylvania.

H. Jane Fried is an assistant professor of Counseling Psychology and coordinator of the Student Personnel and Counseling Program at Northeastern University in Boston, MA. Dr. Fried has also been director of residential life at the University of Hartford and coordinator of student development, staff training, and research in the residence hall system at the University of Connecticut. She has been a member at large of the Executive Council of the American College Personnel Association, chair of the Standing Committee on Women, chair of the Affirmative Action Committee, and a member of the Ethics and Professional Standards Committee, of the Directorate of Commission I (Leadership), and of the editorial board of the *Journal of College Student Development*. She is the editor of "Education for Student Development," "Teaching and Training," a chapter in *Student Services: A Handbook for the Profession*. She is the author of numerous articles on affirmative action, on ethics in student services, on women's issues, and on issues of concern to new professionals, all of which have appeared in *Developments*, the newsletter of ACPA. She earned her doctorate from Union Graduate School, worked under the supervision of Burns B. Crookston at the University of Connecticut, and earned her master's degree in student personnel work at Syracuse University.

Shanette M. Harris is assistant professor in Educational and Counseling Psychology at the University of Tennessee as well as a licensed clinical psychologist. She was previously associated with the Counseling and Psychological Services Center of Duke University. She received a doctorate from Virginia Polytechnic Institute and State University, a master's degree from Western Carolina University, and a bachelor's degree from Howard University. Her research interests include minority student retention and adjustment, program evaluation, gender-role behavior, and stress and coping.

Jeanne L. Higbee is assistant professor of counseling in the Division of Developmental Studies at the University of Georgia. Previously she held the position of associate dean of student affairs at Western Maryland College. She has also been affiliated with Johns Hopkins University and the University of Wisconsin-Madison. She received her bachelor's degree from Iowa State University and her master's and doctorate from the University of Wisconsin-Madison.

Leila V. Moore is with the Division of Student Programs, an affiliate associate professor of Counselor Education, and an affiliate member of the graduate faculty at Pennsylvania State University. She has a bachelor's degree from Carnegie Mellon University in English literature, a master's degree from Syracuse University in student personnel administration, and a doctorate from the State University of New York at Albany in counseling and personnel services. She has held faculty positions at SUNY-Albany, Pennsylvania State

University, the College of Saint Rose, and Bowling Green State University. In her current position she is responsible for special leadership education programs, policies governing the Greek system, and staff development for her division. She also teaches in the Student Personnel Program. Dr. Moore is editor of a fall 1990 Jossey-Bass sourcebook, *Evolving Theoretical Perspectives on Students*. She is the author of more than 30 refereed articles, book chapters, and monographs. Her research and writing foci include professional development, cultural pluralism, student development theory, and application of theory to practice. Dr. Moore is president-elect of the American College Personnel Association. At Pennsylvania State University she serves on the Task Force for Student Outcomes Assessment. She is the 1988 recipient of the Pennsylvania College Personnel Association's Outstanding Contribution to the Profession Award.

Mitchell F. Rice is professor of Political Science and Public Administration at Louisiana State University, Baton Rouge. He is the author/coauthor of four books and more than 40 journal articles. His latest book is *Health of Black Americans from Post Reconstruction to Integration, 1871–1960* with Woodrow Jones, Jr. (Greenwood Press, 1990). His research and writings focus on "public policy issues and Black Americans." He holds a PhD in government from the Claremont Graduate School.

Jan-Mitchell Sherrill is assistant vice president for student affairs at Towson State University and the director of the National Campus Violence Prevention Center. He was editor and chapter author of *Responding to Violence on Campus*, Jossey-Bass (1989). Mr. Sherrill holds an MEA from the Writing Program at the University of North Carolina at Greensboro.

James B. Stewart is vice provost and associate professor of Labor Studies and Industrial Relations at Pennsylvania State University. He also serves as editor of *The Review of Black Political Economy*. Dr. Stewart serves as director of the National Council for Black Studies Summer Faculty Institutes and was the 1990 recipient of the Presidential Award presented by the National Council for Black Studies. His writings have appeared in many journals, and he is coeditor with Harold E. Cheatham of the book entitled *Black Families: Interdisciplinary Perspectives*. Dr. Stewart was previously the director of the Black Studies Program at Pennsylvania State University.

Lissa J. VanBebber is currently a PhD candidate in the department of sociology at the University of Notre Dame. Her areas of research are social psychology and the sociology of education. She obtained her master's degree in student personnel work in higher education from Ohio State University. She worked as the coordinator of instruction and training at the University of Maryland, where she designed and taught Resident Assistant, Leadership, and Communication courses. She also served as the director of residence life and housing at Saint Mary's College in Indiana, where she established new training models and did some consulting work in the area of race relations and student development.

Lawrence W. Young, Jr. is director of the Paul Robeson Cultural Center at Pennsylvania State University. Mr. Young earned his bachelor's and master's degrees at Miami University in Oxford, Ohio. His major area was English, which he subsequently taught in the public schools of Cleveland and Middletown. From 1969 to 1982, when he assumed his current position, Mr. Young served at Miami University as assistant director of Black Student Affairs, as director of Educational Opportunity Programs, and as director of Minority Student Affairs. Mr. Young has been involved in a number of organizations, including the NAACP and the National Council for Black Studies. He has had numerous articles published and has been guest editor for *NIP* magazine and American correspondent for *Afromart* magazine. He writes on all matters that affect the Black community. He has lectured to high school and college students and to professionals. He recently completed a workshop production on alcohol, advertising, and African Americans. Future plans include completion of doctoral studies, writing a novel, and visiting a free Azania (South Africa).

INTRODUCTION

Harold E. Cheatham

This book, *Cultural Pluralism on Campus*, is addressed primarily to higher education personnel responsible for design, implementation, and evaluation of campus programming that ensures the creation and preservation of a culturally plural—as contrasted with a culturally diverse—environment. This endeavor is partly responsive to American College Personnel Association members' self-reported "gaps in proficiencies" for providing student programming to serve, specifically, the needs of ethnic minority students. The authors also are responding in this book to the recent national phenomenon referred to as *the resurgence of racism on campus*. Also termed *the new American dilemma*, racially motivated intimidation and violence have reawakened the nation to the need to address systematically the lingering effects of racial discrimination.

From some campuses there is a reported sense that the intrusion of racial politics on campuses has created a distraction from the process of student educational and intellectual development. Such analyses suggest that the ivy-covered ramparts need staffing against further invasion. From other campuses comes the sense that programs and policies of the past two decades have been sufficient to promote racial diversity. Those responses suggest public confusion and lack of appreciation of the campuses' legitimate efforts and accomplishments. From still other campuses comes a sense that sustained efforts to address the matter of creating culturally plural environs have yet to be earnestly undertaken. Each of these observations might be tempered by the hard evidence of the momentum lost by ethnic minorities during the past decade (Blake, 1987) and by the demographic projections of ethnic minorities' numerical predominance in the U.S. population early in the 21st century (Levine & Associates, 1989).

Numerous national and state commissions, associations, policy studies institutes, and individual scholars have documented issues related to racial and ethnic inequities in U.S public and higher education. In *One-Third of a Nation* (American Council on Education & Education Commission of the States, 1988), for example, it was noted that ethnic minorities are still burdened by the weight of historical injustice. That report was concluded, as was the U.S. Kerner Commission report (National Advisory Commission on

Civil Disorders, 1968), with the pronouncement that the United States is moving backward rather than forward in its efforts to provide for these citizens' full participation in the national life and prosperity. *One Third's* authors reviewed the brief interlude of progress (partly attributable to the 1960s civil rights legislation), asserted that the formula for success is no mystery, and called for a demonstration of national will of such magnitude that a retrospective of key economic and social indicators of progress 20 years hence would reveal that equity has been achieved.

The challenges from these status reports as well as from those of professional associations suggest that there is an essential and renewed consciousness about the fate of ethnic minorities. There also is some evidence of increased recognition of societal interdependence with women. Neither simple atoning for past ills (Jackson, 1988) nor vigorous and continuous sounding of the alarm (Thomas & Hirsch, 1989) will serve to eradicate historical and continuing injustice. Rather, the current arousal must be used to instate programs and policies that ensure equity. The future of the United States demands no less.

Throughout the history of U.S. higher education, the nation's collegiate institutions have responded, although not uniformly, to calls to pursue aggressively their social obligation to provide educational opportunity. Fortunately, despite some unevenness among higher education institutions' effectiveness in addressing equity issues, and particularly those regarding ethnic minorities and women, there are many notable accomplishments.

This volume was developed to assist as higher education is again called upon to devise—as well as undergird—educational practices that eradicate the lingering effects of discrimination and that thereby enable fullest development of all people. Through focused, empirically grounded discussions, programs and models are presented that are instructive for those charged to provide leadership in deriving pluralistic collegiate environments.

The authors in this volume transcend simplistic, conventional formats to provide discussions of rationale, structure, funding, authority or "control," clientele, and similar factors related to exemplary programs. To accomplish the stated objective (i.e., providing equity), adopted programs ultimately must bear the unique signature of the institution. In that regard, the programs and models advanced in this volume are discussed in the context of institutional mission statements. Many institutions have reframed or extended their published mission statements to amplify an institutional commitment to cultural diversity and cultural pluralism. Special emphasis is placed on these "contemporaneous mission statements" that have spawned some existing and emerging programs to address ethnic minority student concerns. In complementary presentations, the authors discuss institutional roles and responsibilities as well as the dynamics and characteristics of the clientele.

There remains the critical need in this society to address ethnic minority issues while ensuring that cultural specificity between and among groups is not ignored. Simultaneously, it is critical to develop workable formats that enable maximum popular choice and involvement for all students on campus. Thus, to produce a single volume addressing ethnic minority concerns is to risk the charge of arrogance for failing to treat equally the various ethnic groups of concern. Alternatively, there is a hint of arrogance in assuming that through focused treatment of one ethnic or cultural group it is possible to develop knowledge and models that have applicability to other groups' experiences and needs. The authors in this volume have chosen the latter format. In most chapters the experience and quest of African American students is addressed while noting extensions and modifications that might serve other ethnic minorities. This decision resulted from the observation that most prototypes of collegiate ethnic minority programming are primarily responsive to African American students. These have been adapted and extended to serve similar populations. Also, although there remains some disagreement about the politically correct term for describing cocultures whose peoples are of Latino, Chicano, and Puerto Rican heritage, the decision was made to use the imprecise and more familiar term *Hispanic*.

There is a considerable literature that documents the negative history of U.S. higher education. Moving beyond the litany of assaults on institutional integrity, the aim in *Cultural Pluralism on Campus* is to arm colleagues with rationale for, and practical defensible approaches to, programming that accomplishes their institution's long-term and contemporaneous mission of service. And finally, through the discussions and models presented, it is the intent of the authors to move beyond the common demonstrations that predominantly White campuses (simply) are inhospitable environments and therefore are inappropriate choices particularly for African American and, by extension, other ethnic minority collegians. Rather, the emphasis is on identifying, explicating, and transporting workable models for creating pluralistic collegiate environs.

OVERVIEW

Cultural Pluralism on Campus is divided into three parts. Part I addresses the issue of inequality, the sociocultural distinctiveness of ethnic minority students, and useful approaches to shifting the imbalance. In the first chapter, Harold Cheatham explores the concept of affirmative action while advancing arguments to counter the companion notion of affirmative discrimination. In chapter 2 Cheatham addresses minority identity development, reviewing models of development and proposing extensions of these to serve the ethnic minority student's developmental needs. The intent is to address the often posed question, Who are these people, and what do they want, anyway?

In Part II, the authors focus on specific programs to serve the distinct social and developmental needs of ethnic minority students and of the campus at large. In chapter 3, Lawrence Young makes the case for minority culture centers on predominantly White campuses. His central thesis is that these centers are actually consistent with the institutional mission to provide an enriched living-learning environment. Chapter 4 by James Fairweather and Judith Albert is devoted to collegiate programming for disabled students. Their theme is related to James Stewart's in chapter 10, and they demonstrate the differences that characterize programs designed for a specific clientele as opposed to those that are not systematically organized and administered. Jeanne Higbee focuses chapter 5 on the role of developmental education in promoting cultural pluralism. She examines the facts and myths about developmental education and notes the absence of appropriate articulation among the types of higher education institutions. Higbee calls for interinstitutional cooperation to increase access to higher education.

Lissa VanBebber, in chapter 6, provides a rationale for incorporating diversity training into leadership education courses. VanBebber notes that the success of these endeavors depends upon student leaders' being knowledgeable about more than a single culture or racial group. Complementary to VanBebber's presentation, Leila Moore, Art Costantino, and Jane Fried, in chapter 7, also move beyond the theoretical bases for intervention and provide tips and suggestions for creating campus-wide programs to promote cultural pluralism. Moore and her colleagues focus on the practical aspects or the "how to" of diversity interventions. Ethnic minority and particularly African American athletes have long contributed to campus diversity. These athletes have an equally long history of being victims rather than beneficiaries of the collegiate environment. Mitchell Rice, in chapter 8, traces this abuse and explains the intent and effects of the National Collegiate Athletic Associations' efforts in behalf of athletes. Rice prescribes student personnel, interventions that can help in establishing the reality of the concept of the student athlete. Rounding out this section, Camille Clay and Jan Sherrill, in chapter 9, discuss factors related to ethnoviolence and the implications of the racial violence being experienced on college campuses. Clay and Sherrill's report is based primarily on experiences from a national center founded to study campus racial violence.

Part III addresses program funding and program evaluation. James Stewart, in chapter 10, provides a case study of a model devised by a large flagship state university to fund programs to ensure pluralism. He contrasts that model with the same institution's strategic planning model. Finally, in chapter 11, Shanette Harris addresses the reluctance of some practitioners to evaluate programs systematically, and further, she notes the relationship between that reluctance and program demise. Harris provides comprehensive treatment of program evaluation together with an example to demonstrate the steps for implementation.

The editor and authors are grateful to the American College Personnel Association Media Board for undertaking this task. We are also grateful that we have been allowed to serve the profession and our colleagues in their collective endeavors to create and preserve culturally plural collegiate environments. Special thanks are extended to John H. Schuh, editor, and Flo Hamrick, associate editor, of the ACPA Media Board as well as to Mark Hamilton, Elaine Pirrone, Michael Comlish, Laura Sumner, and the rest of the AACD Publications & Communications staff for their contributions and cooperation during the production of this book.

REFERENCES

American Council on Education & Education Commission of the States. (1988). *One-third of a nation: A report of the Commission on Minority Participation in Education and American Life*. Washington, DC: Authors.

Blake, E., Jr. (1987). Equality for Blacks. *Change, 19*(3), 10-13.

Jackson, J. (1989, January 19). Atonement for racist episodes isn't enough. *New York Times*, p. 17.

Levine, A., & Associates (Eds.). (1989). *Shaping higher education's future*. San Francisco: Jossey-Bass.

National Advisory Commission on Civil Disorders. (1968, March 1). *Report of the National Advisory Commission on Civil Disorders*. Washington, DC.

Part I
Resolving Inequality

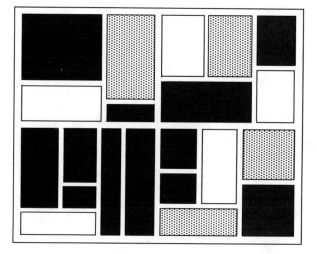

CHAPTER 1

AFFIRMING AFFIRMATIVE ACTION

Harold E. Cheatham

The time has come to transform ideological swords into conceptual plowshares and to risk trusting in the harvest of open dialectical exchange. (Mahoney, 1989, p. 1376)

Although Mahoney's conclusion, cited above, is addressed to participants in a continuing feud among psychological schools of thought, it is nevertheless instructive for those who insist that the complement to affirmative action is affirmative discrimination. More important may be Mahoney's conclusion that through the flexibility that follows a truce between factions, "we will ultimately develop...optimal means for protecting and facilitating the infinite individuality of human development" (p. 1376). That ideal doubtless is more difficult to accomplish than to enunciate, but it is a goal for student affairs practitioners who are dedicated to establishing cultural pluralism within collegiate environments.

A goal in this chapter is to provide a useful perspective of the concept affirmative action and to explore the relationship of this concept to *the resurgence of racism*, a phrase popularly used to identify the increasing incidence of racially motivated harassment and violence directed toward ethnic minority students on predominantly White U.S. campuses. A further goal is to identify and critique briefly the proposition that affirmative discrimination is a necessary result when affirmative action is implemented. The ultimate goal of this chapter is to inform collegiate institutional policies and practices designed to put into place the principles of equity. That goal will be approached through discussion of a historical precedent that called for educational reform while recognizing resistance as a likely response. In reaching the goals of this chapter, it will be argued that the current incidence of racial violence on U.S. campuses is a continuation of racism rather than a resurgence, and that equity is achievable only where administrators and practitioners forsake simplistic formats and interventions in favor of clearly articulated actions undertaken with compassion and resolve.

It should be noted that in this chapter the terms *ethnic* and *ethnicity* are used in preference to or (as need for clarity dictates) in combination with *race* as a descriptor referring to a group's shared sociocultural and sociohistorical experiences. This distinction is advanced because it is concern with the latter (i.e., group heritage) that is the focus of this volume. Further, the distinction is consistent with Miles' (1989) persuasive argument regarding the imprecise, political, and unscientific use of the concept of race. He noted that sorting the world's people by race is an 18th-century European convention reflecting socially *imagined* realities. Discussing the historical correlation between the emergence and development of capitalism and racism, Miles wrote:

> *The emergence of the idea of "race" marks an important transition, followed later by the ascription of this idea with a biological content and by the "scientific" legitimation of a biological hierarchy. Although subsequent scientific work exposed the falsity of these arguments, the idea of "race" remains, and some "scientists" continue to claim a biological or genetic substance to it. (p. 3)*

Miles concluded that "...social scientists...have, perversely, prolonged the life of an idea that should be explicitly and consistently confined to the dustbin of analytically useless terms" (p. 72).

RACISM ON U.S. CAMPUSES

Numerous reports appearing in contemporary popular and professional literature document the phenomenon termed *resurgence of racism* or *new racism*. The incidents of racially motivated violence and aggression to which the terms referred have not resulted simply from the presence on campus of students more representative of the nation's racial and ethnic diversity. These students' numbers on predominantly White U.S. campuses are not sufficient to pose real threats to Whites' privileged status. African Americans, for example, comprise 13% of all college-age youth and only 9.5% of all undergraduates (Mingle, 1987), and among that cohort they have a considerably less than 50% likelihood of completing college. It seems to follow that if the incidence of violence were related to the numerical incidence of racial and ethnic minority students on campus, violence would have peaked with these students' enrollment figures and now be in concurrent decline. The new racism seems instead to be the age-old intractable attitudes and behaviors frequently rationalized on campuses and in the larger society as a response to affirmative action legislation and programs.

Affirmative action per se is not responsible for campus violence directed to ethnic minority students. The phenomenon instead is the result of symbolism—of destructive and calculated appeals to the nation's history of racial oppression and exclusion. The phenomenon also is the result of the fact that the nation and higher education, in general, are ill-prepared to exploit positively the cultural diversity that has been achieved in the past two decades. Conservative politicians and scholars have been successful in calls for widespread opposition to affirmative action, in part because "cultural pluralism" is a contradiction in a society organized and perpetuated in service of majority culture. In U.S. society, privilege has been maintained partly through exploitation of the myth that affirmative action simply stigmatizes and fills African Americans with self-doubt (Steele, 1990) while "doing in" (i.e., reverse discriminating against) the solid citizens who made this nation what it is.

Brief mention of some of the more familiar sites of protracted campus racial violence serves to identify some of the incidents: University of Massachusetts at Amherst, Dartmouth College, Michigan State University, Pennsylvania State University, University of Pennsylvania, and the University of Michigan. At this writing, each of these institutions is actively addressing the racially motivated clashes and the climate on their campuses in efforts to create genuine community.

AFFIRMATIVE ACTION: THE CONCEPT

Affirmative action consists of sets of institutionalized policies, procedures, and programs designed and implemented to ensure the eradication of past negative actions through which certain citizens were denied equal opportunity for full participation and success in all U.S. societal institutions. Affirmative action is an intentional good-faith effort to reverse the ills of the past. It is, as Washington and Harvey (1989) suggested, the corollary of benign neglect.

Affirmative action is intended to change the configuration of U.S. societal institutions. The forerunner to affirmative action policies appears to be President Roosevelt's Executive Order 8802 in 1941 requiring nondiscrimination by employers receiving government defense industry contracts. The earliest direct reference to the concept of affirmative action apparently is in President Lyndon B. Johnson's "Great Society" speech delivered in 1965 at Howard University, a traditionally Black institution in Washington, DC. In proposing an economic reconstruction, Johnson's intent was to move the nation from equality as a concept to equality as a fact. He apparently was advancing Roosevelt's conception and reinstating a policy enunciated by President Harry S. Truman based on the findings of the President's Commission on Higher Education (also called the Truman Commission).

The Truman Commission was concerned with the role of higher education and with the pervasive perception that American citizenry was not being adequately prepared to deal with what it called world citizenship (President's Commission on Higher Education, 1947, p. 16). It noted that:

It is commonplace of the democratic faith that education is indispensable to the maintenance and growth of freedom of thought, faith, enterprise, and association. Thus the social role of education in a democratic society is at once to insure equal liberty and equal opportunity *[italics added] to differing individuals and groups, and to enable the citizen to understand, appraise, and redirect forces, men, and events as these tend to strengthen or to weaken their liberties. (p. 5)*

The Commission also placed specific emphasis upon development of the individual:

The first goal of education for democracy is the full, rounded, and continuing development of the person. The discovery, training, and utilization of individual talents is of fundamental importance in a free society. To liberate and perfect the intrinsic powers of every citizen is the central purpose of democracy, and its furtherance of individual self-realization is its greatest glory. (p. 9)

President Truman called for affirmative *action* to ensure that disfranchised U.S. citizens would have equity in access to higher education.

It should be noted that there were two Truman Commissions; the other addressed segregation in the U.S. military. Although the president's authority ended with petitioning for an end to discrimination in educational opportunity, through the 1948 Executive Order 9981, President Truman ordered an immediate end to segregation in the military. (Although the primary purpose here is to address higher education, the interested reader may observe elsewhere the comparative progress of the U.S. military and U.S. higher education in providing equal opportunity since 1948 [Cheatham, 1988; Cheatham & Seem, 1990]).

Four decades after that proclamation, the discovery, training, and utilization of individual talents remains a distant ideal steeped in complexity that ought to be easily resolved in a notable educational system. As we prepare for the 21st century we are embroiled in argument about whether to require college-level coursework in cultural diversity. It is interesting to note that the Truman Commission concluded that such training was critical: "We must learn to admit the possible worth of human values and ways of living we ourselves do not accept" (p. 17). The report continued—and emphasized:

In the past the liberal arts college has stressed the history, arts, and institutions of Western culture without giving much time or attention to the kinds of civilization that exist in other parts of the globe. In the new world it is not enough to know and understand our own heritage. Modern man needs to sense the sweep of world history in order to see his own civilization in the context of other cultures. (p. 17)

Some who oppose renewed national interest in recognizing our rich cultural diversity as we move toward cultural pluralism have dismissed as "political" and "faddish" the debate that asserts a continuing need for multicultural understanding. That resistance seems to have been anticipated: The Commission, in its argument against piecemeal adjustments and "superficial curricular tinkering," warned about the importance of diversity in our national life. The Commission summoned the citizenry to a heightened perception of the rich advantages of cultural diversity, although also acknowledging that this challenge bore irritation and fright for those of "provincial mind" as opposed to reward and stimulation for those of a "cosmopolitan and sensitive mind" (p. 8). "We must," the Commission entreated, "develop a deep sensitivity to the emotions, the hopes, and the needs of human beings everywhere and so come to accept, not merely in abstract terms but in concrete forms, the manhood and interdependence as well as the individuality of all men" (p. 17). Finally, the Commission noted the tardiness and timidity with which institutional change is undertaken, and it concluded that the called-for changes in institutional policies were likely to occur only under legal compulsion. Legal imposition then of the concept of equity has provided the stage upon which opponents charge that the will of the majority has been scuttled by the courts (e.g., Glazer, 1975).

AFFIRMATIVE ACTION OR AFFIRMATIVE DISCRIMINATION?

Resistance to affirmative action is as old as the policy itself. Although affirmative action began in the early 1960s, it was reported as early as 1968 that 75% of White respondents believed that the progress of African Americans was too fast (Hastings, 1969). Despite perceptions of progress resulting from affirmative action legislation, despite the fact that opportunities opened for many individuals throughout the 1960s, African Americans as a group remained in the lower levels of the labor force (Blauner, 1989). Moreover, their unemployment rate remained twice as high as that of Whites although the ratio of median income for African American families improved from 55% to 62% of that for White families.

Similar statistics depict the slow progress of ethnic minorities in attaining parity in U. S. higher education. African American participation rates in higher education rose from 35% to 48% between 1967 and 1985, dropped to 44% in 1985, and rose again to 47% in 1986. Similar advances and declines have been experienced by Hispanic and American Indian students. More telling statistics, however, are that 55% of Hispanic students and 43% of African American students are attending 2-year institutions, and that fully 18% of African Americans in higher education are attending traditionally Black colleges (Green, 1989).

Part of the task of preparing U.S. campuses and citizenry for our new world, as contrasted to the world characterized by the 1947 Truman Commission, is to promote understanding of affirmative action in a comparative context—that is, understanding of affirmative action as an attempt over the past 25 years to offset the sufferings of African Americans during 375 years, of American Indians during the confiscation of lands and the abrogation of treaties, and of other ethnic minorities during their briefer histories in the United States.

Promoting this view of affirmative action frequently evokes the defensive response that current generations are being called upon to atone for others' past sins. What is called for, however, is not atonement but rather recognition and acceptance of the proposition that to redress such expansive injustices requires time, commitment, and some disaccommodation of those who have historically been privileged. Affirmative action continues as a necessary convention in our ethnically diverse society in which issues of merit and qualifications still enjoy political and philosophical precedence over issues of equity and fair process (Washington & Harvey, 1989).

Washington and Harvey noted that U.S. higher education institutions are implicated in the state of affairs because they have been content to go along with rather than challenge policies and practices that historically have resulted in the disenfranchisement of ethnic minority people. They note further that experience to date does not confirm the expectation that those occupying the citadels of knowledge will be free of the prejudices and irrationalities characteristically ascribed to the less well educated and will value intellect over race/ethnicity. Instead of providing leadership in the resolution of one of our major social problems, collegiate institutions essentially have passively reflected the values and attitudes of the society at large.

GOALS AND TIMETABLES

Rallying arguments by opponents charge that what is wrong with affirmative action is that it flies in the face of public policy, policy that must be exercised without regard to race/ethnicity, color, or national origin (Glazer, 1975). Other opponents of affirmative action call for race-neutral social programs in which equity will be derived by the affected group through targeting individual recipients. An unfortunate aspect of affirmative action is that its implementation to date has been based upon ethnicity and gender group identity rather than upon heightening individuals' potential for contributing to the society. Affirmative action programming targeted to group membership and past history of disenfranchisement has resulted in the adoption of numerical indices or goals to implement and assess the effects of affirmative action. There is nothing inherently evil about goals and timetables per se, but when employed as tools to achieve affirmative action, the perception and charge soon follow that target groups are receiving more than equal opportunity.

Implementation of affirmative action policy has faced decades of stubborn opposition. Opponents have been tenacious in characterizing affirmative action as a practice that scuttles the basic and revered American principle that honors merit. Some conservative African American scholars have joined the battle against affirmative action (Sowell, 1989; Steele, 1990). Among their arguments is that affirmative action has promoted campus racial antagonism, that it confers a sense of inferiority on African Americans, and that it confers preferential treatment which, in the long run, is injurious. They and other opponents have interchanged, sometimes carelessly, sometimes calculatedly, but mostly to this advantageous effect, the terms *goals, quotas, timetables, preferential treatment*, and *entitlements*. Such interchanging subverts the intended purpose of affirmative action and easily persuades many Americans that they are victims of reverse discrimination. But preference and entitlements are not peculiar to affirmative action; numerous societal institutions have used these to accomplish stated recruiting goals. One example is the federal government policy of enabling resettlement of members of U.S. Armed Forces through benefits and veterans preference policies in employment, education, and home-buying. Another example is collegiate admissions policies (or practices) favoring "chips," or "legacies" (i.e., alumni/ae offspring), and graduates of private preparatory schools with which an institution has articulation agreements. And there is scarcely a college or university with competitive athletic teams that has not used entitlements and set-asides to accomplish recruitment goals.

According to Executive Order 11246 issued by President Johnson in 1965, nondiscrimination simply required elimination of all discriminatory practices toward present or potential employees. The intention was that there must be some form of positive action, aimed at undoing the grossest inequities of past discrimination, a schedule for how such actions are to take place, and an honest appraisal of what the plan is likely to yield. Goals, then, were accompanied by timetables intended to serve as gauges for assessing progress toward the stated goals. Such goals are not unlike those enunciated in the strategic plans of both corporations and higher education institutions. Recently a university official explained the president's definition of the roles of two staff members, one appointed for strategic planning, the other for assessment. The former was described as the *vice president for where we're going*, the latter as the *vice president for are we getting there?* The intent in setting goals for affirmative actions, for where we are going, is to be able to assess whether we are getting there.

Goals are where we want to go. A goal is not a quota. A quota is not a goal. Quotas, however, are rigid numerical ceilings that specify a maximum number of persons to be admitted to an experience, to be allowed to reach a goal. When used as the complement of *goal*, the word *quota* serves as a rhetorical device for antiaffirmative action crusaders. Capricious, arbitrary actions taken against any group or individuals violate the sense of fundamental fairness. Once goals are confused with quotas, opponents of goals can engage in "quota-bashing," deftly enlisting the full force of the citizenry and societal institutions, including the courts, as has been done in recent federal government administrations.

The tools for implementing affirmative action programs and measuring their effectiveness could be identified by any of several terms. They happen to be termed goals, and that term lends support to the notion that time-honored standards have been violated, that is, that reverse discrimination has simply replaced age-old discrimination.

To interchange the terms *affirmative action* and *preferential treatment* and conclude *reverse discrimination* from that process is to suggest that those who benefit from affirmative action are not subject to the same standards of evaluation. Undoubtedly, legions of fully qualified *individuals* have benefited from affirmative action in the form of an institutional goal to admit an appropriate complement of individuals from previously underrepresented groups. Frequently, however, opponents argue that unqualified groups have been favored when in actuality it is *members* of certain groups that have been examined against some standard of qualification and then admitted to the experience.

Getting colleagues in higher education to understand, accept, and champion the intent and appropriateness of affirmative action requires reinstatement of the actual meaning of terms that have become encumbered by negative connotations. Also required is an attendant shift away from emphasis on group membership toward emphasis on individual and societal needs.

INSTITUTIONAL AND INDIVIDUAL RACISM

In general, attention is called to racism observable at the institutional level rather than at the individual level. Policies and practices incorporate into the institution's routine organizational procedures that yield an institutional pattern of responding are said to be *institutionalized*. Jones (1983) suggested that institutional racism generally refers to practices that do not require verification beyond the demonstration that there are patterns of outcomes that affect people according to their race/ethnicity.

Institutional and individual racism are both forms of social control: They work to deny the value of cultural distinctiveness and to create a climate suggesting that cultural distinctiveness does not matter thereby effectively negating other cultures. "Insisting on a narrow range of acceptable values and behavioral styles, and basing equity (rewards and resource allocation) decisions on them is one of the most conspicuous and damaging ways in which cultural bias operates" (Jones, 1983, p. 145). When cultural bias or racism is detected and charged it is seldom clear who is at fault. Derrick Bell (1990) identified this pattern in an essay on the exploitation of fear of crimes perpetrated by African Americans. He wrote:

> Conservative policy makers find it relatively easy to shift the [W]hite public's attention from the lack of opportunity and uneven distribution of wealth to the latent fears about Blacks moving too fast—fears that these days are couched in antiaffirmative action language. Whites at every level share racial fears and stereotypes to some degree....
>
> There is, of course, a long-running debate about whether discrimination and disadvantage account for Black crime or whether the tragic statistics result from inherent inadequacies of Black people. This discussion is able to survive all manner of Black achievements. [The actual perpetrator's] bold effort to shift the blame for his deed is an American tradition that virtually defines the evil that is racism. (p. E 23)

The cultural diversity of U. S. society is an undeniable fact that transcends the "melting pot" metaphor. Recognizing and authenticating diversity is a precondition to achieving cultural pluralism that incorporates rather than negates the broader range of human potential and contributions.

COLLEGIATE AND SOCIETAL RESPONSE

U. S. higher education has not achieved the reform called for by the 1947 Truman Commission. Despite dogged opposition, this nation has come to another point in its history when clearly the national interest will be best served by the opponents of affirmative action reassessing and amending their position. Demographers project that early in the 21st century ethnic minority persons will numerically predominate in U.S. society and in U.S. higher education (Levine & Associates, 1989). It is a troublesome proposition that those comprising the labor force and responsible for sustaining the gross national product may not be able to do so due to inadequate educational preparation. Beyond the troublesomeness are other reasons for ensuring equity of opportunity and outcomes, the most important of which is the need to support the basic American ideal of humane treatment of all people.

To ensure the future of this nation, we must succeed in educating our citizenry and institutions that affirmative action is intended as a remedy for problems created by racism and sexism and by the consequent inequity in U.S. society. The relationship among the nation's productivity and vitality and its citizenry must be perceived. Social control has been the tool of conservatives, and social control continues today through benign neglect and through benign programs aimed at minority recruitment without companion programs devised to ensure minority retention. Conventions that are devised to serve the distinct needs of ethnic minority students but that are not integral to institutional collegiate programming goals and missions abet racism, bigotry, and isolation. They also provide approval of the status quo. Ethnic minority persons can neither change doctrine nor eradicate its vestiges. In providing affirmative action the task is to recognize, accept, and incorporate the values and cultural contributions of ethnics into our culture, which so far has not adequately valued those contributions. This means that the interpretive framework must address the nature, form, character, and self-definition of those being evaluated (Jones, 1983). The evaluative standard needs to be shifted from equity in simple numerical terms to equity in terms of exalting all humanity.

Implementation of affirmative action is complicated by issues of moral authority as a basis for making whole again a people decimated by legal statutes and by sanctioned exclusionary practices in U. S. society. In addition, implementation is complicated by transactions in which the notion of moral authority is preceded by charges of inferior morality or, worse yet, of immorality on the part of those not endorsing proposed affirmative action remedies.

Despite the absence of widespread chaos and the presence of the naive, ahistorical proposition that it is better to be African American in the 1990s, inequality remains a serious social problem. To the extent that affirmative action is based on political as opposed to humanistic motives, the nation misses the opportunity to redress past wrongs and hasten the arrival of cultural pluralism.

Observing the demographic shift toward a predominately ethnic minority population, Toffler (1981) called for new institutions sensitive to the rapidly shifting needs of changing and multiplying minorities (p. 422). Perhaps what is needed is a restructuring of present institutions so that they relinquish their exclusive orientations and adopt policies and practices that value all of society's cocultures. Collegiate as well as all other U.S. institutions must come to regard accommodation of all people as necessary and appropriate, rather than as just another capitulation to avoid further troublesome dialogue.

CONCLUSION

The most savage forms of discrimination against racial and ethnic minority persons has ended, yet the effects of those earlier times are with us. Affirmative action was invented to provide relief or equity for victims of negative action. Equality of opportunity and outcome remains a distant ideal, if not a myth; affirmative action has brought predictable resistance from those who see it as a continuation of discriminatory practices.

In June 1990, the United States Supreme Court again reversed its position (by a 5-to-4 vote) in the matter of the use of preference to achieve an affirmative action goal (*Metro Broadcasting Inc. v. FCC*, 1990). Reinstating the notion of "compelling government interest," the Court ruled in favor of the Federal Communications Commission (FCC), which had been sued over its "minority preference" policy in awarding broadcast station licenses. The Court termed the practice "benign" (that is, noninjurious to nonminorities who hold 98% of all FCC licenses) and ruled that using race/ethnicity as a factor is constitutional when certain governmental objectives are served. Again, it should be noted that preference in this case does not mean that minorities are not qualified to own and operate broadcast stations. Rather, the FCC in adopting the preference policy had noted that despite qualifications, ethnic minority applicants tended to be noncompetitive on other dimensions that are not easily overcome. Further, it had noted that the interests of ethnic minorities are not adequately served by majority-owned broadcast stations.

The issue of how to deliver equity is far from resolved; only one justice reversed positions in this argument about whether affirmative action necessarily results in reverse or affirmative discrimination. Despite the passionate debate evoked by this contemporaneous issue, the future of this nation depends on the eradication of barriers to the full participation of some of its citizens. U.S. higher education has a societal obligation to contribute to the resolution of this dilemma.

The momentum in progress for some members of previously disenfranchised groups owed to the 1960s civil rights movement and enabling legislation is a fact that requires no particular illumination. So also is the precipitous decline in these gains a fact that requires no illumination. Rather, what is needed is analysis of both the progress and decline to enable the necessary revisions of the current course.

U. S higher education largely reflects the values of the society. Meyers (1989) suggested that education for African Americans has passed through five stages of public policy: (a) prohibition (pre-1860), (b) development (1865-1896), (c) segregation (1896-1954), (d) desegregation (1954-1973), and (e) enhancement. In this latter stage, effected by the *Adams v. Richardson* rulings, (1972, 1973), U. S. higher education is called upon to exercise leadership that finally delivers equal educational opportunity.

Conservative political opponents have mounted attacks upon affirmative action as if its history has delivered equity or even enduring advantages to ethnic minority groups. In their attacks these opponents charge that policies aimed at achieving collegiate enrollments reflective of the larger society (i.e., high school graduates) result in preferential treatment for less academically qualified students and that such remedies result in changing the fundamental character of the university, in lowering of academic standards, and in discrimination against the most able students. In that regard, Bunzel (1988) noted that the effects of affirmative action were to provide real or alleged victims redress by discriminating against them. Such analyses do not adequately account either for the structure of U. S. society or of U. S. higher education and particularly not for the collegiate environmental factors that by some accounts (Hughes, 1987; Mallinckrodt, 1988; Trippi & Cheatham, 1989) figure more critically into African American student attrition than academic failures. The Bunzel (1988) analysis ends with the notion that the real issue is *either* setting goals based on racial composition of high school graduating classes *or* emphasis on individual merits and potential regardless of race/ethnicity. The real issue is really not an either/or proposition. It is both (Astin, 1984).

The Truman Commission concluded the preamble to its 1947 report by asserting that "It can be done." It argued, as have other commissions (Green, 1989), that the intelligence and ability to transform America exists. What is needed is will, courage, and wholehearted commitment. The 1947 report concluded:

> *Colleges must accelerate the normally slow rate of social change which the educational system reflects; we need to find ways quickly [of] making the understanding and vision of our most farsighted and sensitive citizens the common possession of all our people. (p. 23)*

The task before us is not new; the challenge is supreme. Will we revise and revitalize U.S. education by intent or by default? What is new is the time frame in which we must function.

REFERENCES

Adams v. Richardson, 351 F. Supp. 118 (D.D.C. 1972).

Adams v. Richardson, 356 F. Supp. 92 (D.D.C. 1973).

Astin, A. W. (1984). A look at pluralism in the contemporary student population. *NASPA Journal, 21,* 2-11.

Bell, D. (1990, January 14). Stuart's lie: An American tradition. *The New York Times,* p. E. 23.

Blauner, B. (1989). *Black lives, White lives: Three decades of race relations in America.* Berkeley: University of California Press.

Bunzel, J. H. (1988). Affirmative action admissions: How it "works" at U C Berkeley. *The Public Interest, 93,* 111-129.

Cheatham, H. E. (1988). *Gender and racial equity in U.S. military occupational distribution* (DEOMI Report No. 88-4). Patrick Air Force Base, FL: Defense Equal Opportunity Management Institute

Cheatham, H. E., & Seem, S. E. (1990) Occupation equity: A Black and White portrait of women in the United States military. *The Review of Black Political Economy, 19*(1), 1-12.

Glazer, N. (1975). *Affirmative discrimination: Ethnic inequality and public policy.* New York: Basic Books.

Green, M. F. (Ed.) (1989). *Minorities on campus: A handbook for enhancing diversity.* Washington, DC: American Council on Education.

Hastings, M. (1969). *The fire this time: America's years of crisis.* New York: Taplinger.

Hughes, M. S. (1987). Black students' participation in higher education. *Journal of College Student Personnel, 28,* 532-545.

Jones, J. M. (1983). The concept of race in social psychology: From color to culture. In L. Wheeler & D. Shaver (Eds.), *Review of Personality and Social Psychology* (Vol. 4, pp. 117-150). Beverly Hills, CA: Sage.

Levine, A., & Associates (1989). *Shaping higher education's future.* San Francisco: Jossey-Bass.

Mahoney, M. J. (1989). Scientific psychology and radical behaviorism. *American Psychologist, 44,* 1372-1377.

Mallinckrodt, B. (1988). Student retention, social support, and dropout retention. *Journal of College Student Development, 29,* 60-64.

Metro Broadcasting Inc. v. FCC, Nos. 89-453 & 89-700 (1990).

Meyers, S. L. (1989). *Desegregation in higher education.* New York: University Press of America.

Miles, R. (1989). *Racism.* New York: Routledge.

Mingle, J. R. (1987). *Focus on minorities: Trends in higher education participation and success.* Denver, CO: Education Commission of the States.

President's Commission on Higher Education for American Democracy (1947). *A report of the President's Commission on Higher Education: Vol. 1. Establishing the goals.* Washington, DC.

Sowell, T. (1989, February 13). The new racism on campus. *Fortune,* pp. 15, 116-118, 120.

Steele, S. (1990, May 13). A negative vote on affirmative action. *New York Times Magazine,* p. 46.

Toffler, A. (1981). *The third wave.* New York: Bantam Books.

Trippi, J., & Cheatham, H. E. (1989). Effects of special counseling programs for Black freshmen on a predominantly White campus. *Journal of College Student Development, 30,* 35-40.

Washington, V., & Harvey, W. (1989). *Affirmative rhetoric, negative action: African American faculty at predominantly White institutions* (Report No. 2). Washington, DC: George Washington University.

CHAPTER 2

IDENTITY DEVELOPMENT IN A PLURALISTIC SOCIETY

Harold E. Cheatham

The central thesis for this chapter is that the unique sociocultural and psychosocial experiences of ethnic minority persons are too little appreciated and thus have not been incorporated into collegiate programming that would serve these persons. There is a specific and unique history and set of attendant expectations that ethnic minority students bring to campus; these are rooted in the dynamics of the family and culture and in the repertoire which develops as a function of the complex interactions between family members and the external environment. Ethnic minority students' social and intellectual development will be better served when their distinct cultures and experiences have been identified and intentionally incorporated into campus life.

Many collegiate institutions have sought to increase enrollment of ethnic minority students, particularly of African Americans, but many external and internal barriers remain (Edwards, 1988; Gibbs, 1973; Madrazo-Peterson & Rodriquez, 1978; Wharton, 1986). Further, many institutions have attempted to educate ethnic minority, specifically African American, students while ignoring their sociocultural reality. Despite a near universal perception and expectation of education as the vehicle to upward mobility, African American students report that the climate for learning at predominantly White institutions (PWIs) operates against their academic success (Fleming, 1984; Gibbs, 1974; Hughes, 1987).

African American students in PWIs frequently have noted the scarcity of African American faculty, of appropriate and responsive support systems, and of curricular and cocurricular conventions that make collegiate environment "legible" (i.e., assist the student in translating and understanding institutional policies and procedures). Edwards (1979, 1988) concluded that much of the failure to provide equity resides in deficiencies in the environment, or in "structural discrimination," which Hill (1990, p. 91) defined as unintended, adverse consequences of societal trends. The outcomes related to functioning in such collegiate settings include higher sensitivity to discrimination, comparatively lower academic performance, and lower satisfaction with college.

African American students believe that White faculty are prejudiced toward them (Semmes, 1985), a perception that contributes both to lowered expectations of these students' academic performance and to low-quality faculty interaction with and responsiveness to African American students. Mingle (1978) reported that White faculty consciously interact less frequently with African American students than with White students and that these faculty also harbor the perception that the African American students have entered the institution under different standards. The persistence of indifference and hostility on PWI campuses was noted by Lunneborg and Lunneborg (1985), who reported that minority students feel isolated and ignored, that the university is "cold," and that they are subjected to racism, prejudice, and patronizing attitudes. In their look at the durability of normative systems on U.S. campuses, Loo and Rolison (1986) reported greater sociocultural alienation for minority than for nonminority students, and that fewer minority students felt that the university reflects their values. Madrazo-Peterson and Rodriquez (1978) reported similar perceptions and adjustment issues for Hispanic students attending a PWI.

Those barriers to cultural pluralism that are reported to pervade PWIs, contravening minority students' sense of self, provide a stark contrast to African American students' reported experiences in historically Black colleges (HBCs). Researchers generally have concluded that the HBC provides a unique educational environment (Allen, 1986; Cheatham, Tomlinson, & Ward, 1990; Fleming, 1984; Hughes, 1987). These environs are supportive and better assist students' psychosocial adjustment and development of self-efficacy (Bandura, 1982, 1986). Specifically, in regard to their adjustment and experiences, students at HBCs report comparatively less loneliness and isolation, and higher quantity and quality of interaction with peers and with faculty and staff. Further, Baratz and Ficklen (1983) reported that HBCs produce graduates with greater cultural awareness than their PWI counterparts, yet of equal competitiveness in the U.S. labor market.

There is much that can and must be done to enable ethnic minority students'—and, indeed, all students'—optimal functioning at PWIs. Negative experiences notwithstanding, some African American and other ethnic minority students continue to achieve within PWIs—and particularly in institutions where students experience higher levels of interaction with other African Americans. A heightened incidence of interaction with Whites is an apparent consequence of increased interaction with one's ethnic peer group members. In that regard, Smith and Allen (1984) reported a correlation between African American students' success and a characteristic within PWIs that they termed "institutional quality." Smith and Allen called upon undergraduate educators to observe the connection among the institution's agents and agencies, its operating procedures, and the resulting influence of these conventions on African American students' academic performances.

The point advanced in these observations is that depending upon institutional climate, with its historical, social and cultural antecedents, students' development is either enhanced or impeded.

INSTITUTIONAL CLIMATE

Recent reports (see chapter 9 by Clay and Sherrill in this volume) herald the resurgence of racism and violence directed toward members of ethnic minority groups in the larger U.S. society and on U.S. campuses. These reports fly in the face of the position that openly espoused, ideological racism has all but disappeared. For all of its post-civil-rights-era adjustments, U.S. higher education has failed to meet the educational and developmental needs of ethnic minority Americans (Egerton, 1982; Nettles & Baratz, 1985; Wharton, 1986). Actually, there is some speculation as to whether U.S. higher education understands the needs of its consumers, in general (Katchadourian & Boli, 1986).

These citations of the disposition of ethnic minority students on PWIs do not imply universality. Numerous U. S. colleges and universities enjoy enviable success at recruiting and retaining ethnic minority students, notably African Americans; an even greater number boast of success within specific programs. The haunting question is, With the significant amount of human and capital resources and scores of programs directed to African American students attending PWIs during the last two decades, how can the record continue to be so uneven? A partial answer has been advanced in the charge that many institutions have continued business as usual after acting to relieve rather than excise the pain. If the purpose in attending to ethnic minorities' educational quest is to aid the individual goal of self-actualization, that is one thing. And perhaps that self-actualization can be achieved within the existing institutional structure once the normative, Eurocentric model of cultural intervention has been appropriately criticized and refined. If, however, ethnic minority pesons' quest extends beyond self-actualization and onward to education for social utility, the quest collides with traditional barriers. Education that liberates and promotes personal authenticity presumes systemic change and adaptation that do not depend upon initiatives of those to be served. Rather, collegiate institutions must make an unqualified commitment to developing enduring multicultural environs. The quality of the institutional climate is indispensable to the matriculation, development, and graduation of ethnic minority Americans.

From a review of two decades of research on African Americans in U.S. higher education, Sedlacek (1987) suggested that perhaps the noted success is attributable to a Hawthorne-like effect (cf. Lindzey & Aronson, 1969). He concluded that although researchers have provided contradictory conclusions, positive—even if inconsistent—efforts to serve the needs of African American students have contributed to retention. Academic persistence has been linked to the student's integration into and affiliation with the institution (Tinto, 1975; 1982), contact with faculty outside of the classroom (Braddock, 1981; Nettles, Thoeny, & Gosman, 1986), preventive or special counseling services (Carroll, 1987; Trippi & Cheatham, 1989; Trippi & Cheatham, 1991), institutional environment (Smith & Allen, 1984), and to the complex interaction of institutional characteristics and student characteristics (Spady, 1970).

HISTORICAL, SOCIAL, AND CULTURAL ANTECEDENTS OF THE BLACK SELF

African American/ethnic minority students have been variously characterized as "strange and formidable" (Calia, 1966, p. 100), guarded, diffuse, inhibited, aggressive, of high *and* low self-concept and self-esteem, optimistic, committed, and unrealistic (cf. Fleming, 1984; Gibbs, 1973; Gurin & Epps, 1975; Smith & Allen, 1984; Taylor, 1986). Efforts to identify commonality, let alone universality, among African Americans is indeed risky; the diversity implied by the preceding descriptors persuades that African Americans/ethnic minorities are not monolithic. Blackwell (1975) noted that except for the consequences of racism and the pervasiveness of color consciousness in America, there is no experience universal to African Americans.

African Americans and other ethnic minorities, in general, share related sociohistorical experiences that are based upon negative attributions to their ethnicity and color and, in the case of African Americans, upon the vestiges of the "peculiar institution" of slavery (Stampp, 1956). Mathis (1978) and Nobles (1974) contended that African Americans, in response to enforced isolation and disenfranchisement, evolved systems and relationships to meet their needs. Moreover, these scholars contend that these new forms or systems had their genesis in African form and tradition. Included among the transplanted African forms are family pattern, attitudes and behaviors, verbal expression, gender-related role expectations, and epicurean traditions (Blackwell, 1975). This conceptualization argues that the African American community contains elements similar to other social systems, including value consensus. Further, it argues that the African American community is a political, social, and economic entity with shared norms and expectations. African American families are characterized by (a) strong kinship bonds, (b) strong work orientation, (c) adaptability of family role, (d) high achievement orientation, and (e) a religious orientation (Hill, 1972).

In a meticulously documented account of slave community and its legacy to African Americans, Blassingame (1979) contended that the predominant view of the slave community denies that the slave had a meaningful and distinctive culture. That view further obscures the slave's inner life, thought, action, and sense of self. Blassingame demonstrated that the slave held fast to African culture and practiced and enhanced its meaning such that not only was the culture preserved but that it also added to American culture through merging and synthesizing those aspects that had shared similarity. Among those enduring forms exist religion, African linguistic style (i.e., Black English) or "Ebonics" (Asante,1988), and art form. Particularly noted among art forms are music and folktale, the prototypes of which are regarded as most resistant to European forms (Blassingame, 1979).

For our purpose, the summary notion here is that in the exchange and adaptation process African slaves in America retained the African cultural determinants of their status (Blassingame, 1979; Herskovits, 1941). The demonstration of retained African form is basic to the preference here for the term *Africentric*, which suggests continuity, as opposed to *Afrocentric* suggesting instead a form that is a derivative of the African form. This sense of self-efficacy, together with the demonstrated resilience of African cultural forms that were merged with American forms, provides a different and more positive view of the slave's existence and hence of the legacy of African Americans.

Unlike the Western philosophic system, the African tradition has no heavy emphasis on the individual. Rather, the individual being is authenticated only in terms of others. (For a demonstration of the African sense of self, consider, for example, Nelson Mandela's personal triumph over apartheid and *his* triumphant 1990 tour of the United States. Then consider how Mr. Mandela takes no individual or personal credit but refers to self only in the plural form: "While *we* were in prison....") Similarly, African American families generally stress affiliation, collectivity, interdependence, respect for elders, and obedience to authority as preferable to the Euro-American/Eurocentric values of individuation, autonomy, and competition. There is a pervasive awareness of corporate responsibility and collective destiny as epitomized in the traditional African self-concept: "I am because we are; and because we are, therefore, I am" (Nobles, 1974). In this regard, Hughes (1987) noted that the relationship characteristic among African American family members suggests individuation patterns unique to African American students. Contrary to the interpretations and attributions made by those unknowledgeable of African American family form and function, these students do not perceive their familial relationships and reliance on friends as delaying their development of independence. Rather, African Americans' individuation patterns perpetuate the Africentric form that is termed "the extended family."

In sum, scholars have concluded that despite the intent to destroy community and values of African slaves in America, slavery inadvertently ensured that social organization as it existed in the souls of slaves was actualized in African Americans. Social organization—where norms, role ascription, ethical conduct, group solidarity and defense, cooperation, accommodation and conflict, and related sociologic concepts descriptive of peoples and cultures resided in the lives of slaves— forms the legacy of African Americans. This social organization, different from that of free peoples, provided for the traditional functions of group solidarity and family organization in the face of staggering odds.

Thus the truncated view of the culture of African Americans' forebears—and hence of African Americans—leads to unfounded conclusions. Further, for some, this view also justifies interventions that ignore the unique characteristics of the person being "treated." Simplistic interventions result from describing racial and ethnic minority persons *not as they are but as they are different* from the modal individual (McAdoo, 1981). In that comparative context, the emphasis remains on validating the majority experience as opposite to studying the ethnic minority experience. Mathis (1978) observed, "One's ability to understand [B]lack reality is limited if the interpretive framework is based on assumptions associated with non-[B]lack reality" (p. 676). Mathis' essential argument was also advanced by Merton (1968), who suggested that outsiders lack the intuitive sensibility for understanding the target group's culture. Again, it is noted that although this discussion is focused on the African American experience its essence is transportable to other ethnic peoples.

Those embracing intervention models that ignore the unique and vital heritage of ethnic minority persons and treat them rather as deficient Whites reveal an ethnocentric or, more specifically, Eurocentric bias. The conceptualization holding that because of their retention of African form and tradition African Americans ought to be thought of as African in *nature* and American in *nurture* (Nobles, 1978) is termed Africentric. An essential characteristic of Africentric theory or worldview is the belief in simultaneous and harmonious existence of all things.

The Africentric model is advanced here not as universally applicable but rather as a useful alternative to the predominant Euro-American or Eurocentric model, which does not fully accommodate the intellectual and social development of African Americans on White campuses. It is asserted as having validity for understanding the diversity and complexity of the heritage of African Americans. Further, it is presented as useful for fostering African American students' demonstrated strengths so as to enable them to function in the competitive, achievement-oriented environment of the U.S. campus while holding fast to their cultural heritage (see Figure 1). By transporting variables endemic to other cultures, one can extend the utility of this model (Cheatham, 1989).

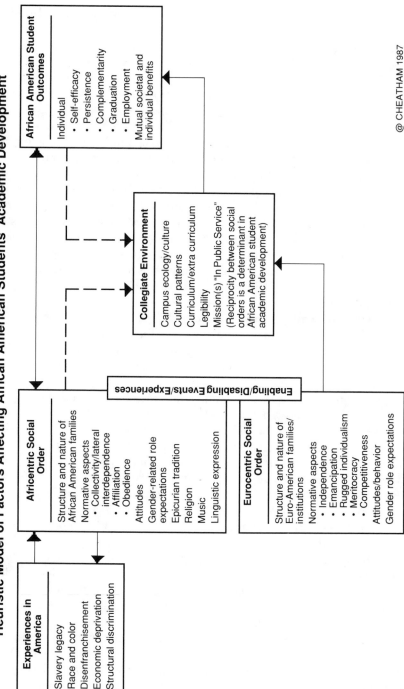

Figure 1

Heuristic Model of Factors Affecting African American Students' Academic Development

African American Student Outcomes

Individual
- Self-efficacy
- Persistence
- Complementarity
- Graduation
- Employment

Mutual societal and individual benefits

Collegiate Environment

Campus ecology/culture
Cultural patterns
Curriculum/extra curriculum
Legibility
Mission(s) "In Public Service" (Reciprocity between social orders is a determinant in African American student academic development)

Enabling/Disabling Events/Experiences

Africentric Social Order

Structure and nature of African American families

Normative aspects
- Collectivity/lateral interdependence
- Affiliation
- Obedience

Attitudes
Gender-related role expectations
Epicurian tradition
Religion
Music
Linguistic expression

Eurocentric Social Order

Structure and nature of Euro-American families/institutions

Normative aspects
- Independence
- Emancipation
- Rugged individualism
- Meritocracy
- Competitiveness

Attitudes/behavior
Gender role expectations

Experiences in America

Slavery legacy
Race and color
Disenfranchisement
Economic deprivation
Structural discrimination

Figure 1's heuristic model depicts aspects of the experience of African Americans in U.S. society as these are effected through synthesis and adaptation of elements from both the Africentric and Eurocentric social orders. Further, the model depicts the empirical evidence that suggests that individuals from each order embody behaviors and characteristics derived from their respective order as well as from the complementary order. The vertical bar connecting these social orders depicts individual options to synthesize, adapt, and even reject social order phenomena that are perceived or experienced as either enabling or disabling of one's functioning in this society. That the collegiate environment is more syntonic with the Eurocentric social order than with the Africentric is illustrated by the solid line from the former and the broken line (to suggest the tentativeness of its influence) from the latter. Some ethnic minority students certainly emerge from this depicted, impoverished environment personally integrated, strong and fully functional. The implication to be drawn from the model, however, is that creating more culturally syntonic collegiate environments (i.e., that reflect and respect ethnic minority cultures) is an appropriate and critical undertaking for societal institutions that proclaim human development among their goals.

The various ways African American students have been described suggests that most are somewhere between the constants depicted in the Africentric and Eurocentric models. The Eurocentric model may be more appropriate to the African American student whose precollege social experience was quite diverse (i.e., racially integrated, cosmopolitan). Just as social and cultural exchange, synthesis and adaptation has resulted in people who are similar in attitudes, beliefs, and values, the sociocultural experiences of some African American students may render them more *or* less amenable to Africentric-focused interventions. No application is automatic, however. Those committed to serving the needs of ethnic minority students and to hastening the arrival of cultural pluralism ought to be familiar with Africentric theory and models as well as with the various theories and models of identity development of other ethnic minority groups' members.

It seems redundant but necessary to suggest that to ignore the cultural specificity of the ethnic minority student while treating him or her as the idealized American is to continue to engender problematic situations on U.S. campuses. A growing body of research and literature substantiates sociocultural experiences and developmental differences distinguishing African American, Asian American, American Indian, and Latino students from their Caucasian American counterparts.

It seems equally redundant and necessary to petition that through observation of and "unconditional positive regard" for that specificity, there is much that many traditionally White collegiate institutions have done and that others can do to enable ethnic minority students to function optimally and emerge with an intact, validated self.

STUDENT DEVELOPMENT THEORY

Student development theory is a specific psychology derived from theories of human development with a special focus on developmental changes occurring throughout the phase of the life cycle of one termed "student." Chickering (1981) proposed that student development is an *intentional* intervention that promotes such capacities as clear values, integrity, communication skills, critical thinking and synthesis, a sense of tolerance and interdependence, empathy, understanding and cooperation, and a capacity for intimacy that goes beyond mere competence and tolerance. In sum, he proposed the development of a basic sense of personal identity, neither superimposed nor mediated but conscientiously facilitated through appropriate programmatic interventions. He conceptualized collegiate institutions as developmental communities and recognized that students are not homogeneous but are instead developmentally different from one another. (Chickering's theory and schema is but one of several available postulations of student development. For a broader presentation of college student development theory and practice, see Creamer & Associates, 1990, and Knefelkamp, Widick, & Parker, 1978.) Chickering posed the question of the consequence of taking this human development as the unifying purpose of higher education as well as of the consequences that accrue to the individual and the society when there is greater awareness of the interactions between self and system.

Chickering's model is interactionist. It contains seven vectors: (a) developing competence, (b) managing emotions, (c) developing autonomy, (d) establishing identity, (e) freeing interpersonal relationships, (f) clarifying purpose, and (g) developing integrity. The collegiate environment then is postulated as providing the conditions that facilitate students' development along the vectors. Among the experiences postulated as focusing and nurturing behavior and, in turn, provoking introspection and growth are (a) clarity and consistency of objectives, (b) redundancy that occurs as a function of institutional size, (c) choice and flexibility in curriculum, teaching, and evaluation, (d) residence hall arrangements that foster interpersonal relationships, (e) positive faculty-student and student-administration interactions, and (f) a student culture that complements a positive academic environment (Knefelkamp et al., 1978). These experiences, it should be noted, are central to the themes of the chapters in this volume.

The Student Development Task and Lifestyle Inventory (SDTLI) (Winston, Miller, & Prince, 1987) and its predecessor, the 1979 Student Development Task Inventory based on Chickering's widely applied theory, assess college students' psychosocial development. Despite the "...considerable evidence to support the contention that college students as a *group* [italics added] share common challenges and that development is coherent and predictable" (Miller & Winston, 1990, p. 102), there exists little evidence that the identity development of African American and other ethnic minority students is accounted for in the aggregate data. In a study of student socialization, Nettles & Johnson (1987) found that African American students ranked higher than White students on peer group relations and lower on academic integration and satisfaction. They concluded that these two student cohorts have different developmental needs and that differential approaches are necessary in collegiate institutions addressing ethnic group members' socialization needs.

Developmental differences have been reported in two studies using the SDTLI to assess African American students. Both reported gender differences not shown in studies of White students.

In the first study, Jordan-Cox (1987), in a cross-sectional design study of African American students in three HBCs in the same city found African American women preceding their male counterparts in interpersonal relationships, autonomy, and life purpose. She suggested that these differences might be a function of the type of collegiate environment (i.e., one was historically a women's college). She also noted that first-year students differed on 9 of 12 variables whereas seniors differed from each other on only three variables—all three concentrated in the interpersonal relationships area. There is a hint in her conclusions that this diminishing of differences may have resulted as a function of the characteristics of the collegiate environs. This notion, moreover, is consistent with the nurturing experiences postulated by Chickering (cited in Knefelkamp et al., 1978).

In the second study, Cheatham, Slaney, and Coleman (1990), also using a cross-sectional design to study African American students in an HBC and a PWI in the same state, found seniors, regardless of institution, preceding other students in Educational Involvement, Career Planning, and Life Management. SDTLI results yielded three main effects for institution: PWI students reported greater incidence of Cultural Participation and posted higher scores than HBC students on Emotional Autonomy. The results of the Salubrious Lifestyle (i.e., sense of well-being) favored students at the HBC.

Although the role ethnic and cultural influences play in psychosocial development is not yet clear, it is certain that the characteristics that distinguish ethnic minority students from their counterparts must be taken into account in student development conceptualizations and programs. From the aggregate research it seems safe to conclude that identity development is a specific task faced by ethnic minority students and as such ought to be incorporated into stage development theory.

Several writers have provided evidence that African American students are responsive to a variety of interventions, particularly to those that authenticate the student's sense of self and that provide the students with a sense of genuine community on White campuses (c.f. Carroll, 1987; Jackson, 1985; Jones, 1985; Locke & Zimmerman, 1987). Locke and Zimmerman reported that a program predicated on a theory of human development promoted significant growth in ego development in African American students. Those student volunteers trained as peer counselors registered positive gains in moral reasoning. Locke and Zimmerman noted that counseling about racial issues triggered more intense responses among peer counselors and resulted in less objective levels of reasoning. That effect noted, they concluded that psychological growth among African American students may be a key to enhancing these students' success on White campuses.

Trippi and Cheatham (1989) identified six areas of concern that dominate counseling interactions with an African American cohort of students served in an academic assistance program for differentially prepared students. They reported that 70% of 1,620 counseling contacts addressed academic concerns, academic skill deficiencies, course scheduling, financial need, introductory interviews, and legibility or understanding of institutional procedures and norms. They also found that African American freshmen for whom counselors unilaterally scheduled subsequent appointments were significantly less likely to persist to second-year status than were students who independently initiated follow-up appointments or with whom no specific follow-up appointments were scheduled. Using a cross-sectional design, they found that the number of in-person counseling contacts was the independent variable most related to persistence of African American first-year students. In a longitudinal study of this same cohort (Trippi & Cheatham, 1991), they reported legibility as the single most important variable in student persistence in college.

SUMMARY AND CONCLUSIONS

Certainly not all efforts to recruit and retain ethnic minority students have been poorly conceived nor met by dismal failure. What is evident is that after two recent decades of bold, new societal efforts for providing equity in U.S. higher education the retention and graduation results are uneven and unenviable. Most African American students are enrolled in PWIs and continue to be at some risk as casualties of these institutions (Wharton, 1986). Berrian (1982) contended that, contrary to lore, PWIs *once committed* succeed in developing ethnic minority students. Of critical importance in this observation is the institutional climate and the student's experience of that climate. There is evidence suggesting that although African American students express a preference for a counselor from their own ethnic group they rate the counselor's education, attitudes and values, age, and personality as being more important than similar ethnicity (Atkinson, Furlong, & Poston, 1986). Negative learning environments—aside from perpetrating a disturbing and disgraceful waste of psychic energy—totally contradict the purposes of education in a democratic society.

This appraisal ushers the conclusion that there is much that can and must be done to provide positive educational and developmental experiences for ethnic minority students on White campuses—and beyond that to hasten the day when equity and, even more critically, cultural pluralism is a reality in U.S. higher education and society. Collegiate officials cannot homogenize ethnic minority students amidst proclamations that color and ethnicity are of no consequence. Even in the optimal situation where the culture accepts unconditionally the members of its cocultures, to proclaim that ethnicity and sociocultural experience are inconsequential would be to impede the growth of ethnic minority persons. Color and ethnicity are critical dimensions of how one defines self and particularly so in a society that has placed such importance on color and "race." The critical prerequisite to serving fully the developmental needs of ethnic minority students is to reconceptualize development theory and models with ethnic minority identity development as a specific developmental task.

Investigations of factors affecting minority students' academic success have focused on the characteristics of the student, of the institution, and on the complex interaction of the two. The discussion of those factors in the preceding sections provides premises from which to suggest that notable success has been registered by some institutions, whereas others have yet to undertake modifications of institutional policies and practices. Unfortunately, some institutions' lack of progress is traceable to their investment in narcotizing rhetoric suggesting that without a cadre of committed ethnic minority professionals they cannot fashion an environment conducive to minority student development. Jones (1985), specifically addressing counseling service delivery but in a context relevant to our purposes, noted that no research to date demonstrates that all minority clients view all White counselors as inappropriate sources of help. It follows that although staffing that is representative of the institution's various ethnic groups is a desirable convention, institutional commitment should not await that event.

The thesis for this chapter is that the sociocultural or psychosocial experiences of African Americans, and indeed of all ethnic minority groups, are not adequately appreciated and accommodated in theoretical postulations and programmatic interventions designed to serve these groups' members. There is a specific and unique history and attendant set of expectations that the African American and the ethnic minority student, in general, bring to campus. These are rooted in the psychosocial dynamics of the family and in the repertoire that develops as a function of the complex interaction among the family's members and the external environment. Those who would be helpful to ethnic minority students on U.S. campuses must increase their knowledge and appreciation of these students' sociocultural and sociohistorical legacies.

There is no easy resolution of the complex task of how to ensure cultural pluralism on U.S. campuses. There is faith that the issue will yield to the concerted efforts of principled, committed educators—both those responsible for the curricula and those responsible for the cocurricula. There also is impressive evidence that many institutions have made significant inroads. Review of the relevant literature suggests, further, that not just the prestigious or quality institutions (i.e., those characterized by diverse curricula, resources and annual budget, and sometimes even by the date and place of founding) are reporting some success. Rather, impressive accomplishments are reported by diverse institutions that are attuned to the society's rapidly changing needs and are addressing with integrity the complementary mission of service to the nation. The characteristic common among these institutions is the will to challenge the normative system and its assumptions.

REFERENCES

Allen, W. R. (1986). *Gender and campus race differences in Black student academic performance, racial attitudes, and college satisfaction.* Atlanta, GA: Southern Education Foundation.

Asante, M. K. (1988). *The Afrocentric idea.* Philadelphia, PA: Temple University Press.

Atkinson, D. R., Furlong, M. J., & Poston, W. C. (1986). Afro-American preferences for counselor characteristics. *Journal of Counseling Psychology, 33,* 326-330.

Bandura, A. (1982). Self-efficacy mechanism in human agency. *American Psychologist, 37,* 122-147.

Bandura, A. (1986). Fearful expectations and avoidant actions as coefficients of perceived self-inefficacy. *American Psychologist, 41,* 1389-1391.

Baratz, J. S., & Ficklen, M. (1983). *Participation of recent Black graduates in the labor market and in graduate education.* Princeton, NJ: Educational Testing Service.

Berrian, A. H. (1982). Toward desegregation and enhancement. In R. Wilson (Ed.), *Race and equity in higher education* (pp. 137-153). Washington, DC: American Council on Education.

Blackwell, J. E. (1975). *The Black community: Diversity and unity.* New York: Harper & Row.

Blassingame, J. (1979). *The slave community: Plantation life in the antebellum South.* New York: Oxford.

Braddock, J. H., II. (1981). Desegregation and Black student attrition. *Urban Education, 36,* 15-23.

Calia, V. F. (1966). The culturally deprived client: A reformulation of the counselor's role. *Journal of Counseling Psychology, 11,* 100-105.

Carroll, J. (1988). Factors affecting academic success and dropout behavior among Black freshmen at a predominantly Black urban community college. *Journal of College Student Development, 29,* 52-59.

Cheatham, H. E. (1989). Reversing the decline of African American enrollment in U.S. higher education. *Southeastern Association of Educational Opportunity Program Personnel Journal, 8,* 14-22.

Cheatham, H. E., Slaney, R. B., & Coleman, N. (1990). Institutional effects on the psychosocial development of African American college students. *Journal of Counseling Psychology, 37,* 453-458.

Cheatham, H. E., Tomlinson, S. M., & Ward, T. J. (1990). The African self-consciousness construct and African American students. *Journal of College Student Development, 31*, 492-499.

Chickering, A. (1981). *The modern American college*. San Francisco: Jossey-Bass.

Creamer, D. G., & Associates (1990). *College student development: Theory and practice for the 1990s*. Washington, DC: American College Personnel Association.

Edwards, H. (1979). Sport within the veil: The triumphs, tragedies, and challenges of Afro-American involvement. *Annals of the American Academy of Political and Social Science, 445*, 116-127.

Edwards, H. (1988). The single-minded pursuit of sports fame and fortune is approaching an institutional tragedy in Black society. *Ebony, 43*, 138-140.

Egerton, J. (1982). Race and equity in higher education. In R. Wilson (Ed.), *Race and equity in higher education* (pp. 1-27). Washington, DC: American Council on Education.

Fleming, J. (1984). *Blacks in college*. San Francisco: Jossey-Bass.

Gibbs, J. T. (1973). Black students/White university, different expectations. *Personnel and Guidance Journal, 51*, 463-469.

Gibbs, J. T. (1974). Patterns of adaptation among Black students in a predominantly White university: Selected case studies. *American Journal of Orthopsychiatry, 44*, 728-740.

Gurin, P., & Epps, E. (1975). *Black consciousness, identity, and achievement: A study of students in historically Black colleges*. New York: Wiley.

Herskovits, M. (1941). *The myth of the Negro past*. New York: Harper.

Hill, R. B. (1972). *The strengths of Black families*. New York: Emerson Hall.

Hill, R. B. (1990). Economic forces, structural discrimination, and the Black family. In H. E. Cheatham & J. B. Stewart (Eds.), *Black families: Interdisciplinary perspectives* (pp. 87-105). New Brunswick, NJ: Transaction.

Hughes, M. S. (1987). Black students' participation in higher education. *Journal of College Student Personnel, 28*, 532-545.

Jackson, G. G. (1985). Cross-cultural counseling and the Afro-American. In P. Pedersen (Ed.), *Handbook of cross-cultural counseling and therapy* (pp. 231-237). Westport, CT: Greenwood Press.

Jones, E. (1985). Psychotherapy and counseling with Black clients. In P. Pedersen (Ed.), *Handbook of cross-cultural counseling and therapy* (pp. 173-179). Westport, CT: Greenwood Press.

Jordan-Cox, C. A. (1987). Psychosocial development of students in traditionally Black institutions. *Journal of College Student Personnel, 28*, 504-511.

Katchadourian, H., & Boli, J. (1986). *Careerism and intellectual change among college students*. San Francisco: Jossey-Bass.

Knefelkamp, L., Widick, C., & Parker, C. (1978). *Applying new developmental findings* (New Directions for Student Services, No. 4). San Francisco: Jossey-Bass.

Lindzey, G., & Aronson, E. (Eds.). (1969). *The handbook of social psychology* (Vol. 5, 2nd ed.). Reading, MA: Addison-Wesley.

Locke, D., & Zimmerman, N. A. (1987). The effects of peer counseling training on the psychological maturity of Black students. *Journal of College Student Personnel, 28*, 525-531.

Loo, C., & Rolison, G. (1986). Alienation among ethnic minority students at a predominantly White university. *Journal of Higher Education, 57*, 58-77.

Lunneborg, P. W., & Lunneborg, C. E. (1985). Student-centered versus university-centered solutions to problems of minority students. *Journal of College Student Personnel, 26,* 224-228.

Madrazo-Peterson, R., & Rodriquez, M. (1978). Minority students: Perceptions of a university environment. *Journal of College Student Personnel, 19,* 259-263.

Mathis, A. (1978). Contrasting approaches to the study of Black families. *Journal of Marriage and the Family, 40,* 667-676.

McAdoo, H. P. (1981). *Black families.* Beverly Hills, CA: Sage.

Merton, R. (1968). *Social theory and social structure.* New York: Free Press.

Miller, T. K., & Winston, R. B., Jr. (1990). Assessing development from a psychosocial perspective. In D. G. Creamer & Associates, *College student development: Theory and practice for the 1990s* (pp. 99-126). Washington, DC: American College Personnel Association.

Mingle, J. (1978). Faculty and departmental response to increased Black student enrollment. *Journal of Higher Education, 49,* 201-217.

Nettles, M., & Baratz, J. C. (1985). Black colleges: Do we need them? *Change, 17* (2), 58-60.

Nettles, M., & Johnson, J. (1987). Race, sex, and other factors as determinants of college students' socialization. *Journal of College Student Personnel, 28* (6), 512-524.

Nettles, M., Thoeny, A. R., & Gosman, E. J. (1986). Comparative and predictive analyses of Black and White students' college achievement. *Journal of Higher Education, 57,* 289-318.

Nobles, W. W. (1974). African root and American fruit: The Black family. *Journal of Social and Behavioral Sciences, 20,* 66-77.

Nobles, W. W. (1978). Toward an empirical and theoretical framework for defining Black families. *Journal of Marriage and the Family, 40,* 679-688.

Sedlacek, W. E. (1987). Black students on White campuses: 20 years of research. *Journal of College Student Personnel, 26,* 484-495.

Semmes, C. E. (1985). Minority status and the problem of legitimacy. *Journal of Black Studies, 15,* 259-275.

Smith, A. W., & Allen, W. R. (1984). Modeling Black student academic performance in higher education. *Research in Higher Education, 21,* 210-225.

Spady, W. (1970). Dropouts from higher education: An interdisciplinary review and synthesis. *Interchange, 1,* 64-85.

Stampp, K. M. (1956). *The peculiar institution: Slavery in the antebellum South.* New York: Vintage Books.

Taylor, C. A. (1986). Black students on predominantly White college campuses in the 1980s. *Journal of College Student Personnel, 24,* 196-202.

Tinto, V. (1982). *Defining dropout: A matter of perspective.* Washington, DC: Jossey-Bass.

Tinto, V. (1975). Dropout from higher education: A theoretical synthesis of recent research. *Review of Educational Research, 45,* 89-125.

Trippi, J., & Cheatham, H. E. (1989). Effects of a special counseling program for Black students on a predominantly White campus. *Journal of College Student Development, 30,* 35-40.

Trippi, J., & Cheatham, H. E. (1991). Counseling effects on African American college student graduation. *Journal of College Student Development, 32.*

Wharton, C. R., Jr. (1986, July). *Public higher education and the Black American: Today's crises, tomorrow's disaster?* Plenary address to the National Urban League Conference, San Francisco, CA.

Winston, R. B., Jr., Miller, T. K., & Prince, J. S. (1987). *Assessing student development: A preliminary manual for the Student Development Task Inventory (rev. 2nd ed.) and the Student Developmental Profile and Planning Record.* Athens, GA: Student Development Associates.

PART II
DEVELOPMENTAL NEEDS

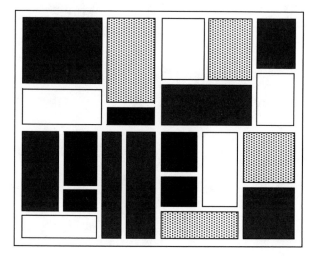

CHAPTER 3

THE MINORITY CULTURAL CENTER ON A PREDOMINANTLY WHITE CAMPUS

Lawrence W. Young, Jr.

Over the last several years, college campuses across the country have witnessed unsettling incidents of intolerance. These have focused the attention of administrators and faculty on the need to examine and modify the nature of the campus environment that a historically White university provides for minority students. The recognition and acceptance of the demographic data spelled out in the report *One-Third of a Nation* (American Council on Education & Education Commission of the States [ACE & ECS] 1988) has led to some soul searching. Campus personnel have debated issues related to whether and how campuses will be able to meet the needs and demands of the African Americans, Native Americans, and Asian Americans who will constitute a significant portion of the population by the year 2000. Central to many of these discussions is the question of whether the creation or expansion of a minority cultural center adds to the quality of campus life for *all* students or whether such centers constitute a "resegregation" of the academy.

This chapter will present the case for the introduction, development, and incorporation of ethnic minority cultural centers on predominantly White campuses as a vehicle for creating a comfortable and compatible facility environment for ethnic minority students. Further, it will be argued that these centers are important instruments to advance the academy's mission of creating intercultural understanding and acceptance within the total collegiate community.

Most academicians are familiar with the following scenario: On a relatively peaceful college campus, there occurs an act of blatant bigotry. The victimized group mobilizes support and loudly protests to the university administration that something must be done. Meetings are held and embarrassment about the incident is expressed. Statements of solidarity with the protesters are issued, and promises are made to "do something." If no further incidents occur and something is done, the campus returns to its former relatively peaceful state.

Campus officers and administrators should not be misled into believing that a return to tranquility is a resolution to the complex problems of interculture friction and intolerance. On many campuses where there is a burgeoning minority student population, there is within those groups a sense of anxiety, alienation, frustration, suppressed and generalized anger, and dissatisfaction. Joseph Feagin (1989) calls this "impotent rage," which may well up and overflow as a result of what may be perceived by others as an innocuous incident. Although most campuses have been spared the trauma of student-to-student warfare, the events of 1986 at the University of Massachusetts at Amherst provide a chilling specter of the potential danger that must be addressed. The effective minority cultural center—one that is appropriately staffed, funded, and viewed as complementary to other institutional programs—provides the institution with an essential tool for the creation of a more tolerant, more accepting community.

The minority cultural center on a predominantly White campus goes to the heart of the unresolved societal issue of providing equity to victims of exclusion and injustice. The unanswered question on campus remains, What shall we do with these new students?

The earliest of these centers were introduced as adjuncts to the African American civil rights movement of the 1950s and 1960s. Genuine efforts at affirmative integration in most predominantly White universities had been a relatively recent phenomenon. The assassination of Dr. Martin Luther King, Jr., however, led some colleges to address their societal roles, commit resources to recruitment, and create cultural centers on campus. These centers were often viewed by minority students and staff as safe havens in an alien and hostile or indifferent environment, particularly at schools with no supportive minority community into which one could retreat. Many in the predominantly White campus community regarded these centers with curiosity, resentment, scorn, and disparagement. Like their academic counterparts—African American Studies, Chicano Studies, Native American Studies, or Asian Studies—cultural centers were considered illegitimate appendages to an otherwise effective, legitimate, established, and accepted order. In some cases, the groundwork for the demise of these structures was incorporated in the plans for their inception. Cynical, reactionary, and even naive administrators undermined these centers while pledging to create a harmonious and supportive community for all students. The similarity between uses of a cultural center and its established counterparts such as student unions, the Greek system, art museum, activities office, and program board, seems to have escaped some who petitioned that existing facilities and organizations were adequate to meet *all* students' needs.

An accompanying impediment to these centers' viability was their underutilization by members of the target groups. For some, the need to assimilate into the larger dominant community precluded identification with a minority center or, for that matter, other minority-oriented programs. Some feared that close identification with such a center might negatively affect social and professional opportunities. The antipathy and voiced opposition of the 1970s and the underutilization of the cultural centers by some members of the minority community served as a precursor to the neoconservative responses by majority (and some minority) group members to the companion issues of the 1980s—African American studies, women's studies, curriculum diversity, affirmative action, and, of course, minority cultural centers.

What follows is an examination of the educational soundness and positive social value of ethnic minority cultural centers on predominantly White college campuses. That exposition is preceded by examination of the concept and purpose of minority cultural centers, the existing social climate, and the value of such centers to the ethnic campus community. Finally, a model for minority cultural centers that considers political, fiscal, and educational realities as well as safeguards for the viability of such a center is presented.

THE ETHNIC MINORITY CULTURAL CENTER DEFINED

Ethnic minorities, as used in this paper, refers to those groups who have identifiable racial and cultural ties to the four major classifications—African Americans, Hispanic Americans, Native Americans, and Asian Americans. Though broad in nature and encompassing a number of subcategories, these classifications, consistent with federal guidelines, provide the general framework for most universities' attempts to support underrepresented populations. Some campuses have established a minority affairs office, sometimes without appropriately trained staff. This is generally an administrative office that may have responsibility for recruitment, retention, and intervention on behalf of ethnic minority students. A minority affairs office is often viewed as a mediation unit working to make the mechanics of the institution legible to the minority student so that those students might gain maximum benefit from the collegiate experience. This office and its staff also work to interpret to and intercede with the central administration on behalf of minority students in an effort to ensure that decisions and policy making incorporates a pluralistic viewpoint. This simultaneous mission of working between and across two or more somewhat overlapping publics has no precise parallel in other student affairs units.

As distinct from a minority affairs office, an ethnic cultural center should have as its primary mission the presentation and preservation of the cultural manifestations of a specific group. On a college campus, this mission assumes a decidedly educational focus. A cultural center should be regarded as complementary to such areas as student or faculty recruitment, retention, financial aid, and scholarships. The substance of a cultural center should be closely focused on the specific representation of cultural groups in a broad and extensive fashion.

Culture can and does have a variety of meanings. Julius Waiguchu (1971) has defined culture as "the totality of all the attributes which make up a way of life of a people in a given period of history" (p. 66). This "way of life" for most Native Americans, Hispanic Americans, and African Americans differs from that of their European American counterparts. Cultural centers, in part, facilitate recognition and acceptance of this fact. And although there may be variations within the subgroups of European Americans in areas like dialect and food, there is considerable agreement in such areas as art, dance, standard language, social arrangements, and politics.

An ethnic minority cultural center on a predominantly White campus should be a clear manifestation of the presence and the validity of a cultural group and a representation of the academy's acceptance of that group as an important and viable contributor to the community of teachers and learners.

RATIONALIZING THE CULTURAL CENTER

One Third of a Nation (ACE & ECS, 1988) clearly spelled out the challenges, the threats, and the opportunities that lie before institutions of higher education. The incisive report detailed the "lost ground" suffered by racial and ethnic minorities in higher education. It stated that in the last 10 years, "...when the pool of minority high school graduates was becoming bigger and better than ever, minority college attendance rates initially fell and have remained disproportionately low" (p. 11). The report continued:

> *If we allow these disparities to continue, the United States inevitably will suffer a compromised quality of life and a lower standard of living. Social conflict will intensify. Our ability to compete in world markets will decline, our domestic economy will falter, our national security will be endangered. In brief, we will find ourselves unable to fulfill the promise of the American dream. (p. vii)*

In suggesting strategies for progress, the report first challenged America's institutions of higher education to renew and strengthen their efforts to increase minority recruitment, retention, and graduation and to make a commitment to "create an academic atmosphere that nourishes minority students and encourages them to succeed and create a campus culture that values the diversity minorities bring to institutional life" (p. 22).

Recently, as director of a university cultural center, the author accepted a challenge to debate the rationale for an African American cultural center. The challenger charged that such a facility was discriminatory because no German American or French American cultural centers exist and those cultural heritages were as rich and valuable as the African. The exchange that followed was an example of perceptual differences or "trained incapacity" (Kinget, 1975). It was explained that most people have been trained, educated, and socialized to see things in only one way, but that as people learn to see things in a different way they can open up new worlds of possibilities. Actually, the differing perceptions were reconciled in the agreement that the German American cultural center on campus was called the German Language Department and that it had far greater staff, resources, facilities, and support than did any minority cultural center. Additionally, it was agreed that the department was part of a nationwide network of German American departments that often acted collectively to promote, protect, preserve, and present German culture.

One view of the academy might be that most are centers of European American culture. From Amherst to Yale, the American university has exalted and preserved European culture. A study of 20 predominantly White colleges and universities (Young & Green, 1989) revealed the imbalance for the European tradition in literature, history, art, and languages. For example, the University of Massachusetts at Amherst offers 184 courses in European and American literature and one each in African and African American literature. Harvard offers 152 courses in European and American history, 5 in African American history, and 8 in African history. At Pennsylvania State University, 58 different courses are listed in art history, but all except 5 are on European art. Only "Arts of Africa, Oceania, and Indian America" incorporates Africa.

Pennsylvania State University, which offers the standard language courses in French, German, Portuguese, and Spanish, also offers Arabic, Chinese, Greek, Hebrew, Japanese, Latin, Serbo-Croatian, Slavic Polish, and Russian. But there is only one African language course, in Swahili, which is offered as a self-instruction course. At the University of Michigan, 229 courses are offered in European languages and a number in Asian languages, but none in African languages.

This brief survey demonstrates that major universities' course offerings, particularly in the humanities, are Eurocentric in focus—a perspective that poorly serves the educational needs of minority *and* majority students in a changing and culturally diverse society.

In a dualistic thought process, for someone to gain, someone must lose. This thinking has been the basis for much of the negative reaction to affirmative action and curriculum restructuring. However, the majority do not lose when minority groups are allowed to be full participants in all aspects of society. The majority do not lose when ethnic minority cultures are represented within the academy. The majority do not lose when there is opportunity for understanding and greater familiarity with the cultural contributions to civilization of minority groups. In actuality, through the processes of exchange, adoption, and synthesis, all are allowed to gain.

In the register of failed initiatives, there is ample evidence that recruitment of minority students without undertaking alterations of social climate is an effort in futility. Some administrators, faculty, and alumni have used this experience as an argument for discontinuing recruitment programs for minorities. The underlying assumption is that students, new to this environment, must either assimilate, leave, or stay and face isolation and alienation. All campuses employ a variety of social support systems for the benefit of students, and on predominantly White campuses those systems have a decidedly Eurocentric focus. There is university support for the "traditional" glee club but rarely for a gospel choir. Bridge lessons and tournaments are organized, but seldom are games more traditional to the minority communities accommodated. Campus concert committees define popular music by the standards of Music Television (MTV) and ignore the music popularized by the Black Entertainment Television Network (BET). Even those ethnic minority students who are willing and able to forego familiar cultural support system find the new trappings and rituals to be frustrating. Most are unwilling to make that sacrifice:

> ...many Blacks have difficultly adjusting to a White oriented campus and drop out of school. They feel like Ralph Ellison's "Invisible Man." Everyone and everything is oriented in another direction. Minority students are left out. The outcome for a minority student on such a campus is negative. (DiCesare, Sedlacek, & Brooks, 1972, p. 319)

A properly functioning and effective ethnic minority cultural center can provide the dual service of intervening for minority students and of introducing cultural pluralism to majority students. These processes ideally should be part of the function of every agency of the university, but the reality at this time is that those roles are assigned to a minority cultural center.

History and Reality

The ethnic minority student entering a predominantly White collegiate environment walks into a figurative "wonderland" where new rules, new norms, and new expectations apply. Recent reports have discussed the decline in the enrollment of some ethnic minorities in higher education. It is not unusual to find minority student enrollments of under 5% even though the United States is quickly approaching a day when ethnic minorities will constitute 33% of its population. The environment on campus is influenced by an overwhelmingly White student body, faculty, administration, and curriculum. In this circumstance, the ethnic minority student must struggle to carve out a relevant environment or submerge his or her cultural heritage while attempting assimilation.

The ethnic minority cultural center provides an outlet for healthy expression and representation of the identity of members of a specific group. Some still will question the rationale for units or entities on campus that are believed to be "special interest," separatist, or discriminatory. Some people will describe these centers as unnecessary or even subversive to the academy's mission. These, of course, are people who may mainly view instilling conformity to the dominant vision as a major mission of the academy. The creation of special-interest areas or even whole universities for special-interest groups is not new. In this country, higher education was originally the province of a special-interest minority group—that consisted of the sons of wealthy landowners. Religiously distinctive schools, often termed "parochial" or "Hebrew," also serve a special interest. Their role is to preserve, protect, and promote a particular culture while preparing group members for professional and economic assimilation into the mainstream. At the center of this educational process is a reinforcement of values, ideology, and beliefs that facilitates acculturation. In a similar mode, historically Black colleges, the offspring of a society that institutionalized separation by race, have served as a primary source of African American acculturation. Founded almost exclusively out of political expedience, the historically Black colleges also served as a barrier between African Americans and the pervasive and debilitating discrimination rooted in code and custom in American society.

The historically Black colleges contributed to the creation of a relevant environment for African American students and were among the few formal institutions (the African American church being another) to stress and nurture pride, identity, self-respect, and reverence for African American culture.

All evidence seems to support the acceptance of the cultures of ethnic minority students within the academy as we accept the presence of ethnic minority students. That acceptance would necessitate some formal structures whose mission and purpose is to protect, collect, promote, and present manifestations of that culture in an educationally relevant and responsible fashion. Such a pronouncement is consistent with most existing institutional mission statements. The available and rational vehicle for achieving that end is the ethnic minority cultural center.

Relevance and Value

Educators recognize the centrality of the in-class experience to the learning process. They also have come to recognize and accept the value and relevance to the learning process of out-of-class components. Indeed the cocurriculum administered by student affairs personnel includes imparting understanding, appreciation, values, leadership skills, cooperative interactions, management and organization, responsibility, and interpersonal skills. The educational role of student affairs personnel does not compete with the central role of the academy. Indeed, this educational role complements the academic. In a world and a society rapidly changing in composition, it is urgent that all educators be cognizant of the concepts and constructs of pluralism and be willing to incorporate those concepts into the learning/teaching process. Stepping into this brave new world will not be without problems. The nay-sayers and voices of reaction will petition, saying "too much," "too fast," "unnecessary." Many conservative opinion makers already have decried academic and social alteration as an attack on the foundation of the academy.

Still, there is the important concept of educational justice, which presupposes the existence of a social order that conforms to certain principles of fairness, goodness, and virtue. Educational justice presumes that society will maximize opportunities for the largest number of people to realize their fullest potential, thereby maximizing the benefit to society. A fundamental principle of American law is that whenever there is a wrong or injury, there should be a remedy. A wrong or injury presumes the violation of some right or claim.

Thus, when the government created the G.I. Bill, which provided access and means for veterans to attend universities and earn degrees, it was assumed that because veterans had made sacrifices during their service they merited some compensation to help them compete with their counterparts who had not served. Providing such an advantage was seen as a way to ensure and promote educational justice. In addition, a point system was devised to give veterans a compensatory advantage among employment applications.

Providing such advantages assumes the existence of political and moral foundations for acting affirmatively to correct or remedy a past wrong or injustice. These actions make clear that groups and classifications of people have a right to seek relief from wrongs that may affect them.

In addition to being educationally sound and sensible additions to the campus support system, ethnic minority cultural centers contribute to the establishment of educational justice within the academy. Educational justice transmitted through minority cultural centers not only remedies the wrongs done historically to members of ethnic minority groups but also remedies wrongs done to members of the majority, whose lives and learnings have been restricted to a Eurocentric prism. These centers provide those who utilize them with the necessary knowledge, values, skills, and attitudes to live and prosper in a multicultural, multiracial world. These centers neither displace nor replace the established order; rather they seek to occupy their rightful role in the academy—a role that complements the learning process.

The extent of the task at hand is revealed in the answers to an Afro-American Cultural Center Survey of major universities in the eastern, midwestern, and southern states (Young & Krohn, 1989). Of the 176 colleges and universities that received the survey, 48% returned the completed instrument. Only 38% of those responding reported the existence of a center on campus, but 44% of those without a center indicated that the desire for such a center had been expressed by students (58%), staff (36%), and faculty (32%). The ability and the willingness of the academy to address these expressions may be, in the long run, a testament to its willingness to create the learning environment necessary for tomorrow.

ESTABLISHING THE ETHNIC MINORITY CULTURAL CENTER

The first ethnic minority cultural centers to appear on predominantly White campuses were established in the mid-1960s in response to the alienation and isolation expressed by the first wave of racially conscious and secure African American students. In many instances, those centers had few philosophical underpinnings and were viewed by many with suspicion, if not hostility. The isolation, anger, depression, and apathy expressed by African American students on campuses has been documented extensively by several researchers (cf. Epps, 1972; Fleming, 1984; Sedlacek & Brooks, 1986).

The correlation of psychological environment to retention rate has also been documented by Fleming (1984), who reported that African American students in predominantly White institutions showed evidence of intellectual stagnation and frustrated achievement in the senior year.

African American students perceive a personal indictment in the Eurocentric curriculum and extracurricular activities and in the overwhelmingly White population and environment in which they are psychologically and physically isolated. For these students, the cultural center need have no broader philosophy than to serve as a refuge, a retreat, and a respite from the perceived and experienced hostility to their presence on campus.

Over time and with careful nurturing by students, faculty, and staff, the general university community has been encouraged to see the ethnic minority cultural center as having educational value and a place in the structure of student activities, services, and programs on campus. Although some universities established centers without sound theoretical underpinnings, others saw the establishment of such centers as part of their commitment to educating all students and implementing educational justice.

Structure and Location

Ideally, the model cultural center should be a free-standing facility located within reasonable proximity to the center of campus and thus accessible to the entire community. The location and the quality of the facility should provide both latent and manifest messages of commitment. Size will be a local variable, but the facility should have adequate space for administrative offices, meeting rooms, a gallery or display area, a library or resource space, audio-visual facilities, student organization space, an auditorium, a kitchen, lavatories, and storage space.

The idea of a self-contained, self-sufficient center should be viewed as empowering for minority students. Some students may view this potential for isolation as an opportunity to wrap themselves in a kind of protective cultural cocoon.

Although this kind of retreat may have some momentary salutary effect on student attitudes and emotions, educators are aware that this is not the purpose or intent of the center. Smith, in his 1980 report entitled "Admission and Retention Problems of Black Students at Seven Predominantly White Universities," stated:

> Universities should encourage not discourage Black student aware-
> ness of their heritage in all of its positive aspects. Black students need
> their own organizations and cultural activities as important means to
> deal with hostile environments and ensure the development of healthy
> attitudes toward themselves and other Black people. (p. 17)

The location of the center in the administrative structure of the university will also be a local variable. If the center is viewed primarily as a program-ming unit then it will probably be located in student affairs. Others may adopt the Schomburg model and be a part of university libraries. Whatever the location, the center will require a full-time director with adequate support staff and equipment. Where it is feasible, students should be employed in the center.

Mission

The specific programs and activities of the ethnic minority cultural center might include representative visual exhibits, educational programs, cultural celebrations, social interaction events, relevant film and video tape screen-ings, lectures and discussions, and opportunities for study. The programs and activities presented will be impacted upon by available staff, budget, and other resources. The cultural center can be a crossroad where a spectrum of cultures meet to share views, customs, ideas, and values.

Ethnic minority cultural centers should not only maintain their service mission but also function with an education mission. These emphases were advocated by the first group of African American cultural center directors, who were shaped by events of the 1960s and 1970s and who were well versed in the literature of Third World groups. These professionals, often working in isolation, saw the centers as a natural community extension of the intellec-tual thrust of ethnic studies and as a support for these studies. The centers of the future will have to do more, although instilling pride, forging identity and assisting with preparation will still be important parts of each center's service mission. The centers will have to fill the huge gaps in teaching and tolerance that have been neglected in other curricula. They will be front-line agents in the battle against bigotry in society.

The leaders of these ethnic minority cultural centers and other student affairs professionals have seen the need to help young people on the campuses develop a different, less self-indulgent, more caring ethic. Through the presentation of alternative views of the world, ethnic minority cultural centers provide the opportunity for the psychological liberation of all students from archaic and dysfunctional forms of thought and behavior. Ethnic minority students often complain of suffering from a form of cultural starvation on predominantly White campuses. A major function of the ethnic minority cultural center is to supplement the campus diet of cultural fare.

The Bolinga Black Cultural Center at Wright State University affirms in its mission statement that:

> It is not our responsibility only to promote an understanding of who we are and where we are going, but more importantly to equip Black children with the knowledge and wisdom necessary for them to continue on from that foundation and to acquire critical skills which will help to assure the survival of Black people in America. (pamphlet n.d.)

The Black Cultural Center at Purdue University states its mission as follows: "Our purpose here is to destroy myths for both Black and White people and to acquaint all people with the heritage of Black America" (pamphlet n.d.).

Colgate University's Cultural Center has the broad mission of "...raising cultural awareness in all students about people of color in the United States and abroad" (pamphlet n.d.). According to Elleni Tedla (personal communication, April 1990), the Coalition for a Better World Program at Colgate builds involvement in the center by bringing in students from across the campus to discuss such broad issues as peace, campus or societal racism, the environment, poverty, and homophobia as they relate to people of color.

Dignity, pride, integrity, intellect, respect, and responsibility are the hallmarks of ethnic minority cultural centers. Respect is such an important aspect of these cultural centers that students and other leaders would choose to name many centers after their cultural heroes and heroines. Martin Luther King, Jr., Paul Robeson, Black Elk, Cesar Chavez, Gwendolyn Brooks, and Malcolm X each have cultural centers dedicated in their honor. This process is logical and rational because it provides the needed recognition of minority group heroes and heroines for the total population in an intellectual learning environment. Respect and understanding begins with recognition of the humanity of others.

CONCLUSION

There can be little doubt that there will be increased pressure on predominantly White college campuses to institute or upgrade ethnic minority cultural centers and to alter the living/learning environment to accommodate those who were formerly excluded. In developing minority cultural centers, directors and students will be required to think introspectively to determine the direction the center may take. Two models derived from the continent of Africa are often considered. Both models may be functional, but one is preferable to the other in accomplishing the educational mission of the center and the university.

In the first model, the ethnic minority cultural center is a safe haven for ethnic students who, feeling alone, isolated, and under attack, adopt the *laager* or siege mentality of the Afrikaners of South Africa. If the hostiles—the others, the aliens—are allowed in, they will take everything. The ethnic students must huddle together to ward off any intruders and protect the perimeter. In the safe haven model, every effort is made to preserve the self-perceived purity of the culture and to resist at all costs any alteration of the status quo.

In the second model, the ethnic minority cultural center is an oasis, and all are welcome to refresh themselves in its invigorating waters. In this model, all who come and partake not only leave things of value behind but also take away treasures to share with others. Because the cultural center has so much to offer, its facilities are shared willingly with everyone and are the property of all who seek them out. In the oasis model, which can be employed with confidence in the power it embodies, the ethnic minority cultural center is viewed as a place of relief from the surrounding sameness, as a place where cultures meet, exchange, interact, and then emerge renewed, refreshed, and made stronger by the sharing.

Ethnic minority cultural centers on predominantly White campuses can help minority students to discover who they were, who they are, and who they should become while concurrently addressing the institution's stated missions. These centers offer a pathway for the creation of a truly democratic and educationally just academy and contribute to the establishment of a relevant environment and a tolerant society. These centers will promote rather than impede the process of discovery—discovery of others as well as discovery of self. Educators focused on the future will see the value and soundness of such centers and will serve as major proponents.

REFERENCES

American Council on Education & Education Commission of the States. (1988). *One-third of a nation: A report of the Commission on Minority Participation in Education and American Life.* Washington, DC: Authors.

DiCesare, A., Sedlacek, W. E., & Brooks, G. C., Jr. (1972). Nonintellectual correlates of Black student attrition. *Journal of College Student Personnel 13*, 319-324.

Epps, E. G. (1972). *Black students in White schools*. Worthington, OH: C.A. Jones.

Feagin, J. (1989, May). *The future of Blacks in america: Race and class in American cities.* Lecture at Cleveland State University.

Fleming, J. (1984). *Blacks in college*. San Francisco: Jossey-Bass.

Kinget, G. M. (1975). *On being human: A systematic view*. New York: Harcourt, Brace, Jovanovich.

Sedlacek, W. E., & Brooks, G. C. (1976). *Racism in American education: A model for change.* Chicago: Nelson-Hall.

Smith, D. (1980). *Admission and retention problems of Black students at seven predominantly White universities*. Washington, DC: National Advisory Committee on Black Higher Education and Black Colleges and Universities.

Waiguchu, J. (1971). Black heritage of genetics, environments, and continuity. In R. Goldstein (Ed.), *Black life and culture in the United States* (pp. 64-84). New York: Thomas Crowell.

Young, L., & Green, K. (1989). [A survey of diversity in the fine arts and liberal arts courses at 20 major universities]. Unpublished raw data.

Young, L., & Krohn, J. (1989). [A survey of Afro-American cultural centers]. Unpublished raw data.

Chapter 4

Organizational and Administrative Implications for Serving College Students with Disabilities*

James S. Fairweather and Judith J. Albert

Before the 1970s, disabled youth historically had limited access to higher education. Many of these youth were denied admission to colleges and universities because of their disabilities (Angel, 1969; Fonosch, 1980). Others gained admission only after intervention by an influential individual, such as a physician (Stone, 1983). Once enrolled, disabled students found few accommodations and often were confronted by architectural barriers and by programs inconsistent with student needs (Angel, 1969).

Section 504 of the Rehabilitation Act (Section 504) of 1973 and the Education for All Handicapped Children Act (PL 94-142) of 1975 provided legal and financial means to increase access to postsecondary education for disabled youth. Section 504 prohibited discrimination in college admissions on the basis of disability and required colleges and universities to make facilities accessible to all individuals. PL 94-142 focused on programmed interventions during elementary and secondary schooling to better prepare disabled students for postsecondary education. As a consequence, the number of special education students graduating from high school has increased dramatically in the past decade (Office of Special Education and Rehabilitative Services, 1988). The percentage of special education students that attend 2- or 4-year colleges also has increased since 1978 (Astin, Hemond, & Richardson,

*Most of these data appeared in the *Journal of College Student Development, 31*(5), September 1990.

1982; Hippolitus, 1986; Kirchner & Simon, 1984a; McBee, 1982). Disabled youth, however, still lag well behind their nonhandicapped counterparts in access to postsecondary education (15.1% versus 56.0%) (Fairweather & Shaver, 1990).

Understanding disabled students and their experiences contributes to our understanding of cultural pluralism, particularly in expanding educational opportunities to all students because the difficulties experienced by disabled students in the transition from high school to college and in remaining in college until completion of the degree are similar to those of other underrepresented groups. In particular, the "middle class" model, which assumes that attaining a high school diploma leads naturally to admission to college and prepares the student for completion of the degree, does not hold true for this population. Instead, the "hand-off" from the high school to college is problematic with a much lower than expected percentage of disabled students making it into postsecondary education (Edgar, Horton, & Maddox, 1984). Further, the difficulties faced by the few disabled students who make it into college in obtaining needed services often forces them to exit early (Fairweather, in press). These distressing patterns should sound familiar to practitioners concerned with the recruitment and retention of other underrepresented groups.

Moreover, the composition of the disabled student population is disproportionately low income and minority (Fairweather & Shaver, 1990). Attempts to redress the difficulties faced by disabled students might coincide with efforts to assist other disadvantaged groups.

Once a disabled student makes it to campus, the campus administrator must confront the following question: What must I do to identify and ensure delivery of necessary services? Although some evidence suggests that the number of programs available to assist disabled students has grown (Jarrow, 1987; Thomas, 1986), little evidence exists about the most effective ways to organize and deliver services in postsecondary educational institutions. Effective service delivery in postsecondary institutions is further complicated by program administrators depending on students to self-identify needs and to initiate requests for services (Fairweather & Shaver, 1990; Heliotis & Edgar, 1980). Lacking crucial information about specific student needs and about alternative means of delivering services to disabled students, program administrators have relied primarily on extensions of traditional student services, attempting to fit client needs into existing programs rather than offering client-specific services.

The purpose of this chapter is to provide an answer to the question of how to organize the delivery of services to best meet the needs of disabled students. These recommendations have applicability to any administrator interested in increasing the retention of underrepresented groups. Recommendations are based on a case study of the delivery of services to disabled students at a major research university identified by the Higher Education and the Handicapped Resource Center (HEATH) as exemplary. Recognition by HEATH is based on the extent of services and the existence of a formal structure to deliver them. Particular attention was paid to the constellation of programs and services made available to disabled students, the needs of students, and the match among student needs, services, and the method of delivery.

THE CASE STUDY

The Setting

The major research university under study is a public doctoral-degree granting, northeastern institution with an enrollment above 25,000. Services to disabled students are provided primarily through the Office of Disability Services (ODS), the Office of Vocational Rehabilitation (OVR), and a variety of separate, special university-sponsored programs.

Office of Disability Services

In 1975, the university president's Commission on the Physically Handicapped Student recommended formalizing services for disabled students. Before this declaration, some services for these students were available but not coordinated at a central level. After a period of debate about the structure and substance of services, in 1981 the Office of Disability Services was established, and a full-time coordinator was appointed to serve students with all types of disabilities. Supported by the Vice Provost Fund for Disabled Students and Equipment, ODS provides to virtually all disabled students general academic assistance including help with registration, classroom changes, testing accommodations, notetakers, interpreters, tape recorders and other assistive devices, laboratory assistance, orientation, referrals, and follow-up. ODS also assists disabled students in obtaining dormitory modifications, special parking permits, transportation, medical consultations, academic counseling, library assistance, and special financial aid considerations. Career-vocational and other personal services are provided through regular university channels, such as the health center and Career Development and Placement Services.

The ODS coordinator is the only full-time disability service administrator on campus. In 1988, the coordinator was assisted by a graduate student and by 83 students working part time.

All entering freshmen receive information about ODS during registration. Referrals to ODS also are made through the Freshman Intake Counseling and Advisement Program, the Office of Vocational Rehabilitation, the State Bureau for Blind and Visual Services (BBVS), and professors, advisers, and resident assistants.

Office of Vocational Rehabilitation

Although located on campus, the Office of Vocational Rehabilitation is officially under the auspices of a supervising counselor from the District Vocational Rehabilitation Office located 50 miles away. Unlike the more formal development of ODS, the placement of OVR on campus resulted from interpersonal agreements between faculty in the Department of Rehabilitation Counseling and officials in the State Vocational Rehabilitation Agency. In the initial agreement, a faculty member traveled to the state office to provide counseling services in the local region. Eventually, the services were moved to the university to ease administration and to gain access to additional faculty. The evolution of the OVR-university relationship and the resulting placement of OVR on campus appear to be unique to this university.

Despite its location on campus, however, OVR remains an independent organization. Eligibility for services is determined prior to and separate from the university admissions process on the basis of state criteria. Students with physical or sensory handicaps are the principal clients of OVR. Once a student who is eligible for OVR assistance has been admitted to the university, an OVR counselor and the student work together to prepare an individualized education plan (IEP) prior to the start of classes. Written IEPs clarify career goals and the academic programs necessary to reach them. Financial assistance and eligibility are determined based on the recommendation in the IEP. IEPs are reviewed and updated annually.

Although the OVR counselor is legally responsible for ensuring the delivery of services to eligible students, the counselor does not have a formal position in the university and can only direct the student to ODS and other service providers as appropriate. The counselor can intervene in campus financial matters when conflicts between OVR and the university arise.

The OVR office at the university is staffed by the supervising counselor 30 hours per week. The counselor is assisted by a secretary from the regional office, who travels to the university 1 day per week.

Other Services

Several other services for disabled students are provided through discrete offices. Established in 1963, *adapted physical education* services assist students who could not otherwise participate in physical education. The *library* provides a staff member to assist visually impaired students. Eligibility for services is determined by two external agencies, Recordings for the Blind and the Regional Library for the Blind and Visually Handicapped. The *computer laboratory* provides computer equipment to disabled students, primarily those with visual disabilities. Originated in response to local requests from parents and formalized after receipt of a federal grant in 1983, the *learning disabilities program* provides tutorial assistance, including a diagnosis of the disability, a written IEP, and assistance with social skills development. The program serves 80 students and employs 30 students who serve as clinicians in the program. Finally, the *physical plant* makes buildings accessible to disabled students, although special adaptations for the handicapped must compete with other requests for capital expenditures.

Summary

The programs for disabled students originated through various channels. Several were initiated by individual faculty. On the other hand, the ODS was initiated by the central administration. External agencies, such as OVR and the Regional Library for the Blind and Visually Handicapped play crucial roles. The interrelationships of these various organizational components and their effectiveness are examined below.

The Investigation

This study combined case study interviews with both administrative personnel and disabled students with a survey questionnaire mailed to disabled students to examine the "complex network of cultural, social, institutional, and psychological variables" (Parlett & Hamilton, 1976, p. 145) integral to the delivery of services to disabled students at the university. Of the population of 444 served by ODS and/or OVR during the fall semester, 1988, 24 students (13 served by ODS and 11 served by OVR) encompassing each of the 11 categories of disability defined by the U. S. Department of Education (Office of Special Education and Rehabilitative Services, 1988) were purposely selected for interviews. The remaining 420 students were sent mailed questionnaires. Of these, 228 completed and returned the questionnaire (response rate of 54.3%).

In addition, to gather information about service provision, personal interviews were conducted with the 24 university administrators directly or indirectly involved in providing services to disabled students.

Instrumentation and Data Collection

Interviews with administrators focused on (a) the origin of existing services (Mangrum & Strichart, 1983), (b) the individual's role or position in the office under study (McBee & Cox, 1974), (c) how students obtained services from the office under study (Edgar, et al., 1984; Kirchner & Simon, 1984b; McLoughlin, 1982), (d) the manner and extent of service provision (Bevilacqua & Osterlink, 1979; McBee & Cox, 1974; Minner & Prater, 1984), (e) legislative influences on service provision (Kirchner & Simon, 1984b; McBee, 1982), (f) resource allocations to disability-related services and programs (Stilwell & Schulker, 1973), (g) obstacles to effective service provision (Fonosch, 1980; Penn & Dudley, 1980; Stone, 1983), (h) the needs of disabled students (Brolin & Elliot, 1984; Fonosch, 1980), (i) coordination and cooperation with other offices and/or agencies (Brolin & Elliot, 1984; Cavanagh, 1983; Edgar et al., 1984; King, 1982; Smith-Davis, 1983), (j) the role of the office as advocate (Brolin & Elliott, 1984), (k) personal perception of disabled students and service philosophy (Jacques, 1962; Penn & Dudley, 1980), and (l) the assessment of program effectiveness (Edgar et al., 1984).

Interviews with and the survey of students gathered information about (a) age, sex, and disability (or disabilities) (Hartman & Redden, 1985; Fairweather & Shaver, 1990; Mangrum & Strichart, 1983); (b) academic major, length of time at the university, and current student status (Fairweather & Shaver, 1990; Fasteau, 1979; Hartman & Redden, 1985; Mangrum & Strichart, 1985); (c) the reason(s) for enrolling at the university (Penn & Dudley, 1980); (d) preenrollment and current disability-related needs (Fasteau, 1979; Mangrum & Strichart, 1985); (e) unmet needs (Mangrum & Strichart, 1985); (f) services received (Fairweather, 1986; Kirchner & Simon, 1984b); (g) the location of services obtained (Fairweather, Stearns, & Wagner, 1989); (h) the manner of service delivery (Bryan & Becker, 1980; McBee & Cox, 1974); and (i) the manner in which contact was made with service providers and how services were obtained (Brolin & Elliott, 1984; Mithaug, Horiuchi, & Fanning, 1985).

Service Provider Groups

To examine the impact of programs and services, students were classified into four groups based on primary service provider: (a) receiving services only from ODS or ODS-related units (ODS group, 34.0%), (b) receiving services only from OVR or OVR-related organizations (OVR group, 47.1%), (c) receiving services from both ODS and OVR (ODS-OVR group, 13.6%), and (d) receiving services only from a program or organization other than ODS and OVR (other service provider group, 5.3%).

For the most part, the ODS group consisted of students with *latent educational disabilities* (conditions that are not readily apparent but can adversely affect academic performance, such as learning disabilities). The OVR group consisted primarily of students with *manifest disabilities* (conditions that are long term and visible, such as wheelchair-bound or blind) or with *latent physical disabilities* (newly diagnosed conditions that result in intermittent, visible difficulties, such as mobility-impaired without a wheelchair). The ODS-OVR group and the other service provider group contained a mixture of students with these distinct types of disabilities.

Organization and Delivery of Services

Structure of Service Delivery

The functions of disability-related services at the university vary by the location of the program or service within the institutional service delivery structure (see Figure 1). Programs housed within academic units (e.g., speech and hearing clinic) reflect the loosely coupled, collegial atmosphere prevalent in that system. These services were developed and directed by experts who designed programs to meet individual student needs. Serving only a small portion of the population of disabled students, services often are available on a one-to-one basis in these programs.

Programs operating within the administrative structure are tightly coupled, bureaucratic entities. The ODS, for example, establishes student eligibility, provides services, makes referrals, and consults with other units about disability-related issues. Other units operating within the administrative branch of the university require ODS approval before granting requests for assistance. These service channels are strictly defined and observed.

Other service providers operating within the administrative hierarchy at levels equal to or above ODS are not linked to that office. The health center and library, for example, establish their own standards for eligibility and provide assistance to disabled students independent of ODS. To enable students to move freely among these service providers, these independent operations are informally linked with ODS for consultation and referral.

Functional differences among programs contribute to service fragmentation, resulting in independent rather than interdependent operations. Programs located within the administrative hierarchy (e.g., ODS, health center) provide general services with a wide range of activities; Corson (1975) calls these "generalist suborganizations" (pp. 78-81). In contrast, programs and services with origins in academic departments (e.g., learning disabilities program) provide a more narrow range of services for a more specific clientele.

Outside agencies, even when located on campus, act as external influences, affecting the service milieu indirectly. As an example, the OVR, situated on campus but governed independently, functions primarily as a referral agent for eligible students. OVR provides direct financial assistance, but other organizational units deliver the services supported by OVR funds.

Availability of Services

Eligibility must be established through formal channels in order for disabled students to obtain special services. For some services, such as the learning disabilities program, eligibility must be kept current through ongoing diagnostic assessments. Other units, such as the library, require students to submit formal applications for services that must be approved by off-campus organizations before services are rendered.

ODS services are typically available on request by disabled students who can demonstrate need. Although the number of students served by ODS

Figure 1
Organizational Diagram of Disability-Related Services

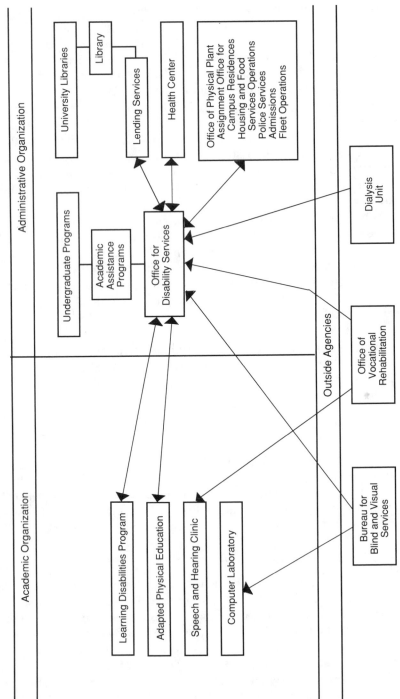

doubled between 1987 and 1988, the number of staff and the resources available have remained constant. This has resulted in students using informal means to obtain assistance, such as contacts with other students.

With respect to type of disability, students with manifest and latent-physical disabilities were the most satisfied with the availability and adequacy of services. In contrast, students with latent-educational disabilities found services more difficult to obtain. In particular, students with learning disabilities felt that few service providers understood their condition and the services required to assist them in making academic progress. Similarly, administrators report that students with latent-educational disabilities were the most difficult to assist. Inadequate diagnostic assessments and educational records, dependence on self-referral, hesitancy by the student in seeking assistance, and the array of services needed on a continuing basis by these students made service delivery difficult.

Table 1

Most Frequent Services Currently Received by Students With Disabilities

Service Provider Group	Service	% Receiving Service
Receiving services only from ODS (N=70)	Financial assistance	30.0
	Testing accommodations	27.1
Parking	25.7	
Tutors	18.6	
Housing	15.7	
Tape recorders/other assistive devices	14.3	
Receiving services only from OVR (N=98)	Financial assistance	80.4
	Housing	20.6
Career counseling	10.3	
Receiving services from both ODS and OVR (N=28)	Financial assistance	57.1
	Parking	39.3
Tutors	32.1	
Notetakers	25.0	
Receiving services from another service provider (N=11)	Testing accommodations	54.5
	Financial assistance	36.4
Tutors	27.3	
Contacting professors	27.3	

Student interviews and survey results demonstrated that students with latent-educational disabilities felt inadequately informed about service availability. In contrast, students with manifest or latent-physical disabilities, most of whom were served by OVR, had less difficulty in obtaining assistance. Many of these students had discussed needs and service alternatives before entering the university. OVR, for example, developed an individualized educational program with each eligible student prior to enrollment in college. The IEP provided diagnostic information and recommended services to guide action by the supervising counselor.

Table 2

Principle Method for Students to Obtain Disability-Related Services

Service Provider Group	Service	% Using Source
Receiving services only from ODS (N=70)	Financial assistance	30.0
	Testing accommodations	27.1
	When arrived on campus	48.5
	Help from family	29.4
	Wrote for information	22.1
Receiving services only from OVR (N = 98)	Financial assistance	30.0
	OVR provides all services	50.0
	OVR helped locate services	25.0
	Help from high school counselor	25.0
Receiving services from both ODS and OVR (N=28)	OVR helped locate services	34.0
	Visited beforehand	22.0
	When arrived on campus	22.0
	Suggested by professor/ adviser/counselor	22.0
Receiving services from another service provider (N=11)	Suggested by professor/ adviser/counselor	30.7
	Visited beforehand	23.1
	When arrived on campus	23.1
	Other	23.1

Table 1 shows the survey results concerning the variety of services received by disabled students at the university by service provider group. More than one-half of all disabled students received some level of financial assistance. In addition to financial assistance, students supported by ODS received help with testing accommodations, handicapped parking, tutors, housing assistance, and assistive devices. OVR-supported group students additionally received help with housing and career counseling, and students supported by both ODS and OVR received assistance with handicapped parking, tutors, and notetakers. Students supported by other service providers, students who largely comprised the learning disabled cohort and were supported by the learning disabilities program, received assistance with testing accommodations, tutors, and contacting professors.

The interview and survey results showed that the manner in which students obtained services varied by primary service provider (see Table 2). OVR- and ODS/OVR-assisted students relied principally on OVR alone to locate and obtain needed services. Much of the planning was done before arrival on campus. Students served by ODS typcially waited until arrival at the university before seeking assistance, often relying heavily on parents for additional assistance. Students relying on other service providers were more dependent on a faculty adviser or counselor to obtain services.

Adequacy of the Service Delivery System

Student reactions to the adequacy of service delivery were mixed. Students with latent-physical disabilities were satisfied with the financial assistance obtained from OVR. Similarly, students with multiple or manifest disabilities who typically received services from several sources were pleased with the assistance received. In contrast, students with latent-educational disabilities were not satisfied with the current service system. These students were guided through the system neither by an external advocate such as OVR nor by a plan developed before enrollment.

Regardless of disability category, students found the communication among service providers inadequate. Service providers acted as independent entities rather than as parts of a coordinated system. The best served students were those with an easily identifiable set of needs served by a self-contained, self-sufficient program.

The lack of communication between students and administrators was one example of this disjointed service provision "system." Many administrators were unaware that the adequacy of services varied substantially by type of disability and by service provider. Instead, many officials believed the burden rests with the disabled students or with some ill-defined advocate, who would take greater responsibility in identifying needs and in locating services. Students with latent-educational disabilities disagreed, claiming that the lack of a single location for them to express needs led to inadequate access to services.

Discussion

The service milieu for disabled students at the university is an open system (Lewin & Minton, 1986; Quinn & Cameron, 1983). Consistent with Mink, Schultz, and Mink's (1979) description of an open system, the constellation of disability-related services has distinct organizational components—administrative, academic, and external agency—with different service priorities and styles of operation.

At the university, specialized services for disabled students were originally initiated by service providers motivated by personal and professional interests. Later, legal directives and centralized institutional policy led to more formal arrangements and to extended services. More recently, increased availability of external funds has stimulated even more specialized services, a characteristic of open systems identified by Quinn and Rohrbaugh (1983). However, this unplanned, externally motivated expansion has resulted in a haphazard collection of services that are vulnerable to fluctuations in the availability of external funds. Because these externally funded programs often were initiated by individual faculty or administrators without a commitment from the central administration to fund the programs after cessation of external monies, and because these programs were not conceived as part of an overall university plan for services, many of these newer services were not institutionalized (Terreberry, 1968). Without long-term institutional commitment and integration of services, effective service delivery cannot be achieved; efforts to promote cultural pluralism are more likely to be illusory than real.

The organization of disability-related services is characterized by unclear administrative roles and lines of authority. As one example, communication between ODS and other service providers was inconsistent even though ODS is the primary university administrative unit for disability-related services. Although inconsistent flow of information is common in academic organizations, particularly those following a collegial model (Gratz & Salem, 1981), service delivery can be affected adversely if communication is not improved.

Functional differences among subunits have exacerbated service fragmentation, reinforcing independent rather than interdependent operations. External agencies, such as OVR, on the one hand tend to provide individualized and active assistance, incorporating preenrollment planning and diagnoses to assist students in obtaining relevant services. Internal agencies, on the other hand, have adopted a more passive approach, waiting for the students to identify needs before reacting to them.

Success in obtaining services is a function of entry point into the service provision system. Students entering through department-related programs were the least satisfied, feeling alienated from the variety of services available throughout the university. Students entering through administrative units had better access to a variety of services. Students receiving assistance from external agencies, such as OVR, before enrollment were the most likely to obtain useful services.

Type of disability also affected acquisition of services. Students with manifest and latent-physical disabilities were more likely to receive assistance from external agencies that either provided for all of their needs or assisted them in locating services from agencies on campus. Students with less visible latent-educational disabilities had difficulty in obtaining services.

Recommendations

The extent of services available at the university supports its classification by HEATH as an exemplary academic institution. Students who located services seemed satisfied with them. In less exemplary institutions, the focus of student and administrator comments would be on the lack of services rather than on the delivery of services. This distinction is crucial. Improvement in service delivery can be achieved through better organization and management only if the services are available in one form or another. For most institutions, the lack of services in any form is more crucial than the delivery mechanism (Jarrow, 1987).

Even in the purportedly exemplary environment studied, some approaches to service delivery work better than others. The OVR transition-oriented model seems particularly successful for providing services to disabled students. This model emphasizes an active advocacy role for the service provider. The initial steps, identifying student needs and developing an individualized educational program, are initiated before entry. After enrollment, the service provider actively engages the academic organization in locating needed funds and services, and in matching needs with services. This suggests that services for disabled students can be improved by preenrollment planning, including assessment of needs, and by developing personal educational assistance programs, that is, by an adaptation or an approximation of the OVR model.

Unlike traditional organizational structures in which client satisfaction increases with program specialization (Nowak, 1977), increased specialization and program expansion in disability-related services leads to conflicts within the service system and to poor interorganizational communication. This observation is especially true if growth is not monitored and if the designated coordinating unit for the institution has insufficient authority and resources. Provision of services that fit the needs of students through an easily identifiable central location is more effective than increasing the diversity of programs.

Additionally, too much horizontal expansion decreases the flow of information between students and service providers and among service providers. This lack of communication decreases the ability of students to locate needed services regardless of the human and fiscal resources invested in the service system. Effective midlevel professional managers assisted by sufficient numbers of staff are crucial to effective operation of decentralized programs that combine general and specialized services for disabled students.

Finally, effective service delivery for disabled students is better viewed as part of a transitional process, incorporating both high school and college, rather than as an event taking place only after the student reaches the postsecondary educational institution. Service agencies that identify student needs before enrollment and which pave the way through the system are more effective than traditional college student service models, which attempt to fit existing services to students.

CONCLUSION

Although specific to services for disabled students, many of the lessons of the case study apply to programs targeting any disadvantaged students. Problems such as difficulty in locating needed services, or dropping out before the connection with appropriate services is achieved, confront service directors dealing with many types of students.

The lessons here are listed from the perspective of the senior administrator in charge of student services, or perhaps the senior administrator responsible for academic programs.

The first lesson in enhancing the services for disabled students is to recognize that most of these services have been started by one or two concerned individuals, and that the resulting "network" of services is likely to be disjointed and inefficient. In this context, what is needed to enhance the dependability of communication and to provide reliable access to services is to centralize and standardize services. Such centralizing requires designation of a single organization staff to coordinate all services for disabled students regardless of the funding source or origination of the service.

This central organization must have sufficient professional staff to carry out its mission. Simply designating a unit as "in charge of the problem" without granting sufficient resources will not work. In the case of the study, the designation of an organization as the primary service provider was achieved; but the provision of adequate staff, particularly professional service providers (as distinct from graduate assistants and volunteers), was absent.

The central organization itself need not be a bureaucracy; the provision of services can be dealt with by decentralized units. The coordination of services, however, must lie within a single organization. Thus, a network of services with a single responsible unit might be a better model than one in which all services rest within a single organization. Given the likelihood that services exist throughout the campus in a variety of formats, the centralization of all services for disabled students is probably not possible anyway. Decentralized service provision can also make services more responsive to individual students needs.

The central unit also provides the initial agency for student communication. Making the disabled service agency known to students, and having a single telephone number to call for information or at least for referral, makes it much more likely that students will locate the services they need. As shown in the case study, the problem was often one of accessing available services rather than one of lack of services.

A second lesson in enhancing the services for disabled students is to develop a formal system for receiving student feedback about the adequacy of services relative to needs. Each student requiring special services should receive a formal follow-up, either by personal interview or questionnaire, to monitor the functioning of the service system. In the case study, the lack of personnel and the idiosyncratic nature of the services made such an assessment impossible.

The third and final lesson concerns the nature of services for disabled students who are exiting a secondary school system charged with identifying and meeting their needs but who are now entering a postsecondary system that provides services only on request. If the college or university waits until a disabled student requests services, especially if the request is made by checking an item on a registration form, the likelihood is quite high that the student will drop out before services are ever provided. Active intervention prior to enrollment, such as through the OVR program in the case study, and development of an individualized educational program with required services is much more likely to yield successful results. This plan requires that university services develop outreach programs to secondary schools and, where possible, obtain diagnostic information about services needed by the student. As the case study shows, active assistance in the transition from high school to college is required if disabled students are to enter college successfully and complete an undergraduate degree program.

REFERENCES

Angel, J. L. (1969). *Employment opportunities for the handicapped.* New York: World Trade Academy Press.

Astin, A. W., Hemond, M. K., & Richardson, G. T. (1982). *The American freshman: National norms for fall 1982.* Los Angeles: University of California at Los Angeles, Higher Education Research Institute.

Bevilacqua, T., & Osterlink, F. (1979). Components of a service program for the mainstreaming of hearing-impaired students into regular university programs. *American Annals of the Deaf, 124*(3), 400-402.

Brolin, D. E., & Elliott, T. R. (1984). Meeting the lifelong career development needs of students with handicaps: A community college model. *Career Development of Exceptional Individuals, 7*(1), 12-21.

Bryan, W. A., & Becker, K. M. (1980). Student services for the handicapped student. In H. Sprandel and M. Schmidt (Eds.), *Serving handicapped students* (New Directions for Student Services) (pp. 9-22). San Francisco: Jossey-Bass.

Cavanagh, M., Jr. (1983). Cooperative programming with the schools: A proposal. *Journal of Rehabilitation, 49*(1), 33-36.

Corson, J. E. (1975). *The governance of colleges and universities.* New York: McGraw-Hill.

Edgar, E., Horton, B., and Maddox, M. (1984). Postschool placements: Planning for public school students with developmental disabilities. *The Journal of Vocational Rehabilitation, 26,* 15-18.

Fairweather, J. (1986). *Analysis of a survey of school district practices regarding secondary-level handicapped students and their transition to postsecondary experiences.* University Park: Pennsylvania State University, Center for the Study of Higher Education.

Fairweather, J. (in press). Intervention strategies for postschool transition: Two perspectives. *Journal of Vocational Special Needs Education.*

Fairweather, J. S., & Shaver, D. R. (1990). A troubled future? Participation in postsecondary education by youth with disabilities. *Journal of Higher Education, 61*(3), 332-348.

Fairweather, J., Stearns, M., & Wagner, M. (1989). Resources available in school districts serving secondary special education students: Implications for transition. *Journal of Special Education, 22*(4), 419-432.

Fasteau, S. (1979). Development of a community college program for physically handicapped students. *Rehabilitation Literature, 33*(9), 267-270.

Fonosch, G. G. (1980). Three years later: The impact of Section 504 regulations on higher education. *Rehabilitation Literature, 41*(7), 162-168.

Gratz, R. D., & Salem, P. J. (1981). *Organizational communciation and higher education* (AAHE-ERIC Higher Education Research Report No. 10). Washington, DC: American Association for Higher Education.

Hartman, R. C., & Redden, M. R. (1985). *Measuring student progress in the classroom.* Washington, DC: American Council on Education.

Heliotis, J., & Edgar, E. (1980). Issues in mainstreaming students with cerebral palsy in a community college. *Journal of the Association for the Severely Handicapped, 5*(1), 86-99.

Hippolitus, P. (1986). *College freshmen with disabilities preparing for employment: A statistical profile* (Report No. 181-519/64259). Washington, DC: U.S. Government Printing Office.

Jacques, M. E. (1962). Review of: Guiding the physically handicapped college student. *Rehabilitation Literature, 213*(9), 275-277.

Jarrow, J. J. (1987). Integration of individuals with disabilities in higher education: A review of the literature. *Journal of Postsecondary Education and Disability, 5,* 38-57.

King, W. L. (1982). Student services' response to learning disabled students. In M. R. Schmidt & H. Z. Sprandel (Eds.), *Helping the learning disabled student* (New Directions for Student Services)(pp. 49-58). San Francisco: Jossey-Bass.

Kirchner, C., & Simon, Z. (1984a). Blind and visually handicapped college students—Part I: Estimated numbers. *Journal of Visual Impairment and Blindness, 78*(2), 78-81.

Kirchner, C., & Simon, Z. (1984b). Blind and visually handicapped college students—Part II: Settings and services. *Journal of Visual Impairment and Blindness, 78*(4), 164-168.

Lewin, A. Y., & Minton, J. W. (1986). Determining organizational effectiveness: Another look and an agenda for research. *Management Science, 32*(5), 514-540.

Mangrum, C. T., & Strichart, S. S. (1983). College possibilities for the learning disabled: Part two. *Learning Disabilities, 2*(6), 69-81.

Mangrum, C. T., & Strichart, S. S. (1985). *Services offered by college support programs for learning disabled students.* Washington, DC: National Information Center for Handicapped Children and Youth.

McBee, M. L. (1982). Helping handicapped students succeed in college. *Journal of NAWDAC, 45*(4), 3-8.

McBee, M. L., & Cox, J. L. (1974). Higher education and the physically handicapped. *Journal of the National Association of Student Personnel Administration, 12*(2), 96-99.

McLoughlin, W. P. (1982). Helping the physically handicapped in higher education. *Journal of College Student Personnel, 23*(3), 240-246.

Mink, O. G., Shultz, J. M., & Mink, B. P. (1979). *Developing and managing open organizations*. San Diego: Learning Concepts.

Minner, S., & Prater, G. (1984). College teachers' expectations for learning disabled students. *Academic Therapy, 20*(2), 225-230.

Mithaug, D. E., Horiuchi, C. N., & Fanning, P. N. (1985). A report on the Colorado statewide follow-up survey of special education students. *Exceptional Children, 51*(5), 397-404.

Nowak, S. (1977). *Methodology of social research*. Boston: D. Reidel.

Office of Special Education and Rehabilitative Services. (1988). *Implementation of the Education for All Handicapped Children Act: Tenth annual report to Congress*. Washington, DC: U.S. Department of Education.

Parlett, M., & Hamilton, D. (1976). Evaluation as illumination: A new approach to the study of innovatory programs. In G. V. Glass (Ed.), *Evaluation studies* (pp. 140-157). Beverly Hills, CA: Sage.

Penn, R. J., & Dudley, D. H. (1980). The handicapped student: Problems and perceptions. *Journal of College Student Personnel, 21*(4), 354-357.

Quinn, R. E., & Cameron, K. (1983). Organizational life cycles and shifting criteria of effectiveness: Some preliminary evidence. *Management Science, 29*(1), 33-52.

Quinn, R. E., & Rohrbaugh, J. (1983). A spatial model of effectiveness criteria: Toward a competing values approach to organizational analysis. *Management Science, 29*(3), 363-377.

Smith-Davis, J. (1983). *When handicapped children grow up*. Washington, DC: National Information Center for Handicapped Children and Youth.

Stilwell, W. E., & Schulker, S. (1973). Facilities available to disabled higher education students. *Journal of College Student Personnel, 14*(5), 419-424.

Stone, B. (1983). Students with invisible handicaps. *College Board Review, 127,* 23-27

Terreberry, S. (1968). The evolution of organizational environment. *Administrative Science Quarterly, 12*(4), 590-613.

Thomas, C. H. (1986). *Directory of college facilities and services for the disabled*. Phoenix: Oryx.

CHAPTER 5

THE ROLE OF DEVELOPMENTAL EDUCATION IN PROMOTING PLURALISM

Jeanne L. Higbee

This chapter examines the role of developmental education programs in improving access to higher education for culturally diverse students. The chapter also provides a definition of developmental education as contrasted with remedial and compensatory education and briefly describes course content, program structures, and funding sources. One of the purposes of the chapter is to dispel some of the myths pertaining to programs for underprepared learners in higher education. Factors such as assessment, the development of critical thinking skills, a supportive learning environment, and intrusive counseling and advising are discussed as they relate to success-ful outcomes. Institutions must consider how they train and reward develop-mental educators in order to provide optimum learning experiences. The chapter concludes with a list of characteristics that are likely to contribute to the retention and ultimate graduation of students participating in develop-mental education programs.

Intellectually capable students must not be denied their right to higher education due to inequities that still exist at the elementary and secondary levels. Developmental education programs are designed to facilitate the development of those skills necessary to be competitive academically at the institution in which the student is enrolled. Most developmental education programs do not limit their services to a specific minority population; their function is to provide access for underprepared students from a wide variety of backgrounds, regardless of race or socioeconomic status. The focus is on the prerequisite skills, not demographics. As such, developmental education programs promote cultural pluralism by enhancing access and retention without making assumptions regarding the ethnicity of underprepared learners.

Alexander Astin (1984) suggested that in order to promote student pluralism institutions must explore ways to "meet the special and unique needs" of different copopulations while also "fostering a kind of `peaceful coexistence'" (p. 3). Astin proposed that academically underprepared students are among the cohorts which require special attention:

> *As a matter of fact, I would submit that much of the concern about racial minorities in our student bodies stems from the fact that certain minorities, considered as a group, are less well prepared academically than the typical [W]hite student. These mere* correlations *between race and preparation level have prompted many of us in academia to behave as if all Blacks and Hispanics are underprepared and that all [W]hite students are adequately prepared. Many Blacks and Hispanics are well prepared academically and do not, in fact, want or need any special attention.... (p. 3)*

In other words, *culturally diverse, socioeconomically disadvantaged,* and *underprepared* must not be used as synonymous terms. Furthermore, Astin suggested, "...we should direct our pluralistic programs at *student needs* rather than at demographic attributes" (p. 11). The developmental education model provides an example of a program designed to address the needs of an underprepared cohort of the student body regardless of type of institution.

DEFINITION OF DEVELOPMENTAL EDUCATION

Clowes (1982) provided helpful definitions that distinguish developmental programs from those that are remedial or compensatory. He noted that remedial programs fix academic deficiencies; compensatory programs offset a home environment that is not conducive to educational attainment; developmental education programs are growth oriented and designed to foster achievement of potential. Developmental courses focus on the process of learning as well as the content to be mastered and make fewer assumptions regarding the learner's background and previous academic achievement.

Researchers and practitioners continue to use the terms *remedial* and *developmental* interchangeably. This confusion of terms may provide one of the greatest barriers to institutional acceptance for programs that are conceived and implemented as developmental studies. Furthermore, this confusion between remedial and developmental education places an unnecessary and inappropriate stigma on students participating in developmental programs. The resulting stereotypes serve to segregate developmental education students and to perpetuate the myths surrounding the programs in which they are enrolled. Thus, culturally diverse students, especially on predominantly White campuses, may experience discrimination on two counts: as members of ethnic and racial minority groups, and as participants in a program designed to enhance opportunities for educational equity.

Programs that are developmental in nature must go beyond providing an initial channel for access to the institution; they must provide students with the skills and background knowledge necessary to ensure success in college English, mathematics, and content area courses such as history and the social sciences.

Developmental Courses

Most developmental programs include instruction in English, mathematics, and reading and/or study skills. English courses generally focus on composition, that is, on the same activity basic to freshman English classes. Rules of grammar are reviewed within the context of writing papers. Mathematics courses emphasize problem-solving skills while reviewing algebraic functions. Reading courses assume that the student knows how to read; in these courses the emphasis is on learning how to learn. Students learn to read for underlying meanings, to annotate a text, to build vocabulary in order to enhance comprehension, to analyze and synthesize, and to refine strategies for taking both essay and objective tests. Instructional materials may include novels, short stories, news magazines and other periodicals, and chapters from textbooks in the social, physical, and biological sciences.

Most developmental programs offer courses in English, mathematics, and reading and study strategies, but a few also focus on noncognitive factors that may impede student success. Astin (1984) stated,

> Our analysis of research on programs for poorly prepared students suggests that the most successful programs are those that also deal with the affective side of being a student: poor self-concept, passivity, lack of confidence, fear of failure, lack of interest in subject matter, and so forth. (p. 11)

A number of studies exploring the significance of traditional predictors, such as high school grade point average and standardized test scores, and nontraditional predictors of academic achievement, such as confidence, have indicated differences for African American and White students (Farver, Sedlacek, & Brooks, 1975; Pfeiffer & Sedlacek, 1971; Sowa, Thomson, & Bennett, 1989; Thomas & Stanley, 1969; Tracey & Sedlacek, 1985). Research (Habley, 1981; Trippi & Cheatham, 1989) supports the value of counseling and advising programs in enhancing African American student retention. Developmental education programs that include a counseling or student development component may make the most significant contribution in facilitating cultural pluralism and improving retention rates.

Program Structure

The structure of developmental education programs varies from institution to institution. In some cases the program is a separate entity, housed in its own building, hiring its own faculty and staff. In other programs all developmental education faculty have joint appointments to an academic department or the college of education.

Some programs are offered only in the summer or only for first-term freshmen. At other institutions students remain enrolled in the developmental education program until they successfully exit a sequence of courses in each academic area and are considered prepared for regular coursework in that subject.

Most likely no single model for a developmental education program is the prototype for all institutions. What works best may depend upon what academic assistance services are already available on the campus. There are two overriding and somewhat conflicting concerns that may dictate structure. One is that students participating in the program not be stigmatized or in any way alienated from the general student body; they are not second-class citizenry. To avoid stereotyping of developmental students, institutions may tend to prefer a decentralized model. However, the second overriding concern is ease of accessibility and involvement. A more centralized model encourages communication among students, faculty, advisers, and counselors.

Funding

Funding for developmental education programs varies by institution or by state system of public higher education. Some programs are totally or partially funded by the federal government. Equal Opportunity Program (EOP) funding may limit enrollment to protected populations, for example, to racial and ethnic minorities, first-generation college students, and/or the socioeconomically disadvantaged. New proposals must be submitted for each funding period, and competition for acceptance is intense. Institutions that rely on federal funding for developmental education programs may have to eliminate these programs on short notice if they are unable to supplement federal dollars from within their own budgets.

In some states developmental education programs are mandated by the state government or board of regents for all public institutions of higher education. In some instances the state mandate was initially a response to federal desegregation legislation, whereas other statewide programs reflect voluntary efforts to improve the state's educational system, increase access to higher education, and promote heterogeneity among the students served by state institutions.

Private sources of funding might be an untapped resource for programs that are highly innovative, fulfill a special need in the community, or create a link to business and industry. An institution might fund its own program but seek outside funds for a single component, for example, for summer employment scholarships for students foregoing other income when enrolling immediately upon high school graduation.

FACTS AND MYTHS ABOUT DEVELOPMENTAL EDUCATION

The definitional problem is but one of the barriers to acceptance for developmental education, particularly at 4-year institutions. As noted earlier, the myths associated with programs for underprepared students not only undermine program effectiveness but also stigmatize students.

Myth: Threat to Institutional Quality

Many faculty members, particularly those at research universities, consider developmental education programs a threat to the quality of their institutions. However, the existence of developmental education programs does not jeopardize the quality of education. Students are generally admitted to developmental education programs based on inconsistencies in otherwise promising academic profiles, for example, based on aptitude test scores or high school grade point averages that do not quite meet institutional entrance requirements. Admission, depending upon the nature of the institution and the program, is often highly selective rather than open. Many institutions' developmental programs involve provisional admission status; students must prove themselves in order to remain enrolled. Given this conditional admission, the presence of these students should be less problematic for those who are concerned about ensuring the high academic standards of the institution.

The primary mission of any educational institution is to promote the development of its students. The relative importance of research and public service depends upon the nature of the institution and the population it serves. Many higher education practioners believe that ameliorating academic deficiencies among underprepared students is the function of the community college, not the university. The often misunderstood mission of developmental education programs is not to provide an open door to otherwise more selective institutions but to create an opportunity for access for a specifically targeted group of students who, with special assistance, possess the potential to compete academically with the general student body. Alexander Astin (1985) proposed that educators should be less concerned about the reputations of their institutions and more involved in the business of educating their students. He discussed three perspectives: "The reputational view emphasizes what others *think* of you, the resource view emphasizes what you *have*, and the talent development view emphasizes what you *do*" (p. 76). According to Astin, educators espousing the reputational and resource views regard the underprepared student as a liability, but the educator interested in talent development is able to look upon underprepared students as a challenge.

Myth: Emphasis on Recruitment, not Graduation

One of the arguments against developmental education programs for culturally diverse freshmen is that they may provide an initial channel of access to the institution but are in reality only allowing temporary access. Similar criticisms have been levied at community colleges (Zwerling, 1976). Clark (1960) described one function of the community college as "screening agent," performing a "cooling out" (p. 162) function for "latent terminal" (p. 68) students, that is, for those characterized by a disparity between desire and aptitude. Similarly, some critics may perceive developmental education programs as screening devices. Others insist that these programs are only setting up students for later failure at the institution. To the contrary, the goal of developmental education is to facilitate matriculation within the institution. The success of developmental education programs is ultimately measured by graduation rate.

Myth: Reverse Discrimination

Some critics believe that admission practices for developmental education programs are promoting reverse discrimination. Institutional affirmative action policies may differentiate between African American and White students on criteria for standardized test scores and high school grade point averages for admission to these programs, but exit criteria are the same for all students. Only those students with the ability to achieve exit status should be admitted. Students who then matriculate into regular college courses will have the same qualifications. Thus, developmental education programs can accomplish an equalizing effect, bringing underprepared students up to the level of competence necessary to be successful at the institution.

Admission to developmental education programs is not determined by race, ethnicity, socioeconomic status, or athletic prowess. At all institutions there are some students who are less adequately prepared than the majority, some only in specific subject areas. The gifted writer may not be able to pass a freshman mathematics course. The talented biochemist must be able to communicate scientific findings. Students are placed on the basis of academic preparedness in each subject area.

Fact: Developmental Education as a Means of Promoting Cultural Pluralism

Cultural pluralism must become an integral and valued component of the mission of the entire United States educational system. The community colleges are doing their fair share. Upper division institutions must examine means of complementing the good work already in progress in lower division institutions. Each college or university must develop programs consistent with its own mission and clientele. Developmental education is one means of promoting cultural pluralism, especially in 4-year institutions, by empowering underprepared culturally diverse students to compete successfully and graduate without lowering standards.

The effects of the myths surrounding developmental education programs are detrimental to both students and institutions. Otherwise capable students in need of short-term academic assistance should not be deterred from pursuing higher education at the institution of their choice, yet the stigma often associated with developmental education programs can be a major determinant in the decision to attend another college or university to which the student gains regular admission. Thus, promising students from culturally diverse backgrounds are dissuaded from attending institutions that would benefit from their enrollment. In order to attract these students, institutions must reexamine their commitment to developmental education and then take positive steps to dispel the myths, both internally among the institution's faculty and students and externally in the image presented to the general public.

EVALUATING OUTCOMES: CHARACTERISTICS OF EXCELLENCE IN DEVELOPMENTAL EDUCATION

Numerous articles describe and evaluate developmental programs at various types of institutions throughout the country (Gallini, Campbell, & Hatch, 1986; Greenbaum, 1981; Jackson, 1987; Landward & Hepworth, 1984; Morante, 1986; White, 1984). Kulik, Kulik, and Shwalb (1983) conducted a meta-analysis of published findings regarding the effectiveness of postsecondary programs designed to meet the needs of high-risk and disadvantaged students. They found that these programs generally had a positive impact, whether measured by improved grade point average or persistence. Although these indices are important, they should not be the only yardsticks used to measure the impact of developmental education programs. Thorough assessment is essential to student development and institutional effectiveness.

Assessment

Assessment must be the first step of developmental education. Traditionally limited to testing proficiencies in English, mathematics, and reading, the definition of assessment for this population should be expanded to include measures of those affective variables that may serve as barriers to retention. Research indicates that student goals (Dwinell & Higbee, 1989), locus of control, test anxiety (Allen, Giat, & Cherney, 1974; Dew, Galassi, & Galassi, 1984; Lusk, 1983), mathematics anxiety (Goolsby, Dwinell, Higbee, & Bretscher, 1988), sources of academic and personal stress (Dwinell & Higbee, 1989; Higbee & Dwinell, 1988; Roberts, 1989; Roberts & White, 1989) oral communication skills (Francis, McDaniel, & Doyle, 1987), and progress in achieving developmental tasks for traditional-age students (Dwinell & Higbee, 1990) are factors that have an impact on academic achievement. Among the noncognitive variables determined to be related specifically to African American student performance are realistic self-appraisal and positive self-concept (Tracey & Sedlacek, 1984, 1985, 1987; Trippi & Stewart, 1989). Based on assessment results, students can be targeted for interventions to reduce or eliminate barriers to success. Appropriate counseling strategies might include cognitive restructuring, assertiveness training, time management, career exploration, and systematic desensitization for test and mathematics anxiety.

Dualism and Critical Thinking Skills

Students must confront a wide range of developmental issues. Many traditional-age freshmen still engage in dualistic thinking (Perry, 1968). Adult students may also "retreat" (Perry, 1968) to dualism when confronted with the challenges of academia. Dualistic thinkers approach decisions as right versus wrong rather than being able to judge the relative merits of a variety of options. Faculty members, counselors, and advisers are perceived as authority figures who can provide correct answers to complex questions. The developmental professional must assist high-risk students in learning how to weigh alternatives and make knowledgeable decisions. Assisting students in making the transition to relativism (Perry, 1968) should be one of the major goals of a developmental program. It will be difficult for the student to be successful in the majority of courses in the core curriculum, for example, in literature, philosophy, fine arts, sociology, and political science, as long as the student approaches learning from a dualistic perspective. The development of critical thinking skills is closely linked to movement from dualism to relativism.

Kurfiss (1988) defined critical thinking as "an investigation whose purpose is to explore a situation, phenomenon, question, or problem to arrive at a hypothesis or conclusion about it that integrates all available information and that can therefore be convincingly justified" (p. 2). She characterized critical thinking as "a rational response to questions that cannot be answered definitively and for which all the relevant information may not be available" (p. 2). In developmental English classes students must learn to justify the opinions set forth in their compositions. In reading they must learn reasoning skills appropriate to a variety of disciplines; those skills most valued in one discipline only partially overlap with those considered vital to others (Powers & Enright, 1987).

Ruggiero (1989) asserted that greater emphasis must be placed on teaching students how to think. Educators must acknowledge and facilitate the potential for intellectual development among all students. Ruggiero (1989) proposed that the disadvantaged student may possess an ingenuity that the seemingly advantaged student lacks. When faculty members promote critical and creative thinking skills, they involve students as active rather than passive participants in the learning process. Underprepared students must be given an opportunity to appreciate that learning can be exciting and enjoyable. Numerous resources (e.g., Kurfiss, 1988; Meyers, 1986; Ruggiero, 1987, 1988; Stice, 1987) are available to assist the educator in facilitating the development of critical thinking skills in the classroom.

Fostering a Supportive Learning Environment

The challenges of the course content and the need to develop critical thinking skills must be balanced by a supportive learning environment (Parker, 1978; Widick, Knefelkamp, & Parker, 1975). Structure in the classroom is one important means of providing support. Course goals and objectives, requirements, and examination schedules as well as attendance, homework, and grading policies must be clearly stated in the syllabus. Faculty members must serve as role models, for example, by starting and ending class on time, returning assignments promptly, and keeping scheduled appointments. Although individualization of instruction is critical, a self-paced approach to mastery may allow too much freedom. The unmotivated underachiever is likely to procrastinate; the student who lacks confidence will refrain from asking questions and seeking help. Self-paced instruction can isolate students from faculty and from one another.

Relationships with members of the faculty, counselors, advisers, tutors, and peers can provide another source of support for students enrolled in developmental education programs. For culturally diverse students on a predominantly White campus, the formation of a support network is imperative (Richardson, 1989). Structured study groups such as those implemented in supplemental instruction programs (Blanc, DeBuhr, & Martin, 1983) promote active involvement in the educational process and at the same time recognize that some students prefer interactive modes of learning to the traditional lecture/text teaching format (Anderson, 1989). Other types of academic programs that can spawn support networks include summer bridge and special orientation programs (Fitts, 1979; Richardson, 1989); faculty and/or peer mentors (Bry, Marshall, West, & Zollo, 1975; Groves & Groves, 1981); learning laboratories (Peck, Bulakowski, Buck, Caldwell, & Wilson, 1982); group tutorial sessions (Greenbaum, 1981); and block programming (Jackson, 1987; Smith & McMillon, 1986) or cluster scheduling (Greenbaum, 1981). Perhaps most important, however, are opportunities for interaction with members of the faculty both within and outside the classroom (Astin, A., 1985). Faculty members must be sensitive to the unique needs of individual students and must accept responsibility for initiating positive working relationships.

Intrusive Counseling and Advising

Counselors and advisers must also plan on taking the initiative rather than waiting to be approached for assistance. Underprepared students are not likely to seek help and may resist it when offered (Glennen & Baxley, 1985; Jackson, 1987; Trippi & Cheatham, 1989). Voluntary programs will only reach self-selected students, not the population in greatest need of services.

The intrusive advisement program described by Glennen and Baxley (1985) differs from typical college and university advising programs in that students are expected to see their advisers more than once per term, and contacts are initiated by the adviser. High-risk students, that is, students with a high school grade point average under 2.99, must see their advisers during the first 2 weeks of the semester, whereas all other students make an initial appointment during weeks 3 through 7. Students with midterm deficiencies are required to consult with their advisers during the 8th, 9th, and 10th weeks. All students preregister during the last 4 weeks of the semester. Faculty advisers receive training in interviewing, advising, and maintaining records before the beginning of the term.

Early warning systems, including contacts with faculty to monitor classroom performance, are a critical component of any intrusive counseling or advising program (Glennen, 1976; Habley, 1981; Saunders & Dwinell, 1985). Mandatory "getting acquainted" sessions, whether individual or group, will aid in establishing rapport before a crisis occurs (Higbee, 1988; Higbee & Dwinell, in press).

NEW AGENDA FOR DEVELOPMENTAL EDUCATION PROGRAMS

Developmental education programs should be characterized by an expectation of excellence. Faculty and staff must communicate the expectation that students will achieve. Programs in mathematics and the sciences that have adjusted their focus from remedial to developmental, with an expectation of student excellence, have proven very successful in improving general academic performance of African American and Hispanic students as well as in opening the door to more lucrative scientific careers (Watkins, 1989).

Developmental educators should establish high standards and assist students in setting goals that are challenging yet realistic. Unexcused absences, tardiness, and late assignments must not be tolerated lest the developmental thrust be undermined; classroom participation must be an integral aspect of faculty expectations. Research demonstrates that high faculty expectations of students result in positive effects on performance (Spindell & Dembo, 1976).

Conversely, students enrolled in developmental education programs have a right to expect excellent teaching. Stimulating classes enhance student motivation. Sections must be small, that is, no more than 20 students, in order to provide extended opportunities for interaction between faculty and students. Students must also be enabled and encouraged to play an integral role in evaluating faculty effectiveness.

Professional Development Activities for Developmental Educators

Most faculty members in upper division institutions are ill-prepared to understand the needs of developmental education students (Ashdown, 1979; Gross, 1978), and many do not perceive that their roles as educators include serving this population. For developmental education programs to be successful, they must be staffed by professionals who are committed to the ideal of pluralism within U. S. institutions of higher education (Power, 1976). If it is not financially feasible to hire developmental educators specifically for this function, training and staff development programs must be provided for those faculty who teach developmental courses. Training must include background in student development theory and its implications for the developmental classroom. If appropriate opportunities for staff development are not available on campus, a number of professional conferences, workshops, and institutes have been established to fill this need (e.g., annual conference of the National Association for Developmental Education, Kellogg Institute at Appalachian State University). Some state systems of higher education also sponsor faculty development activities for developmental educators (e.g., annual state system of Georgia developmental studies conference). State and regional conferences provide relatively inexpensive and highly effective means of sharing new ideas and enhancing communication among institutions in the system.

Recognition for Dedicated Service

Faculty members must be rewarded for excellence in teaching and for the time they commit to meeting with students outside the classroom (Astin, H.,

1985). Traditional standards for promotion and tenure may not adequately recognize the contributions of developmental faculty. The solution is not to remove the members of this group from the tenure track and thus deprive them of equal opportunity for job security; neither is it to eliminate research activities from their job descriptions, since research regarding developmental education students is desperately needed. A reward system must be developed that reflects the quality of effort in each aspect of the position (e.g., teaching, advising, publications) proportionate to a realistic appraisal of the amount of time available for each activity.

CONCLUSION

Through developmental education programs culturally diverse students as well as mainstream students who are academically underprepared can gain access to all types of institutions of higher education without threatening quality or undermining the value of degree programs. Developmental education programs that are likely to be successful are (a) committed to cultural pluralism from the top and at all levels of the program and institution; (b) created not as a screening device but as a means of promoting student success; (c) directed at needs, not demographics; and (d) perceived and developed to be growth oriented rather than remedial or compensatory.

To enhance student development, programs should (a) include a thorough assessment program; (b) address affective as well as cognitive development; (c) achieve a realistic balance between challenge and support; (d) foster involvement with faculty, advisers, and peers; (e) develop critical thinking skills; (f) provide an intrusive counseling and advising program, including an early warning system; (g) maintain high standards and expectations of student excellence; and (h) promote and reward excellent teaching.

Developmental education programs can play a significant role in facilitating underprepared and culturally diverse students' access to and graduation from institutions of higher education, but to gain acceptance developmental educators must disassociate themselves from traditionally remedial or compensatory education and strive for empowerment of students and excellence in teaching.

REFERENCES

Allen, G. J., Giat, L., & Cherney, R. (1974). Locus of control, test anxiety, and student performance in a personalized instruction course. *Journal of Educational Psychology, 66*, 968-973.

Anderson, J. (1989, July). *Adding style to teaching and learning: The educational imperative*. Presentation at the National Conference on Student Retention, Chicago, IL.

Ashdown, E. (1979). Humanities on the front lines. *Change, 11*(2), 18-21.

Astin, A. (1984). A look at pluralism in the contemporary student population. *NASPA Journal, 21*(3), 2-11.

Astin, A. (1985). *Achieving educational excellence.* San Francisco: Jossey-Bass.

Astin, H. (1985). Providing incentives for teaching underprepared students. *Educational Record, 66,* 26-29.

Blanc, R. A., DeBuhr, L. E., & Martin, D. C. (1983). Breaking the attrition cycle: The effects of supplemental instruction on undergraduate performance and attrition. *Journal of Higher Education, 54,* 80-90.

Bry, B. H., Marshall, J. S., West, L. M., & Zollo, J. S. (1975). A pilot course for the training of peer counselors for educationally disadvantaged students. *Teaching of Psychology, 2*(2), 51-55.

Clark, B. R. (1960). *The open door college.* New York: McGraw-Hill.

Clowes, D. A. (1982). More than a definitional problem. *Current Issues in Higher Education: Underprepared Learners,* (1), 4-6.

Dew, K. M. H., Galassi, J. P., & Galassi, M. D. (1984). Math anxiety: Relation with situational test anxiety, performance, physiological arousal, and math avoidance behavior. *Journal of Counseling Psychology, 31,* 580-583.

Dwinell, P. L., & Higbee, J. L. (1989). *The relationship of affective variables to student performance: Research findings.* Paper presented at the Annual Conference of the National Association of Developmental Education, Cincinnati, OH. (ERIC Reproduction Services No. ED 304 614)

Dwinell, P. L., & Higbee, J. L. (1990). The Student Developmental Task and Lifestyle Inventory (SDTLI): Relationship to performance among developmental freshmen. *Georgia Journal of College Student Affairs, 5,* 4-8.

Farver, A. S., Sedlacek, W. E., & Brooks, G. C., Jr. (1975). Longitudinal predictions of university grades for Blacks and Whites. *Measurement and Evaluation in Guidance, 7,* 243-250.

Fitts, J. D. (1979). Model of a summer program for college survival. *Journal of Developmental and Remedial Education, 3*(2), 6-7.

Francis, K. C., McDaniel, M., & Doyle, R. E. (1987). Training in role communication skills: Effect on interpersonal and academic skills of high-risk freshmen. *Journal of College Student Personnel, 28*(2), 151-156.

Gallini, J. K., Campbell, J., & Hatch, C. W. (1986). Factors influencing retention in a developmental studies program. *Journal of Research and Development in Education, 19*(2), 42-48.

Glennen, R. E. (1976). Intrusive college counseling. *The School Counselor, 24*(1), 48-50.

Glennen, R. E., & Baxley, D. M. (1985). Reduction of attrition through intrusive advising. *NASPA Journal, 22*(3), 10-14.

Goolsby, C. B., Dwinell, P. L., Higbee, J. L., & Bretscher, A. S. (1988). Factors affecting mathematics achievement in high-risk college students. *Research and Teaching in Developmental Education, 4,* 18-27.

Greenbaum, A. (1981). A holistic approach for assisting educationally underprepared students. *Journal of Developmental and Remedial Education, 4*(3), 10-12.

Gross, T. L. (1978). How to kill a college: The private papers of a campus dean. *Saturday Review, 5*(9), 12-20.

Groves, S. E., & Groves, D. L. (1981). The academic assistants adviser program. *College Student Journal, 15,* 309-314.

Habley, W. R. (1981). Academic advisement: The critical link in student retention. *NASPA Journal, 18*(4), 45-50.

Higbee, J. L. (1988). Student development theory: A foundation for the individualized instruction of high-risk freshman. *Journal of Educational Opportunity, 3,* 42-47.

Higbee, J. L., & Dwinell, P. L. (1988). *A developmental inventory of sources of stress.* Paper presented at the Annual Conference of the American College Personnel Association, Miami, FL. (ERIC Reproduction Services No. ED 298 182)

Higbee, J. L., & Dwinell, P. L. (in press). Factors related to the academic success of high-risk freshmen: Three case studies. *College Student Journal.*

Jackson, J. (1987). Counseling as a strategy for mainstreaming underprepared students. *Journal of Multicultural Counseling and Development, 15*(4), 184-190.

Kulik, C. C., Kulik, J. A., & Shwalb, B. J. (1983). College programs for high-risk and disadvantaged students: A meta-analysis of findings. *Review of Educational Research, 53,* 397-414.

Kurfiss, J. G. (1988). *Critical thinking: Theory, research, practice, and possibilities* (ASHE-ERIC Higher Education Report No. 2). Washington, DC: Association for the Study of Higher Education.

Landward, S., & Hepworth, D. (1984). Support systems for high-risk college students: Findings and issues. *College and University, 59,* 119-128.

Lusk, S. L. (1983). Interaction of test anxiety and locus of control on academic performance. *Psychological Reports, 53,* 639-644.

Meyers, C. (1986). *Teaching students to think critically.* San Francisco: Jossey-Bass.

Morante, E. A. (1986). The effectiveness of developmental programs: A 2-year follow-up study. *Journal of Developmental Education, 9*(3), 14-15.

Parker, C. A. (Ed.). (1978). *Encouraging development in college students.* Minneapolis, MN: University of Minnesota Press.

Peck, A., Bulakowski, C., Buck, B., Caldwell, B., & Wilson, M. (1982). Providing something for everyone through the learning center. *Journal of Developmental and Remedial Education, 5*(1), 15-18.

Perry, W. G., Jr. (1968). *Forms of intellectual and ethical development in the college years: A scheme.* New York: Holt, Rinehart & Winston.

Pfeiffer, C. M., Jr., & Sedlacek, W. E. (1971). The validity of academic predictors for Black and White students at a predominantly White university. *Journal of Educational Measurement, 8,* 253-261.

Power, M. E. (1976). "New students" mean change for colleges. *Journal of Reading, 20,* 237-240.

Powers, D. E., & Enright, M. K. (1987). Analytical reasoning skills in graduate study: Perceptions of faculty in six fields. *Journal of Higher Education, 58*(6), 658-682.

Richardson, R. C. (1989). If minority students are to succeed in higher education, every rung of the educational ladder must be in place. *Chronicle of Higher Education, 35*(18), A48.

Roberts, G. H. (1989). Personal and academic stressors affecting developmental education students. *Research and Teaching in Developmental Education, 5*(2), 39-53.

Roberts, G. H., & White, W. G. (1989). Health and stress in developmental college students. *Journal of College Student Development, 30*(6), 515-521.

Ruggiero, V. R. (1987). *Teaching thinking across the curriculum.* New York: Harper & Row.

Ruggiero, V. R. (1988). *The art of thinking* (2nd ed.). New York: Harper & Row.

Ruggiero, V. R. (1989, July). *Teaching thinking across the curriculum.* Presentation at the National Conference of Student Retention, Chicago, IL.

Saunders, S. A., & Dwinell, P. L. (1985). Monitoring academic performance: Promoting success among underprepared students. *Journal of College Student Personnel, 26*(4), 359-360.

Smith, A. L., & McMillon, H. G. (1986). Counselors as educational facilitators. *Journal of Multicultural Counseling and Development, 14*(4), 167-176.

Sowa, C. J., Thomson, M. M., & Bennett, C. T. (1989). Prediction and improvement of academic performance for high-risk Black college students. *Journal of Multicultural Counseling and Development, 17*, 14-22.

Spindell, W. A., & Dembo, M. H. (1976). The effects of student expectations on academic achievement and attitudes. *College Student Journal, 10*, 303-306.

Stice, J. E. (Ed.). (1987). *Developing critical thinking and problem-solving abilities* (New Directions for Teaching and Learning, No. 30). San Francisco: Jossey-Bass.

Thomas, C. L., & Stanley, J. C. (1969). Effectiveness of high school grades of Black students: A review and discussion. *Journal of Educational Measurement, 6*, 203-216.

Tracey, T. J., & Sedlacek, W. E. (1984). Noncognitive variables in predicting academic success by race. *Measurement and Evaluation in Guidance, 16*, 172-178.

Tracey, T. J., & Sedlacek, W. E. (1985). The relationship of noncognitive variables to academic success: A longitudinal comparison by race. *Journal of College Student Personnel, 26*(5), 405-410.

Tracey, T. J., & Sedlacek, W. E. (1987). Prediction of college graduation using noncognitive variables by race. *Measurement and Evaluation in Counseling and Development, 19*, 177-184.

Trippi, J., & Cheatham, H. E. (1989). Effects of special counseling programs for Black freshmen on a predominantly White campus. *Journal of College Student Development, 30*(1), 35-40.

Trippi, J., & Stewart, J. B. (1989). The relationship between self-appraisal variables and the college grade performance and persistence of Black freshmen. *Journal of College Student Development, 30*(6), 484-491.

Watkins, B. T. (1989). Many campuses now challenging minority students to excel in math and science. *Chronicle of Higher Education, 35*(40), A13, A16.

White, W. F. (1984). A college program to ameliorate developmental lag. *The College Board Review, 133*, 7-9, 29.

Widick, C., Knefelkamp, L., & Parker, C. A. (1975). The counselor as a developmental instructor. *Counselor Education and Supervision, 14*, 286-296.

Zwerling, L. S. (1976). *Second best.* New York: McGraw-Hill.

CHAPTER 6

INTEGRATING DIVERSITY INTO TRADITIONAL RESIDENT ASSISTANT COURSES

Lissa J. VanBebber

This chapter focuses on incorporating cultural pluralism into all aspects of the training courses for students who live and work in residence halls. Diversity as a topic is introduced in many resident assistant (RA) training programs and classes. However, diversity as a process, as an integral component of teaching methods, subject areas, and student knowledge is often not thoroughly examined. This chapter outlines the importance—and necessity—of viewing diversity as a continuous consideration and provides examples of and suggestions on how to restructure current RA training courses to meet this need.

Integrating diversity into a resident assistant course is not simple: It is an undertaking that requires incorporating diversity into content, process, environment, students, and instructor(s). Basic is that all people involved in cultural pluralism training be knowledgeable about more than one culture and race. This requirement, which is often a stumbling block for nonminority instructors, has led to an increased dependence upon African American, Hispanic, and Asian American colleagues to "teach diversity" as well as to a reliance upon a single class period or a few in-service training sessions designed to increase students' awareness of differences. Increasing students' awareness is an important first step, but by itself it is not enough to ensure that student leaders will be able to appreciate, understand, and work successfully with the cultural differences they encounter in their resident assistant positions.

In a survey of courses taught to undergraduate resident assistants in northeastern and midwestern U.S. colleges, it was found that 30 of 35 institutions did not address the topic of diversity in a course setting, and that all but two institutions taught diversity only in a single class session (Lindley & Masiello, 1988). The majority of schools attempting to incorporate diversity into the curriculum were doing so by adding a single class session to the current resident assistant course or by adding an in-service training session to the existing training program. In order to incorporate diversity into a leadership curriculum successfully, it must be integrated into *all* aspects of the course. Although the use of ethnic minority instructors or training sessions devoted to raising students' awareness is helpful, the educational value is decreased when the essence of what is being taught is not continually incorporated into the training model.

Isolating diversity as a separate topic allows students and instructors to avoid many of the difficult issues involved in truly integrating diversity into the entire curriculum. It sends a message that diversity is just a current theme to be acknowledged, a message that diversity does not have to be used in all issues and tasks. This are dangerous messages to send because such messages allow student leaders to rationalize and dismiss many campus incidents of discrimination as isolated, one-time events.

College campuses have recently been the scene of highly visible and disturbing racial conflicts. Most of these have shown that there is a great deal of insensitivity toward, and ignorance of, non-Eurocentric, American culture (Lennon, 1988). Student affairs professionals and concerned others must focus on helping students better understand each other and the multicultural world in which they live. It is essential that students have both the challenge and opportunity to work with issues of diversity in all content areas. For resident assistant courses, this goal means that we must begin to examine the values inherent in the skills, methods, and content areas that are taught. We must search for creative and realistic ways to incorporate diversity into all aspects of training sessions.

Incorporating diversity into all aspects of resident assistant training means that all assumptions must be examined. For example, if a course segment on Power and Confrontation is taught, what is taught and how is it taught? Who authored the materials that are used? Are power differences acknowledged between upper and lower socioeconomic classes, between White and Hispanic individuals in the United States, between faculty and students? Are students encouraged to examine power differentials between Greek-letter and other collegiate organizations? How does class composition influence teacher presentation style? Will instructor presentation style change if the racial composition of the class is 75% African American and 25% White? Such questions are useful in examining current assumptions about leadership training and diversity.

A MODEL FOR INTEGRATING
TRAINING PROGRAMS

Critical to integrating cultural diversity into traditional training courses are assessment of the *instructor*, the *subject or content areas* to be taught, and the *students* enrolled in the class. The instructor must have knowledge of other cultures, the institutional context of the college, and his or her personal biases (Boateng, 1990; Dillon, 1989; Hale-Benson, 1986). The value base of subject materials and the types of examples and characters presented within content areas must be examined and evaluated. The knowledge that the students enrolled in the course have about their own cultural backgrounds and other cultures must also be assessed (VanBebber & Roper, 1987). Each of these areas of assessment will be addressed in turn. Learning is an interaction among student, subject matter, and instructor. Because of the interactive nature of the educational process, it is critical that all parts be examined. It is also critical that all areas be examined thoroughly even though assessing these three areas is a time-consuming process that requires at least a year of advance planning. Making assessments of and changes in only one area, rather than addressing all three areas together, results in a less focused, less cohesive course. Focusing on only one part—subject matter—is a reason why cultural diversity is not fully integrated into most RA courses.

Throughout this chapter, examples are provided to illustrate how diversity in each of these three areas can be integrated within the structure of a resident assistant course. For the sake of continuity, most of the examples focus on the cultural differences between African American and Euro-American cultures. However, many diverse populations live in college and university residence halls, and each RA training course should represent the diversity that is present on the home campus. Special consideration and efforts must be taken to acknowledge and support less visible minority groups. For example, homosexuals are often one of the least supported and most feared populations within the residence halls (Hirschorn, 1987). This fear and lack of support can be countered only by vigorous education efforts on the part of residence life staff and student peers. Thus, highlighting visible *and* invisible minority groups is necessary when planning the integration of diversity into resident assistant courses.

Assessment of the Instructor

Lindley and Masiello (1988) found that RA training courses are taught by a wide variety of individuals, both professional and paraprofessional. These individuals ranged from undergraduate resident assistants to residence life training specialists. Some of the RA courses were co-taught, and some were taught by a single instructor. Currently there are neither acknowledged standards nor set criteria for selecting instructors of resident assistant courses. This absence of concensus means that each residence life program individually determines the criteria for its instructors. Particularly important to set standards for—and to assess—for RA course instructors are (a) knowledge of other cultures, institutional context, and personal biases and (b) diversity of teaching methods and styles.

Knowledge of Other Cultures, Institutional Context, and Personal Biases

Higher education in the United States is typically representative of Caucasian, northern European, heterogeneous, middle-class, male culture (Hall, 1976). It is likely that many individuals who teach RA courses have grown up within this culture, attended predominantly White institutions of higher education, and have not significantly experienced or studied other cultures. This creates problems for students from other cultures. If these educators, like missionaries of the past, are ignorant about the structures of their culture and how those structures and ways of learning differ from other cultures, they may unconsciously impose cultural imperialism upon, and create problems for, their students. Instructors should become familiar with alternative ways of perceiving issues of space, time, communication, reasoning, social roles and other characteristics of the world. Such issues are often overlooked in initial attempts to integrate diversity. Changes occur most often only in the area of curriculum because of the class length of a class (1 hour), the teaching style (teachers teaching students rather than students teaching students or everyone teaching and sharing with everyone), and the reasoning process (analytical) that are so dominant in higher education. When time is not taken to educate instructors about culture and cultural differences, true integration of diversity rarely occurs. Individuals who have not lived within more than one culture are less likely to recognize the strength and depth of their own cultural assumptions. Thus it is important either to develop standards for instructors that require knowledge of more than one culture or to establish instructor training programs that will teach potential instructors about cultural differences that affect teaching and learning.

Excellent resources for learning about cultural differences and the effects of lack of cultural knowledge on our ability to communicate with others are the works of Edward T. Hall. His books, *The Silent Language* (1959), *The Hidden Dimension* (1966), and *Beyond Culture* (1959), focus on interpersonal communication differences that are related to context differences in culture. In *Beyond Culture*, Hall divided features of culture (e.g., time, space and tempo, reasoning, social roles) into two main categories: *low context* and *high context*. Bennett (1989) presented a model of Hall's conceptions that is extremely helpful in understanding the difference between low-context environments like those of American colleges and universities, and high-context environments like those found among the cultures of American Indians, Mexican Americans, African Americans, and some rural Americans. Her examples of these two types of environments within the categories of time, space and tempo, reasoning, verbal messages, social roles, interpersonal relations, and sociopolitical context can be useful in developing alternate views of the RA course and its processes.

Instructors using a low-context culture style, the predominant style in U.S. higher education, are likely to emphasize the importance of being on time, the tight schedule of the syllabus, analytical reasoning, the importance of words, and the values of persuasion and being direct. They are also likely to stress the importance of the residence hall rules, the procedures to follow, and the fact that people are individuals first.

A high-context culture style has values and norms that contrast sharply: Schedules are loose; there are often last minute changes of important plans. Moving in harmony with others is consciously valued, and knowledge is gained through intuition, integration, and contemplation. The importance of feelings (rather than words) is stressed. Customary informal procedures and personal contacts are often more important than formal laws and procedures. Group relationships are more important than the individual.

Although there are variances among high-context cultures just as there are among low-context cultures, the differences in how members of cultural groups learn and relate to each other are real, and these differences have a potential impact on every class session in an RA or student leadership class. It is necessary for instructors to acknowledge the value and legitimacy of the nondominant cultural context. This acknowledgement should occur both through a formal recognition presented in the material and through the informal relations that the instructor has with each student.

Instructors should become aware of the individual biases and prejudices they bring to their classrooms. These biases and prejudices, when coupled with power, can emerge as individual racism, that is, as actions taken by one individual toward another because the latter is identified with a certain group. Actions taken by a social system or institution that result in negative outcomes for members of a certain group or groups produce institutional racism (Sedlacek & Brooks, 1976). It is necessary for instructors to understand not only individual racism but also the difference between individual and institutional racism.

Instructors should always critique their choices of material, examples, and individual policies to ensure that these items are not discriminatory, ethno-centric, or stereotyped. Instructors must also point out any student language or behavior that might be construed as racist, sexist, or anti-Semitic. These steps will help students learn how to recognize, monitor, and eliminate individual discriminatory practices. However, RAs and student leaders are often unaware of the existence and practice of institutional racism, of institu-tional discriminatory practices. As staff members or leaders they are repre-sentatives of a larger institution. In this context, it is necessary for them to examine and critique the policies and procedures that they enforce and teach to other students. Helping students learn about this area is a potentially threatening challenge to the larger department or institution, even when the department or institution is fully commited to ethnic and cultural diversity, because of the unconscious level on which ethnocentrism and racism operate.

An example of an institutional policy that is often practiced and should be examined is the policy that exists for use of a floor lounge. Some institutions adopt the policy of majority rule. Under this policy the purpose of the floor lounge will be whatever a majority of the floor residents want. This discriminates against any minority population (e.g., people who study rather than watch Monday night football). This policy may become reflective of what is charged as institutional racism if it also serves to reinforce other discriminatory procedures.

Although discrimination is often not intentional, institutional or residence hall policies that presume universal applicability (i.e., majority rule on space use) may have the same discriminatory effect. An example common on predominantly White campuses is that of meeting space. Most predominantly White, Greek-letter organizations have houses or suites in which they hold their meetings. Most African American Greek-letter organizations do not. A policy that prohibits the use of lounges for meetings serves to discriminate further against groups that do not have the privilege of an established meeting space elsewhere on campus and do not have a majority number of residents who could change the lounge use policy.

To address issues of institutional racism, instructors must be aware of institutional policies as well as departmental policies. Through a discussion of residence hall rules and policies and their relationship to institutional racism, instructors can help RAs and other student leaders learn to challenge rather than perpetuate policies that are potentially discriminatory and contribute to racism. Instructors will need to help student leaders develop group decision-making procedures that do not use voting procedures or other forms of majority rule. Policies on topics like floor use or quiet hours should be formulated in a way that allows each group to contribute to and shape the final decision. Policies should not result from a "we won, they lost" process.

Facilitating class discussions that help students learn about culture and racism and teaching students how to lead effective group decision-making processes require more than just knowledge about the subject matter. The process (teaching style) used by an instructor is also very important and should incorporate diverse perspectives.

Diversity of Teaching Methods and Styles

Once instructors have become aware of their contextual orientation to culture they can begin to analyze and assess their methods and styles of teaching. This assessment should focus not only on cultural differences but also on personality and gender differences as well as on learning styles.

An instructor's teaching style will probably not meet the needs of all students. Most frequently, individuals teach in the manner in which they best learn, developing their methods and materials in a way that unconsciously reflects their own gender and culture (National Society for the Study of Education, 1975; Silver & Hanson, 1980). If an instructor is going to teach so that *all* students can learn, particular attention must be given to the method of delivery, the methods of goal achievement and evaluation, the structure and organization of class time, the homework assignments, and the social climate of the classroom.

The method of delivery and the methods of goal achievement and evaluation will affect a student's ability to learn. Belenky, Clinchy, Goldberger, and Tarule (1986), for example, described the progression of knowledge and reasoning that is constructed by women. They noted that women, through integrative thinking, formulate a constructed knowledge that combines (instead of polarizes) rational and emotive thought and objective and subjective data. Women who utilize constructed knowledge often utilize themselves and their experiences in their learning. They do not position themselves as outside receivers of knowledge. Thus instructors will need to integrate the subject matter with the experiences and realities of women. Women will also learn better if the teacher/student relationship is constructed so that women feel included in the process, not held to an outside position that discourages questioning and interacting. Goal achievement and evaluation measures should not be solely objective. Students, through an instructor's method of teaching and evaluation, should be encouraged to merge the dichotomies of rational versus emotive knowing and subjective versus objective decision making. Gender differences result from and affect students' experience and interpretation of their environment, and instructors must take care not to value or judge males' experiences, even on an unconscious level, as the norm or more valid measure of how student leaders should operate.

By the same token, women instructors may not completely understand the dynamics and interrelationships faced by a male RA in an all-male hall. Much of the material presented in units on helping skills and communication styles emphasizes care and responsibility to others. The notions of care and responsibility are central to women's ways of decision making and thinking (Gilligan, 1982). For women and men RAs to communicate successfully with their male residents, some adaptation of style and "helping phrases" needs to occur. The successful instructor will not only review material that is to be presented with members of different groups but will also listen closely to student feedback. If students say that a skill or phrase "will never work in the halls" it is important to examine the students' rationales because the skill or phrase may be traced to an unconscious bias (heterosexual, racial, gender) that is present in the method or content of the material.

Personality differences must also be considered when the instructor plans the delivery of the training session. The Myers-Briggs Type Indicator (MBTI) (Myers, 1975) is used in understanding the learning styles of students (Lawrence, 1982) and the preferred teaching styles of instructors (Silver & Hanson, 1980). The MBTI examines preferred ways in which individuals interact with the environment. It focuses specifically on the ways people take in information (the sensing-intuition continuum) and how they come to conclusions based on that information (the thinking-feeling continuum). It also provides a measure of people's preferences for acquiring or using information (the judging-perceiving continuum) as well as an indication of the type of environment in which they prefer to direct their energy (the introvert-extrovert continuum) (Myers & McCaulley, 1985).

Knowledge of students' personality types is helpful in constructing work groups and homework assignments. Introverts, who prefer to think quietly, may benefit from hearing the thought processes of extroverted group members. Judging types, who prefer to make decisions quickly, may benefit from the presence of perceiving types who are inclined to gather as much data as possible before reaching a conclusion. Constructing work groups that balance the four dimensions of the MBTI will expose students to a diversity of learning styles and give them an opportunity to learn different ways of approaching and implementing project assignments. Other applications of the MBTI to the classroom environment are described in detail by Lawrence (1982).

Silver and Hanson (1980) focused on the influence of instructor personality type. In their workbook they provided a self-inventory that assesses an instructor's preferences in the areas of the classroom atmosphere, teaching techniques, planning style, preferred student qualities, and other related areas. Again, once instructors become aware of their preferred way of teaching, it is critical that other methods be learned and incorporated into the classroom so that all types of learners will feel both challenged and supported by the method(s) of delivery.

Research on learning styles and ethnicity suggests that certain learning styles are associated with specific ethnic populations (Bennett, 1986; Fleming, 1985; Hilliard, 1976; Shade, 1982). Individuals who have grown up within an ethnic environment that is outside of the dominant White culture have been found to process information differently than their majority student peers. Hilliard (1976, pp. 38-39), for example, noted the following cognitive and perceptual differences between the high-context culture of African Americans and the low-context culture of White Americans (amplifications are in brackets):

1. Afro-American people tend to respond to things in terms of the whole picture instead of its parts. The Euro-American tends to believe that anything can be divided and subdi-

vided into pieces and that these pieces add up to a whole. [*An example is the typical RA course syllabus.*]

2. Afro-American people tend to prefer inferential reasoning to deductive or inductive reasoning. [*This difference may show up when RAs are asked to explain why they believe that one of their floor residents is the person responsible for harassment on the floor.*]

3. Afro-American people tend to approximate space, numbers, and time.

4. Afro-American people tend to prefer to focus on people and their activities rather than on things. This tendency is shown by the fact that so many African American students choose careers in the helping professions, such as teaching, psychology, and social work, even though a scarcity of jobs exists in those areas and the curriculum is not particularly easy. [*Although some believe it is hard to recruit minority students to RA jobs, low numbers of applicants are more likely to result from the environment of the residence halls and the degree to which hall directors and others understand and support the issues and struggles of African Americans rather than something inherent in the RA position.*]

5. Afro-American people have a keen sense of justice and are quick to analyze and perceive injustice. [*Recognition of an injustice may be followed by a demand for justice and action on the part of administrators; RAs may become impatient with a system that becomes easily bogged down or refuses to take decisive stands on issues of justice within the halls.*]

6. Afro-American people tend to lean toward altruism, a concern for one's fellow humans.

7. Afro-American people tend to prefer novelty, freedom, and personal distinctiveness. This is shown in the development of improvisations in music and styles of clothing. [*Within the halls, this tendency may be exhibited in the formation of floor identity, design of floor t-shirts, programs, and even confrontation and mediation styles.*]

8. Afro-American people in general tend not to be "word" dependent. They tend to be very proficient in nonverbal communications. [*In the classroom, some students will communicate their understanding, confusion, opinions, and emotions nonverbally. Instructors may need to develop their own nonverbal communication skills as well as a level of comfort with and acceptance of students' use of nonverbal communication styles.*]

Another example of cultural differences in processing information can be seen in a group of students learning a new dance in the residence halls. Students who come from a low-context culture are accustomed to learning a task by breaking it up into parts and analyzing those parts, mastering each part and then putting all the separated parts together. When learning to dance, these students will separate arm, body, and feet movements. They will attempt to go step by step, slowly tracing the "proper" movements until they have mastered each area. Students from a high-context culture, who tend to be more relational in their learning style, will focus on the whole movement and its relation to the rhythm or words of the song. They are likely to learn the dance's general form while retaining their own individual style.

It is important for instructors to acknowledge and accommodate these differences in style into their instructional design. Many lesson plans are formulated part by part, and unless the holistic design is also presented, some learners will not fully grasp the meaning of the content until the last segment is presented. These differences also indicate that presentations given by people will be more helpful to some learners than presentations of material through the written word. However, not all communication has to be verbal to be effective. Nonverbal communication by the instructor will be trusted and followed by some learners, and by the same token, they will use nonverbal communication to express some of their thoughts and opinions. Thus, instructors must not only listen to the words that are spoken by students but should also observe their nonverbal gestures and interactions.

Learning differences based on gender, personality, and culture are important reasons for instructors to vary their methods of delivery. It is also extremely beneficial to combine mediums in any presentation of material. Using only a lecture style or only a small group discussion style will not be as beneficial for students as combining lectures, videos, experiential activities, and discussion. A final factor that will contribute to a student's ability to retain and apply information is the perceived relevance it has to his or her immediate situation. Because reality is viewed by individuals through their culture and gender, topics that are presented through theoretical constructs need to be tied to the day-to-day reality and experience of each student by using more than one "real-life" example.

Instructors tend to rely on whatever methods they have previously used and often present material in only one or two ways. But to maximize the learning of all students, different methods and formats should be used in each class. An RA training session should include, for example, (a) literature on the topic, (b) visual demonstration of the topic, (c) examples of how the material relates to and can be applied in the residence halls, and (d) comments by current RAs or student leaders about how this topic has helped them in their leadership role. Such a format combines media, utilizes the practical experience of current student leaders, provides the background and holistic view of the topic, and gives more than one example to help students relate to the information. In every possible situation it is also important to give students the opportunity to personalize the information being taught and to share their views or opinions of the material with others.

Figure 1 illustrates this format, using the judicial system as a sample topic (within a Rules and Procedures unit) and outlining a teaching plan for two 1-hour and 15 minute classes.

Figure 1
Sample RA Training Session Format

<u>Class One</u>: **Moral Development Theory and the Judicial System**

15 min. **I.** Opening discussion/debate on assigned reading material that focused on two different models of moral reasoning and development: This discussion should allow students to share analytical thoughts as well as feelings and reactions to the implications of the two models.

15 min. **II.** Presentation of Kohlberg's and Gilligan's models of moral development: Key concepts and differences between models should be highlighted.

15 min. **III.** Small group work: Groups are separated by gender. Groups should critique the current judicial policies and procedures and assess whether or not the policies are more "male" or "female" in character. Is care and responsibility addressed? Or are the policies built on the basis of justice and individual rights?

25 min. **IV.** Each group should present its results and explain them to the rest of the class.

5 min. **V.** Assignment: Each student should list the "other rules" that operate on his or her floor. What informal policies exist among residents? How are these enforced? Who has the power? How should policies for group programs, use of the lounge, quiet hours, and guests be formulated? Assign reading material that will explain the role of personality type and culture in approach to rules and norms.

<u>Class Two</u>: **Rules, Rights, and Process**

15 min. **I.** Opening discussion on the reading and on answers to assigned questions from the first class.

35 min. **II.** Experiential activity: All students are handed a blank contract on which topics for a hypothetical floor have been listed. The topics could include telephone use, guests, safety, noise, parties/activities. Under each heading are blank lines for the actual rules to be written. Students take turns playing the role of the RA who is to lead the class (hypothetical group of residents) in the discussion and formulation of floor rules. Students are encouraged to participate as they believe actual residents would. *The instructors should observe and note any processes that serve to shut down a minority group member's opinion.*

10 min. Instructors lead a class discussion of the activity and brainstorm potential problems or issues that might arise on an actual residence hall floor.

15 min. **III.** Written reflection paper: Each student should spend the last 15 minutes of class writing a paper listing thoughts, opinions, and feelings about the nature of rules, their contribution to a group living environment, and any biases that were discovered.

The two classes from a Rules and Procedures unit have been designed to combine different teaching techniques and information. As necessary, more or less structure can be added to each segment. Some instructors may want to supply each student with discussion questions, or some instructors may want to tailor the experiential activity to address a current campus or departmental issue. It is also possible to spend less time on theory and concentrate more heavily on the language used in preparing written reports of rule violations because discriminatory phrases, adjectives, and assumptions can often be found in the written accounts of policy infractions.

Overall, it is extremely important to incorporate diversity into the reading and discussion material, the style of presentation, and the activities and requirements that are given to the students. RAs and student leaders should have a clear understanding of how rules and procedures are perceived differently by different cultures and personality types as well as the potentially discriminatory effects of policies that emphasize majority rule and equality at the expense of care and equity. Equality and equity are often assumed to be the same, but students must understand that distributing something *equally* among all individual residents is not always *equitable* because equal distribution means that those residents who already "have" will continue to "have more." Dividing something equitably implies, however, that the end result of the division will be an equality among all residents or groups, and not a continuation of the inequality that already exists.

Assessment of Subject and Content Areas

After instructors (and their supervisors) have assessed their knowledge of cultures and the diversity of their teaching methods they must also assess the content of the course or training program.

Value Base of Topics

Typical topic areas on the syllabus for a traditional resident assistant course include those in the following list. The topics were compiled from *The Resident Assistant* (Blimling & Miltenberger, 1984) and the survey of RA courses by Lindley and Masiello (1988).

1. Ice breakers and acquaintanceship activities (Lindley & Masiello)
2. Self-awareness (often using the Myers-Briggs Type Indicator) (Lindley & Masiello)
3. Student development theory (both)
4. Group dynamics and leadership (Lindley & Masiello)
5. Community development (both)
6. Communication and helping skills (both)

7. Confrontation and conflict mediation (both)
8. Programming (both)
9. The Judicial process (Lindley & Masiello)
10. Values and decision making (both)
11. Student mental health (suicide, eating disorders, alcohol and drugs) (both)
12. Personal concerns for the RA (time, stress and academic work management) (Blimling & Miltenberger).

Using these topics, it is possible to begin an examination of the value bases that are often unknowingly reflected in the traditional RA course curriculum. As illustrated in Figure 1's sample format for two classes on the judicial system within a unit on Rules and Procedures, topics can be examined from many different perspectives. Women and students from high-context groups, for example, may not feel comfortable with a judicial system that is based on Kohlberg's (1984) model and implemented in the manner of a low-context society. Because some units are not taught from a philosophical basis (i.e., they focus primarily on application), they may unintentionally ignore the value base from which they are derived or assume the universality of that base. For this reason, it is important to examine the course content thoroughly before adopting it and teaching it to students.

Examining the First Class

The place to begin this examination is with the plan for the very first class. The first class meeting usually is devoted to an explanation of the course requirements and syllabus. It might also include an acquaintanceship activity. Questions that should be addressed to the introduction of the course are, Is there an overemphasis on the points, deadlines, and procedures associated with evaluation measures? How flexible is the design of the course? If there is a reputed lecturer on campus, and can her or his lecture be substituted for a regularly scheduled class? Does the course content provide ample opportunity for student input? What are the expectations of the students? What are the expectations of the instructor? Are the expectations stated? Is the classroom environment addressed? Are policies of nondiscrimination stated? Does the syllabus serve as an example of open communication? (Or does it fail to address the questions and expectations of the students in the course?)

Clearly, the syllabus can and should serve as a summary of important dates and policies, but it should also address the often unwritten mission and goals of the course and the classroom. Student and instructor expectations and goals should be articulated, and issues such as discrimination, freedom of speech, and the classroom as a place of learning should be clearly spelled out.

In addition to covering the course content and policies, it is also desirable to begin an acquaintanceship process. This process is something that should be built into more than one class and should begin slowly. It is not customary in all cultures to self-disclose to comparative strangers; thus some students might be uncomfortable with activities that seem to probe deeply into such personal topics as family, issues associated with money (e.g., travel), or leisure activities. It is often easier to begin with such basic data as current residence, major, and interest in the RA position.

If a class is fairly homogeneous, the acquaintanceship activity can serve as an introduction to other cultures and lifestyles. An example of how this can be done involves the use of small library centers that provide information on various minority populations. These centers should contain information about minority populations that are present on your campus. Sample populations that might be highlighted are women, African Americans, Asian Americans, Jewish students, disabled students, homosexuals, and student athletes. The only criteria for inclusion in the library are (1) that members of the identified group share a common perception and experience of the campus environment, influenced by their background and their treatment on campus, and (2) that the members' identified experience is different from the majority students' experience.

These centers cannot be adequately created in a short period of time, and the development of each center should be supervised by someone who is knowledgeable about the center's cultural population. Care should be taken that the collection presents an accurate and diverse representation of the culture in any videotape, article of clothing, written material, list of preferred activities, gathering place, or other reference material. Campus resource persons who are willing to talk about the culture should also be included. If these persons are not available to set up and evaluate these centers, consider planning an alternative activity rather than minimizing or stereotyping the chosen cultures.

Once the centers are available, the acquaintanceship activity works by asking each student to become familiar with one group, that is, to learn its values, cultural context (see Bennett, 1986), favorite foods, activities, music, heroes and heroines, contributions to society, dislikes, and problems. Each student should also talk with at least two people on the list of campus resources. In the first class the students can simply talk about themselves and share with the rest of the class which group they have chosen to learn about. In the following two classes, miniassignments can be submitted to the instructor or shared verbally with the class about knowledge gained of different cultural groups. Finally, in the third class, teams of students can prepare and present information to the rest of the class about their group. Especially in this final class, instructors should invite discussion and debate and should be prepared to correct any misinformation. The campus staff and any students who served as resources for the RAs should be invited to participate in this final class. Through the experiences of researching and discussing cultural, racial, and sexual orientation differences, the potential RAs will gain an additional lens or filter through which they can view the rest of the materials and situations in the course.

Done well, this activity can enrich the classroom and the student's experience. Care must be exerted to ensure that written summaries and verbal accounts of learning contain sufficient depth and do not perpetuate negative stereotypes of the researched population.

Examining the Basic Context

After examining the first class, it is necessary to examine the basic content of other traditional topics taught in RA courses. Programming, communication and helping skills, student development theory, and confrontation and conflict mediation frequently appear in traditional RA and student leadership courses. Programming is often taught through a brief lecture that outlines the necessary steps to a successful program followed by an assignment in which the student plans a program and submits his or her plan to the instructor for a grade.

Implicit are the notions that programming has a set of rules that have to be followed, that the individual planning the program is largely responsible for its success or failure, and that the individual assumes the majority of the control in the decision-making process. This interpretation is counter to the ways some ethnic groups and many women learn and prefer to operate. In many populations, it is common for people to express ideas and for others to build, change, or alter the original constructs as the group begins to assume responsibility for and ownership of an activity. In this pattern, activities or programs have basic tasks that need to be completed, but the order and timing of the tasks are often interchangeable and quite flexible. Leaders emerge and fade as different parts of the program are highlighted. The success or failure of the program is more dependent on the group's ability to work together than on any one individual. In order for RAs and other student leaders to gain an appreciation of alternative methods and styles, different cultural norms for structuring an activity need to be incorporated into all classes; topics such as programming should be presented in more than one way.

A unit on Communication and Helping Skills can provide many exercises and discussion opportunities for raising awareness about different communication styles and behaviors. It is important that the traditional White, Eurocentric, male model not be emphasized at the expense of alternative models. Most students, having lived or attended schools in the United States, will be familiar with the communication model that stresses direct eye contact, rapid and direct speech, turn-taking that is not supposed to interrupt the speaker, personal space of about 3 feet, and the various tones of speech and nonverbal behaviors that are associated with White-European-defined forms of passive, assertive, and aggressive communication (i.e., Eurocentric). However, many students will be unaware of the norms for communication valued in other cultures.

In *Assertive Blacks....Puzzled Whites*, Donald Cheek (1976) compared the content, style, and function(s) of African Americans' and Whites' use of language. He noted that when African Americans speak among themselves, slang, laughter, gestures, and idiomatic diction are more likely to be used than when Whites are present. Majority students will often notice that there are communication differences between themselves and members of ethnic groups, but they may have little appreciation or understanding of what is meant, assumed, and communicated among those who are speaking. In many cases this lack of understanding is revealed through derogatory statements, such as "*They* don't speak properly" or "*They* are always out of control, laughing and hitting and touching each other." It is important to teach students that in many cultures, people assume a greater degree of intimacy than is assumed in the Eurocentric model prevalent among Whites. Communication in many high-context cultures is a function for relaxing, getting to know people better, and sharing interests. Communication is not used to get or maintain social or business positions, to gain identification with a certain group, or to promote oneself. The act and style of communication differs according to cultural norms and values.

Much of the work of the RA position is based on the knowlege provided by student development theories. Student development theories describe college-age (18- to 24-year-old) students' development and growth in their abilities to think complexly, formulate commitments, resolve moral dilemmas, and function interdependently with others in society. This body of knowledge has gained increased prominence and use in RA and student leadership courses. Lindley and Masiello (1988) found that Arthur Chickering's (1969) psychosocial model of student development and William Perry's (1970) model of intellectual development were taught to student leaders in the majority of institutions that offered a RA course. For many White males these two models have proven to be fairly accurate for describing their developmental stages of growth. However, women and African American researchers have criticized these models and offered alternative explanations and models of growth.

Straub (1987), for example, concluded that women do not follow the same timelines or sequential order as men in resolving the tasks associated with Chickering's seven vectors of development. The most striking difference found between women and men concerns the vector of autonomy. Women often do not resolve the issues associated with this task until they reach the age of 30 or beyond. Chickering's model, based on men, originally defined women's timelines as deviant, because they differed from men, and attributed women's failure to be fully autonomous by the age of 24 to the societal norm of men (fathers and husbands) taking care of women, thus eliminating the need for women to become autonomous. Further research, however, has shown that the timelines and sequential ordering of developmental vectors varies by gender and culture. It is essential that theories be examined closely and alternative models presented.

An alternative model that goes beyond the work of William Perry and focuses on developmental tasks other than intellectual is the Minority Identity Model (Atkinson, Morten, & Sue, 1979). This model discusses the development of an individual and that individual's attitude toward self, toward others of the same minority group, toward others of a different minority status, and toward the dominant group. Although the stages of this model can not be compared directly with those outlined in either Chickering's or Perry's model, they can be used to help students understand the impact of society on the development of an individual and the way that individual subsequently views the larger, dominant society and the individual's own role.

Use of Examples and Characters Within Presented Material

It would be a mistake to assume that ethnocentrism is found only in theories or other content areas of a training course. The material and method through which the subject matter is presented also convey cultural values and prejudices. A common example can be found in the material(s) that are sometimes used for teaching group decision-making and observation skills. Commonly a group of six to eight students is given a problem in which the students have to work together to arrive at a group solution. A second group of students is assigned to observe and critique the patterns of communication and decision making of members of the first group. The observation task is often facilitated by handing members of the second group a one-page sheet of directions and guidelines that describes possible communication behaviors. The observation sheet usually becomes the method through which the students assess the communication behaviors of members of the first group. If this sheet is constructed with a Eurocentric bias, students from other cultures may be unfairly labeled as disruptive, passive, or nonfacilitative. Figure 2 illustrates an observation sheet that is Eurocentrically biased. Figure 3 is an example of an alternative, open-ended observation sheet.

In the guide sheet shown in Figure 3 observers are free to note anything that appears relevant to them and to interpret their observations using all their knowledge of diversity. Unfortunately, many times, a grid sheet like that pictured in Figure 2 is used to accomplish this same function. When a grid sheet is used, observers are asked to place a check in the box that most resembles the communication patterns that they observe. Although this allows some freedom for each observer to interpret the behaviors of group members, it is always within the limits of the boxes. The boxes are categorized

Figure 2

	Fred	Mei	Marc	Sylvia	Ira	Jeena
Group-Building Behaviors:						
ENCOURAGING: Demonstrates responsiveness to others by being warm, friendly, and smiling.						
HARMONIZING: Initiates reconciliation among individuals. Relieves tension in group.						
GATE KEEPING: Attempts to keep communication channels open, positively facilitates the participation of others.						
Task-Directed Behaviors:						
INITIATING: Accurately and clearly defines group problem; suggests useful procedures for task completion.						
INFORMATION/OPINION SEEKING: Seeks relevant information from others, asks for relevant suggestions, ideas, facts.						
INFORMATION/OPINION GIVING: Offers facts and relevant information; states beliefs conducive to productive resolution of problem.						
Nonfacilitative Behaviors:						
BLOCKING: Tends to be negative, interruptive, stubbornly resistant. Unwilling to compromise.						
RECOGNITION SEEKING: Uses disruptive means to call attention to self; boasts/brags about personal achievements.						
DOMINATING: Monopolizes group, forces direction at the expense of other's viewpoints, gives direction to others.						
SUBMISSIVE: Does not contribute to group resolution; passively accepts others' direction.						

Figure 3
Group Dynamics

WHAT TO OBSERVE IN A GROUP

All of us spend our lives in groups of various kinds—family, gang, team, work group, church group—but we rarely take the time to step back and observe what is going on in the group, or to consider why the members behave the way they do. One of our main goals is to become better observers and better participants. But what do we look for? What is there to see in a group?

1. *CONTENT VS. PROCESS:* When we observe what the group is talking about, we are focusing on the content. When we try to observe how the group is handling its communication, i.e., who talks to whom or how much one talks, we are focusing on the group process. As you observe the following group members note what part of the content each member seems to be focusing on and what the member's contributions to the group solution are.

2. *COMMUNICATION:* Observing the pattern of communication helps us see the group in new ways.

   A. Who talks? How long does each person speak? How often does each person speak?

   B. Whom do people look at when they talk:
      1. individuals, possible supporters?
      2. the group?
      3. no one?

   C. Who talks after whom? Who interrupts whom?

   D. What style of communication is used (assertions, questions, tone of voice, gestures, etc.)?

The types of observations we make about communication patterns give us clues to other important things that may be going on in the group, such as who leads the group and who influences whom.

3. *TASK-MAINTENANCE AND SELF-ORIENTED BEHAVIOR:*

Behavior in the group can be viewed from the point of view of what its purpose or function seems to be. When a member says something, is she or he primarily:
   a. trying to get the group's task completed **(task behavior)**?
   b. trying to improve or facilitate a relationship among members **(maintenance behavior)**?
   c. meeting some personal need or goal without regard to the other group members and the overall group problem **(self-oriented behavior)**?

As you observe, jot down what you think each group member is trying to accomplish through communication and interaction with others. Also write down the information or actions or nonverbal behaviors that led you to arrive at your conclusion.

and labeled. Clearly, values have been attached to the categories of behaviors. These labels are usually indicative of the values of middle-class White Americans. Students who communicate using other styles will often receive several checks in the boxes labeled nonfacilitative behaviors. Organizing behavior and categorizing it is useful when working with large groups; however, there is a great possibility that the categories will reflect the dominant culture only. Therefore, when working with students it is important for instructors not only to use materials that allow all groups to be fairly evaluated but also to explain why different types of evaluative materials are chosen over others.

It is extremely important that critiques and alternative methods and models of content material be introduced to students. When any material is presented as representative of the group known as "students," individuals for whom the material does not "fit" are likely to feel as if, once again, their experiences have gone unrecognized or even trivialized by those who claim to be knowledgeable about college students. Instructors must assess the material they present to students and remain current in recent developments, critiques, and research findings for all the topics they teach.

In addition to examining the basic values and norms upon which content is based, instructors and their supervisors should also examine materials created by those who are teaching. The test questions, study guides, homework assignments, and role-play scenarios are usually products of the instructor(s) of the RA or leadership course. The words that are used in the creation of these additional materials must be considered carefully. The following example of how the type and amount of wording can affect the teaching of diversity comes from a class on roommate-conflict mediation. Each student was given a description of two hypothetical roommates involved in a conflict. The students in the class were supposed to play the role of the RA and, based on the information presented, begin to help mediate the hypothetical roommate conflict. Here is the first instructor-created role-play scenario:

This scenario focuses on the problem of the difference in sleeping/ studying habits, but it misses the chance to develop the characters within the problem so that all the intricacies and real-life differences that exist between roommates are illustrated. Compare it with this second instructor-created role-play scenario for two roommates and their conflict:

Situation: Difference in Sleeping Patterns (Night Owl vs. Early Bird)

Role 1: You are a night owl, and you do your best studying between midnight and 3 a.m. You usually get 5 hours of sleep a night, since your first class is at 10 a.m. You prefer to study in your room where you have snack foods and can use the stereo for background noise. You refuse to use the library this late at night but *might* be willing to use the lounge if your roommate is willing to make some compromises.

Role 2: You have five 8:00 a.m. classes. You go to bed by 11:00 pm. every night and are a very light sleeper. You have complained to your roommate about his or her staying up late but have been pretty inflexible in your insistence about having the lights out at the time you go to bed. You are beginning to retaliate for your roommate's refusal to stop studying in the room at 11:00 p.m. by waking him or her when you get up at 7 a.m.

Situation: Frequent Guests in the Room

Role 1: You are a 17-year-old, Jewish, first-year student from Baltimore City, MD. You come from a small family of three children; the other two are both younger than you. Your parents are going through a divorce, and you are deeply troubled by this. You were a marginal (C+) student in high school and got admitted to the university under the Individual Admissions program. You are determined, however, to succeed in college, and you want to be a pharmacist. You study a lot, about half in your room and half in the library, and you like to get 8 to 9 hours of sleep a night. You have a few friends on the floor, but you are basically shy. It is late September.

Your roommate is a 20-year-old junior, a White, middle-class, Catholic student from Columbia, MD. Your roommate is quite sociable and popular and belongs to a Greek-letter social organization. Your roommate is polite to you but has friends over (both men and women) to your room to visit "almost daily." These folks are also friendly, but noisy, and they often stay past midnight talking and laughing. You're tired of this and just want to be left alone. Things in the room get better for a few days, and then the friends reappear and everything becomes the same. You complain to your RA, and the three of you are now scheduled to talk about these problems.

Role 2: You are a White, middle-class, Catholic, 20-year-old junior from Columbia, MD. You belong to a Greek-letter social organization, and you are quite popular with your house members and the other residents living on your residence hall floor. Your family is very supportive of you, and your mother often fixes dinner for you and your friends so that you can get away from campus and have a home-cooked meal. You invite three or four friends (both men and women) to your room about twice a week for a few hours. Once or twice, you stayed up until 1 a.m. with them. You like your roommate but frankly think that she or he is kind of "nerdy." You've tried to include him or her in activities with your friends, but she or he rarely joins you. You sense that your roommate is upset by your guests, and you have talked it over with him or her. You reduced the number of nights per week that you have guests over and think that you are being a reasonable and considerate roommate. Your RA, however, has informed you that your roommate is unhappy and asks that the three of you meet "to talk things over."

In this second scenario, the conflict is still the central focus, but it has been enriched by the inclusion of details of diversity. Adding diversity to all of our examples by acknowledging differences in race, gender, sexual preference, age, siblings, personality, and lifestyle as well as in religious background and rural, suburban, or city background, is an unobtrusive way to remind students constantly that people are not the same. It is also beneficial in helping students discriminate between important and nonimportant information in any given situation. Many conflicts that involve two people of different religious backgrounds have no connection with religion or religious beliefs, but if this lack of connection is not revealed, many students may assume that the conflict is due to the "hot topic," that is due to religious differences. In other situations, students will operate out of an ethnocentric belief that everyone thinks, values, behaves, and reacts to situations and information just as they do. The more that instructors can do to incorporate diversity into the names they give characters, the family patterns they describe, the response patterns used in role plays, and the content and angles from which they teach, the more students will learn. Additional materials such as role-play scenarios, guidesheets, poems, movies, test questions, and short stories must reflect the instructor's commitment to diversity if integration is to be complete and successful.

In summary, in an RA training program the topic of diversity must be addressed by more than a single class session on the subject of culture or prejudice. It is essential to continue that learning and understanding throughout all the topics of the course. This can be accomplished by setting the stage in the first class and by carefully assessing the models, research, and wording of the topic areas and additional materials used in other class sessions of the course.

The Students (RAs)

This section examines two main areas: the cultural backgrounds of the students in the class and the level of knowledge that each student has about other cultures. The information presented is information that should be collected and introduced in the first weeks of class. It is best to gather this information before students enter class. The knowledge about students that this information provides is extremely helpful in the planning of class sessions and small group work.

Students' Knowledge of Their Own Cultural Backgrounds

The information about the cultural background of each student should be gathered directly. Do not assume that because someone "looks" Asian or Native American that they will culturally identify with that particular group. Some students will not really be certain what "culture" or "cultural identity" means. Therefore it will be necessary to spend part of an early class session on the concept of culture. Bennett's (1989) chapter on "Issues of Race and

Culture on the College Campus" in *The Experienced Resident Assistant* is an excellent source of material to use when introducing the concept of culture. The model on the difference between high-context and low-context cultures, discussed earlier, is a place to begin in helping students identify their own cultural orientation. A questionnaire could also be developed to help students identify some of the direct cultural influences on their behavior. Questions that might be included are (1) What are your usual patterns of leisure activity? (2) What role does your family or home community play in your college life? (3) What is your primary reason for attending college? What are your goals? (4) With whom and where do you socialize? With whom and where do you study? (5) Who are your heroes and heroines? (7) What is your favorite type of food, music, dance? (8) What are the similarities and differences between your life at home and your life at college? (9) What culture do you most identify with?

As students grow more comfortable with you and with each other, they may begin—and continue throughout the course—to ask questions in an attempt to understand the differences that are present. Each student's identification of aspects of his or her own culture begins to shift "culture" from theory and abstract concept to practice and day-to-day reality. In addition, this activity helps students learn that they truly live and work in a multicultural environment.

Helping students understand just how powerful culture has been in their lives and the impact that it can have on their role as student leaders is a more difficult task. Although students often have a lot of fun exchanging information about their backgrounds and cultural norms, it is often done at a rather impersonal level.

Students' Understanding and Knowledge of Other Cultures

What many students do not grasp is the level of ethnocentricity that is often present but not verbalized in their discussions with students from a culture different from their own. Many students feel that it is valuable to share information but become defensive if they feel that any attempt is being made to evaluate the behaviors of their culture negatively, even if their culture is one that does not seem to value or accept others. Teaching students to be open to their own and others' cultures is a long and difficult process that deserves its own curriculum. Nevertheless, this learning can be initiated in a leadership training course through the use of experiential or simulation activities. The simulation game *Bafa, Bafa* (Shirts, 1977) is an example of such an activity.

Bafa, Bafa begins by dividing students into two different hypothetical cultures. The students are instructed to behave according to the cultural rules and norms of their assigned culture. All students are encouraged to visit and discover the behavioral norms of the other culture. At the end of the activity, students are asked to comment on their experiences and their impressions of the other culture. Most students will describe the other culture by using value-laden words that are essentially derogatory, for example, *rude*, *pushy*, or *stupid*. Students are also asked, after the behavioral norms and foundations of each culture have been explained, to pick the culture in which they would prefer to live. In this author's experience with over 500 students, approximately 90% of the students picked the culture to which they were originally assigned.

This activity illustrates just how quickly individuals become biased toward "their" group and against a group that is different. It also demonstrates the tendency to evaluate negatively other people's behavior based on the standards of one's own cultural group and background. When these tendencies are exhibited through the use of an experiential activity, students are shocked at how quickly they unwittingly become prejudiced, and how they use this prejudice to label and describe others.

The understanding of ethnocentrism, gained through an activity using hypothetical cultures, is strengthened if it is applied to actual situations and cultures present on the college campus. One situation that is encountered by most student leaders is confrontation. Most RA classes teach styles of confrontation: Confrontation or "methods of approach" is used by resident assistants when they need to speak to another student about counseling-related matters or issues of policy violation. However, cultural differences and their influence upon the dynamics of the interaction are not always mentioned. The reality of the situation for an African American vs. a White RA or a male vs. female RA might be quite different and is likely to be influenced by their gender or race.

Using the example of two RAs, one African American and one White, the need for students to understand their culture, other cultures, and the multiracial/multicultural environment of the situation can be demonstrated in the following scenario:

Situation: Fifty men live on one floor of a high-rise residence hall. Marvin, the RA, walks out into the hall and observes six of the residents gathered around the window at the end of the hall. The residents are laughing as they fill condoms full of water and hurl them at women whom they perceive to be ugly.

How might this confrontation be different if the RA and the students are of different races? What if the women whom the condoms are being thrown at are of the same race as the RA but different than that of the group of men? What if the RA is homosexual and the residents are heterosexual?

Confrontation is not the same for everyone or for every situation. If the RA, Marvin, is African American or homosexual and the residents at the window and the majority of other residents on the floor are White and heterosexual, he will need to learn skills that will enable him to survive as a minority individual on that floor and enable him to be successful in stopping the behavior. If Marvin is White and the residents at the window are African American, he will have to use a style of confrontation that will be accepted by the group and will stop the behavior. If we teach students that a single style of confrontation is likely to work in every situation, we are ignoring the truth. The intergroup dynamics and the cultural pattern of confrontation familiar to the party being confronted need to be assessed before a successful method of confrontation can be chosen by a student leader.

When teaching any skill, the instructor should design practice sessions that give students the opportunity to examine their usual style, alternative styles, and the environment in which the skill is to be used. It will be helpful for men and women, and members of different ethnic minority groups, to share helpful hints and suggestions that can be used in applying the skill or technique in an environment or situation in which their gender or ethnic group is dominant.

SUMMARY: GUIDELINES FOR INTEGRATING RA TRAINING PROGRAMS

Talking with one another is important for the professionals who design and teach the student courses. The following tips and guidelines are offered as a summary and will have the greatest impact if they are discussed and adapted to each specific institution.

1. Set goals for what you want to accomplish. Don't latch onto the concept randomly. Be intentional in your efforts!

2. Values and culture training often work as a good way to introduce differences naturally. This training can also serve as a team builder.

3. Look at the language you use. Do you talk of heroes and not heroines? What are the names that you use as examples when you are teaching? Do you use Chinese, African, or Mexican names? Do you ever mention the disabled, "inconvenienced"?

4. Give background data to your characters.

5. Develop resource areas with files on the experiences and profiles of the minority student populations at your school. List things such as study habits, motivations for attending college, social gathering places, style of dress, religious habits/traditions, family characteristics, hair styles, social customs, famous people.

6. Have each student research a different culture. Invite the students to share what they have learned in different classes.

What happens when diversity is introduced by the students? What is discussed?

7. Think about the group of instructors. What diversity exists within this group? How can you highlight this diversity? What do you currently do to mask this diversity?

8. There is diversity everywhere. How can you bring what you see daily into the classroom? Think about how diversity is or is not integrated into your life and the life of your campus: What do you notice?

9. Integrating diversity and teaching diversity requires that you learn about diversity and not about stereotypes. Find out what you do not know and learn the history.

10. Keep at least one class period devoted to in-depth learning about the minority student populations on your campus. Students need to know beyond simple statements. (I.e., it would be correct to say that many African Americans are Baptist, but this does not explain to a student that the Baptists were the only group that did not require a preacher to have a school education. Thus, many slaves could practice preaching and become successful ministers.)

Diversity is a fact of life. It is not something that can be taught in a single class session. Diversity must be infused into all areas of a student leadership training program. To teach diversity successfully is to examine oneself openly and thoroughly as an instructor, to learn and apply methods and materials that affirm minority cultures, and to encourage students to discover and understand their own culture and the cultures of people around them.

This chapter should be used as a guide for the formation or redesign of RA training programs. It is important, however, that any formulation of an RA training program accurately reflect the cultural environment of the home campus. Although some of the examples provided here might need to be adapted for different cultural groups, the model itself should apply to all training programs. Assessing each component of the interaction between student, instructor, and material is essential and will expedite the realization of cultural pluralism within the RA training program.

REFERENCES

Atkinson, D.R., Morten, G., & Sue, D.W. (1979). *Counseling American minorities, a cross-cultural perspective*. Dubuque, IA: Wm. C. Brown.

Belenky, M., Clinchy, B., Goldberger, N., & Tarule, J. (1986). *Women's ways of knowing: The development of self, voice, and mind*. New York: Basic Books.

Bendet, P. (1986, September). Hostile eyes: What is behind the anger and fear triggered by homosexualtiy? A report on homophobia on American campuses. *Campus Voice.*

Bennett, C. (1986, November). *Teaching intercultural competence and informed citizenship.* Paper presented at the Annual Conference of the National Council of the Social Studies, New York, NY.

Bennett, C. (1989). Issues of race and culture on the college campus. In G. Blimling (Ed.), *The experienced resident assistant* (pp. 39-64). Dubuque, IA: Kendall-Hunt.

Blimling, G., & Miltenberger, L. (1984). *The resident assistant* (2nd ed.). Dubuque, IA: Kendall-Hunt.

Boateng, F. (1990). Combatting the deculturalization of the African American child in the public school system: A multicultural approach. In K. Lomotey (Ed.), *Going to school: The African American experience.* Albany, NY: State University of New York Press.

Cheek, D. (1976). *Assertive Blacks... puzzled Whites.* San Louis Obispo, CA: Impact.

Chickering, A. (1969). *Education and identity.* San Francisco, CA: Jossey-Bass.

Dillon, D.R. (1989). Showing them that I want them to learn and that I care about who they are: A microethnography of the social organization of a secondary low track English-reading classroom. *American Educational Research Journal, 26*(2), 227-259.

Fleming, J. (1985). *Blacks in college.* San Francisco, CA: Jossey-Bass.

Gilligan, C. (1982). *In a different voice: Psychological theory and women's development.* Cambridge, MA: Harvard University Press.

Hale-Benson, J.E. (1986). *Black children: Their roots, culture, and learning styles.* Baltimore, MD: Johns Hopkins University Press.

Hall, E.T. (1959). *The silent language.* New York: Doubleday.

Hall, E.T. (1966). *The hidden dimension.* New York: Doubleday.

Hall, E.T. (1976). *Beyond culture.* New York: Doubleday.

Hilliard, A. (1976). *Alternatives to IQ testing: An approach to the identification of gifted minority children* (Final report to the California State Department of Education). In J. Hale-Benson, *Black children: Their roots, culture, and learning styles* (p. 42). Baltimore, MD: Johns Hopkins University Press, 1986.

Hirschorn, M. W. (1987, April 29). Homosexual students report on a backlash against them as AIDS gains attention; at Chicago virulent attacks. *Chronicle of Higher Education,* pp. 32.

Kohlberg, L. (1984). *The psychology of moral development: Vol. 2. Essays on moral development.* San Francisco: Harper & Row.

Lawrence, G. (1982). *People types and tiger stripes.* Gainsville, FL: Center for the Application of Psychological Type.

Lennon, T. (Writer & Producer). (1988). *Racism 101: A documentary* [videotape]. Boston, MA: WGBH Education Foundation.

Lindley, P., & Masiello, C. (1988). *Assessment of resident adviser training courses taught in the northeast and midwest regions of the Association of College and University Housing Officers—International (ACUHO-I).* Unpublished manuscript.

Myers, I.B. (1975). *Manual: The Myers-Briggs Type Indicator.* Palo Alto, CA: Consulting Psychologists Press.

Myers, I.B., & McCaulley, M.H. (1985). *Manual: A guide to the development and use of the Myers-Briggs Type Indicator.* Palo Alto, CA: Consulting Psychologists Press.

National Society for the Study of Education. (1975). *Teacher education: The 74th yearbook of the National Society for the Study of Education.* Chicago, IL: University of Chicago Press.

Perry, W. G., Jr., (1970). *Intellectual and ethical development in the college years: A scheme.* New York: Holt, Rinehart & Winston.

Sedlacek, W.E., & Brooks, G. (1976). *Racism in American education: A model for change.* Chicago, IL: Nelson-Hall.

Shade, B.J. (1982). Afro-American cognitive style: A variable in school success? *Review of Educational Research, 52*(2).

Shirts, R.G. (1977). *Bafa, Bafa: A cross-culture simulation.* Del Mar, CA: Simile.

Silver, H. F., & Hanson, J.R. (1980). *Teacher self-assessment* (Dealing with Diversity Series, Manual No. 1). Moorestown, NJ: Hanson Silver & Associates.

Straub, C.A. (1987). Women's development of autonomy and Chickering's theory. *Journal of College Student Personnel, 28*(3), 198-205.

VanBebber, L.J., & Roper, L. (1987, February). *Design issues within a multiracial classroom/training environment.* Workshop presented at the Maryland Student Affairs Conference, College Park, MD.

CHAPTER 7

PLANNING PROGRAMS FOR CULTURAL PLURALISM: A PRIMER

Leila V. Moore, H. Jane Fried, and Arthur A. Costantino

Getting started with activities and other interventions leading to campus-wide goals for cultural pluralism seems to be an overwhelming task for many institutions. Institutions struggle over who should initiate the programs, who should fund them, and how students and others should be encouraged to attend. Planning sessions range from chaos as we are first full of good ideas to silence as we are then overwhelmed by the size of the task.

The purpose of this chapter is to introduce and discuss an approach to the process of starting programs and activities in support of cultural pluralism. Included are ideas for enhancing campus acceptance and support of programs, gathering basic resources, and convening a group of persons interested in planning and presenting activities. Suggestions are included for marketing programs and expanding program options. Specific approaches to the design and content of programs are discussed. Following a summary of the suggestions presented in the chapter, the authors have included an annotated resource list based on their experiences with the items noted.

This chapter deals primarily with initial steps in creating a campus-wide program for cultural pluralism, and it includes discussion of the process of getting started as well as the content of the programs, policies, or activities that might be developed in support of cultural pluralism. The material is presented in the form of a series of tips or suggestions for the practitioner.

THE PROCESS: GETTING STARTED

In initiating cultural pluralism programs, many practitioners make the mistake either of diving right into activities without adequate or complete plans, or of planning strategies without simultaneously conducting some experimental programs to see how they are received. Neither approach is helpful. This section presents and briefly explains some first steps in moving beyond rhetoric toward achievement of the goal of cultural pluralism. The suggestions, which are intended to moderate the extremes of programming without planning and planning without programming, represent ideas for the planning process involved in getting started. They do not include important information about program evaluations, developing longer range goals, or expanding programs to include all campus populations. The suggestions reflect a fairly conservative approach to the process of getting started. They are offered within the constraints of a low-to-nonexistent budget, and they rely heavily on the concept of priming the pump as a strategy for producing more programs and activities.

Acquire Support

Beginning a campus-wide effort requires institutional support *at some level*. At many institutions, seeking presidential support at the outset may be unrealistic, but the support of a particular office is important. The office of student activities, commuter programs, and the office of student life are potential sources for initial support. These offices typically have responsibilities for more educational and developmental programs than for service delivery activities. The staff members from these offices often have considerable expertise in the mechanics of successful programming. They know how to advertise, design, and evaluate programs. Their design work is often excellent because they understand different ways to engage students.

Other offices that might be considered for initial support are those that specialize in program development and implementation for underrepresented groups. Examples include the Center for Women Students and the African American Cultural Center. Because of their expertise with specific student cohorts, staff members from such offices often have greater understanding of the content area related to their special population.

For initial program efforts, students may appreciate less content and the opportunity to interact or to explore their values. Consequently, an office that serves the entire campus will create a more forceful statement to the campus about the importance of cultural pluralism and the institution's commitment to it.

The more specialized office may be a better choice if planners anticipate that the issues raised by participants will require more in-depth knowledge. Students who have become committed to learning about pluralism may also be better satisfied with the depth of information provided by specialists.

The ideal situation is, of course, a partnership between the two types of offices. When such a partnership exists, the programs can benefit from careful attention to both process and content.

In addition to securing expertise and cosponsorship, other support is also needed. This support can take many forms, but the most basic for developing a campus-wide program is the time to do the job. At least one full-time professional staff member should rearrange or reinterpret his or her job description so that it reflects the responsibility for designing and implementing a campus-wide program for cultural pluralism. That staff member's director should place a high priority on the implementation of the program. Inclusion in a professional staff member's job description and priority placed on cultural pluralism programs by at least one office constitutes the basic administrative support needed to begin.

Funding is also a consideration in gathering support. However, although funding ultimately may be required, program initiation should not be automatically presumed to require funding—and especially not "new" funds. Time, rather than funding, is the most critical element during the early stages of program development. In addition, a request for new money in most institutions will require some proof that the programs have been tried and are effective for the campus populations. Developing the proof comes later in the process, after a program strategy has been developed.

It is also important to develop a commitment to the goals of the intervention on the part of at least one group whose composition by gender, ethnicity, or culture reflects that of the audience for whom the intervention is intended. The purpose of the intervention should be explained, input should be solicited, and a public endorsement sought. For instance, a manual designed to assist faculty in promoting cultural pluralism in the classroom is more likely to be used if endorsed by respected members of the faculty or by a faculty governing council.

Even at the most basic office or program level, institutional support is sometimes hard to secure. In these instances, cultural pluralism program planning can begin with the support of student government. Very often a student-sponsored program, particularly on the topic of cultural pluralism, will emerge as a campus priority. A staff member who is working with a student-government-sponsored program should be able to use the suggestions here in working with a student group.

Gather Resources

Gathering resources first includes selection of a theoretical perspective to guide efforts and suggest realistic outcomes. A theoretical perspective about identity development provides adequate descriptions of persons in various stages of their awareness as persons with a cultural heritage. These descriptions offer a means of diagnosing awareness levels for target groups and of creating reasonable expectations for learning outcomes. Articles by Jackson and Hardiman (1983) and Downing and Roush (1985), for example, provide clear explanations about identity development. A third resource is Helms

(1984), who has proposed racial identity development stages for African American and White populations. According to Helms, there are four or five primary stages of identity development. For African Americans, the first stage is Preencounter. In this stage African Americans may tend to deny their Blackness or to criticize their Blackness. At the same time, they idealize Whiteness, and identify with White attitudes and practices as they understand them. For Whites, the first stage is Contact. In this stage, Whites first become aware of the existence of African Americans. There is a sense of curiosity and naivete in their early awareness. In this stage, there is also no awareness within the White person of himself or herself as a racial being.

Helms' second stage of identity development for African Americans is the Encounter stage. Often, African Americans enter this stage because of a negative experience with Whites, or because of a particularly positive experience with African Americans. The dominant feeling is a strong acceptance of oneself as African American. For Whites, the second stage is Disintegration. In this stage, Whites become aware of themselves as racial beings, and of the existence of racism. The negative attributes of the White culture pose a dilemma for the White person in this stage: One could attempt to protect African Americans from the racism by adopting a parental attitude toward African Americans, or one could take on the attributes of the African American culture and ignore the White culture, or one could retreat farther into the White culture, thereby ignoring the existence of racism.

The third stage of development for African Americans is Immersion/ Emersion. In this stage, African Americans devalue the White culture. There is a sharp awareness of racism and racist attitudes, and a rejection of the White culture as inferior. The third stage for Whites is the Reintegration stage. Here, the White person develops an animosity toward African Americans, tends to deny any similarities between the African American and White races, and insulates himself or herself from any interactions with African Americans.

The fourth and final stage for African American identity development, proposed by Helms, is Internalization. In this stage, African Americans emerge from their wholehearted focus on their identity as African Americans and adopt a broader view that includes wholehearted acceptance of self as African American as well as an acknowledgement of the White culture. In the Internalized stage, African Americans are also sensitive to oppression against others in addition to African Americans. Experiences with oppression are not forgotten, but they are no longer the focal point of the individual's self-awareness. For Whites, the fourth and fifth stages are Pseudo-Independence and Autonomy. In these stages, the White person develops first a somewhat passive, intellectual view of racial differences. The naivete of the earlier Contact stage is gone, but the curiosity about and acceptance of differences remains. In the Autonomy stage, the person becomes both intellectually aware of racial similarities and differences and accepting of the differences.

There is no need for the differences to be eliminated in this stage, and in fact, the White person seeks opportunities and interactions that reflect the differences because they add richness to his or her perspective.

In addition to the resource of a theoretical perspective, gathering resources also includes identifying programs already in place on campus. Identifying existing programs can be accomplished by reading student newspapers and faculty newsletters. Programs or courses identified in these publications should include the name of the presenter or instructor. A consultation with existing program presenters or instructors serves two purposes: It provides an opportunity to obtain program course outlines and materials to form the beginning of a training resources library, and it becomes the foundation for a core group of persons who have a knowledge base in cultural pluralism.

Finally, gathering resources includes conducting an inventory of campus-owned videotapes and films that might be used in programs. Obtaining campus-owned instructional materials, particularly films and videotapes that can be shown and followed by a discussion, can be accomplished by contacting the campus audio-visual service for consultation or for catalogs. Materials can also be gathered by contacting selected academic departments for listings of materials they use and make available to other campus offices.

Convene a Small Group of Interested Staff, Faculty, and Students

From the list of existing programs, certain names will surface as frequent program presenters or instructors. Using this group as the beginning of a pool from which to draw a small group, the staff member with responsibility for cultural pluralism can add the names of staff or students who may be less experienced as presenters but who have a deep concern for achieving cultural pluralism. The staff member should select and convene a group of 10 to 15 people who represent experience as well as commitment to the goal, and who also represent diversity in cultural heritage, age, role on campus, and level of identity development.

Sooner or later, most efforts to promote pluralism will extend to off-campus environments. Thus, to the extent possible, it is important to include members of the community in which the campus is located. Support for off-campus initiatives is more likely to occur if community leaders have been included from the start. In many urban settings ethnic minority communities will have a keen interest in the campus effort.

The purposes of this small group of program presenters are (a) to provide diverse thoughts for the planning of a campus-wide effort, (b) to serve as a forum for new program ideas, (c) to form a coalition of potential facilitators/workshop presenters for whatever plan is developed, (d) to develop a shared commitment to the effort, (e) to identify and possibly advocate for needed policy changes, and (f) to provide a source of support for each other, particularly during the early stages of planning and inevitable resistance to the changes inferred in this plan.

Establish a Rationale for Participation

Initial program offerings are likely to depend heavily upon voluntary participation. Campuses report that programs are often attended by those individuals who are among the best informed. Although appeals to the social conscience of potential participants should not be eliminated, there is often ambivalence or even hostility and a refusal to be identified as a possible advocate with issues of equity. Consequently, appeals based solely upon commitments to equity may not be sufficient. Attendance often can be increased by outlining how increased awareness can contribute to success in the workplace. Offerings can also be described as opportunities to develop new skills or to complement and challenge existing learning.

Increase Visibility

The visibility of programs can lead to the development of other programs and to the development of a wider audience for existing programs. Suggestions for increasing visibility include providing regular press releases about existing programs as well as about the establishment of the cultural pluralism planning group described above. Following these initial public information efforts, establish a regular source of publicity about the campus-wide cultural pluralism efforts. The content of the publicity will vary as the program develops, but a regular column containing information about the program is the goal. This regular column should appear in both the student newspaper and in the faculty/staff newsletters. Topic possibilities for this column might include features on workshop presenters; announcement of new programs and courses; a "suggestion box" for readers to provide ideas for new programs, suggest new policies, comment on the existing effort, and suggest improvements; a place to feature information about popular films that have a cultural pluralism theme or tone; and a "wish I'd said that" feature, offering well-stated responses to local incidents of bigotry.

Begin New Programs on Friendly Territory

As existing cultural pluralism programs and courses give rise to more programs or parts of courses, schedule inaugural efforts with friendly faces. The staff or student groups related to members of the planning group might be willing to serve as audiences for these new programs and to assist in any fine-tuning by suggesting revisions. Those who are singled out as a testing group for new programs to be offered to the campus may experience two effects: First, they may become more involved in the education of the campus by passing along what they have learned. Second, because they have experienced the content of the program, they may be able to suggest other audiences for the program. Their input should also benefit the planning group by providing more diverse opinions about program content.

Imbed Programs Within Established Efforts

New interventions to foster pluralism have a greater likelihood of being accepted if they are incorporated into existing programs that have already proven successful. Not only will the new initiative benefit from the established reputation of the existing program, but such an approach also reinforces the notion that promoting cultural pluralism should be an integral part of all ongoing efforts. Opportunities for imbedding programs are likely to be numerous. On many campuses cross-cultural communications training or awareness-building programs are being incorporated into the services of personnel departments. At institutions with ongoing commitments to community service, new projects can be chosen that both serve the community and promote an appreciation of cultural differences. Leadership education conferences can include workshops or program series devoted to empowering underrepresented groups, and trainers can be encouraged to revise the content of established programs.

Avoid Highly Resistant Target Groups — At First

Program planners can often agree on which target groups "need the most attention." These groups, however, can also be the most intimidating when it comes to developing effective interventions. When one's own level of awareness is considerably greater than the group targeted for programs, it is easy to design interventions that have the effect of a sledge hammer. Members of the target group may learn to "duck the blow" in such a case, but they generally don't learn what the presenters hoped they would.

As the planning group gathers experience in producing learning from the interventions with friendly groups, their perceptions of the "needy" group will change. As the planners assess their strategies for this type of group and begin to see the potential for learning rather than the need to punish the group for its lack of awareness or participation, they will be ready to develop a plan for approaching the group. Initial contact with these "bastions of bigotry" may be one-to-one interactions with a planning group member. These one-to-one contacts may yield information about the best future approaches to take with the group. Program planners need to remember that the more resistant a group is to learning, the longer the process. Working with a resistant group can be frustrating, time consuming, discouraging, and sometimes debilitating to the planners. The presence of a trainers' support group can be particularly helpful when working with resistant audiences.

Prepare a Moderate Number and Variety of Workshops/Programs and Repeat Them Throughout the Year

Programs or workshops that can be repeated periodically will reduce resistance from presenters who may only have time to do a program requiring minimal or no new preparations. Programs that are well developed initially and that have been well received on a trial basis can also be used to familiarize new facilitators with several stable program designs for their own future use.

THE CONTENT

On most campuses, the struggle to get started with interventions supporting cultural pluralism reflects a naiveté about cultural differences. "What is a cultural difference, and why do I need to know about this anyhow?" This naiveté may be motivated by a lack of exposure to differences, or by any number of other variables, including resistance to learning new information. In the authors' experiences, the task of getting started on most college campuses involves awareness training, that is, the provision of basic information about cultural differences. This section rests on the assumption that getting started involves reaching this naive and unaware target group, including faculty, staff, and students, as well as the group of faculty, staff, and students who are somewhat aware but not sure of how to contribute to the goal of cultural pluralism. To these ends we offer ideas for program content, ideas for reaching the resistant and the "willing but not yet able" groups on campus. As in the preceding section, the focus is on getting started rather than on the longer term goal of designing a comprehensive program that affects the campus as a whole.

Develop Alternative Methods of Presenting Information

In most instances, reading material or lectures efficiently convey information about cultural pluralism but do not promote learning. In order to maximize learning about cultural pluralism, trainers must rely more on visual presentations, create opportunities to relate personal experiences to the information, and, above all, repeat the information by presenting the same content in a variety of ways. The annotated list of training resources included in this chapter contains recommendations for a basic library of films, videos, simulations, and similar media that can be used in awareness training.

Make Use of Campus, Local, or National Current Events

The student newspaper or a local paper contains many examples of both bigotry and pluralism. These items can be used as powerful teaching tools because it is easier for students to relate to campus or local situtations. Keeping a current file of accounts of such incidents will provide the planning group with timely topics for informal discussions. The same accounts can be developed into case studies for more formalized discussions with student groups or for classroom presentations.

Recognize and Reward Responsible Reactions to Bigotry on Campus or in the Community

Personalizing responsible reactions can be a powerful motivator to continue the rewarded behavior. For example, a letter of commendation might be sent directly to a student group that responds effectively to an act of violence on campus. Another suggestion is to create a caring person award and present it weekly via the student newspaper. Other ideas include writing an open letter to a community business that participates in a cultural awareness activity, or writing feature articles on student and faculty groups that have made a special effort in the name of cultural pluralism.

Capitalize on Existing Events and Activities to Heighten Cultural Awareness

A controversial speaker can be followed by a debate that presents many views of the controversy. Contact instructors who may be planning to cancel a class because they will be out of town. Ask these instructors to have the class meet in their absence to participate in a discussion about pluralism and provide facilitators for the discussion.

Target Student Orientation Programs

Each semester, new student orientation programs provide a good opportunity to introduce the importance of pluralism. These programs serve to set a new tone or new expectations on campus about pluralism. They can be particularly powerful programs in terms of their influence on students.

Be Ready for Increased Conflict and Controversy as Awareness Increases

Experience on numerous campuses suggests to the authors that conflict increases as cultural awareness increases. As individuals become more sensitive to bigotry, they tend to express their opinions more often. If accused of insensitivity, individuals respond angrily and defensively. Anonymous acts such as defacing posters with racist or sexist comments and racist or sexist graffiti on campus will probably increase. This inevitable increase in conflict can be turned into an opportunity. Residence staff, Greek-letter organization advisers, and peer counselors are groups that can be prepared for the increased conflict. Workshops and case discussions on how to respond to situations such as these should occur frequently. Staff and students alike need many opportunities to "practice" their responses to increased conflict. Role plays using campus incidents as the scenarios are easily enacted and usually generate considerable interest among those who participate in the role plays. The use of actual campus incidents for these situations, rather than developing abstract "what if" situations, is a more powerful and engaging method for educating. Discussion of the effect of various approaches to the conflicts are most beneficial in helping "front line" staff become more comfortable in the presence of conflict.

Keep an Annotated List of Resources That Are Available for Programs and Activities on Cultural Pluralism

At least one person should be responsible for scanning new materials on cultural pluralism and acquiring those that seem suited to awareness training. Included in this chapter is a training resources list that contains suggestions for films, videos, simulations and other activities that are useful for getting started with an awareness program. Given for each suggested item is a description, recommendation for use, and indication for most effective use. Cautions are also noted. This training resources listing should be viewed as a starting point for campuses in developing their own lists. It is not meant to be all-encompassing; the criterion for inclusion is the authors' experience with the item. The reader should observe that not all cultures are represented equally in the material. Although the authors collected many other resources, it was determined that if evaluation of the item's use could not be made, it would not be included.

Special Notes to Trainers and Facilitators Developing the Content for Cultural Pluralism Programs

Cultural awareness is slow to develop in a person. Trainers who succeed in helping people begin the process of understanding individuals from other cultures must accomplish two specific tasks. First, trainers provoke a paradigm shift in the trainees by helping trainees empathize both cognitively and affectively with those about whom they are learning. This shift and move toward empathy is not easily or quickly accomplished. The best methods combine challenge and support and seem to procede incrementally until something akin to the "aha" experience occurs. Second, the trainer must know how and when to challenge and how and when to support. The various "isms" are learned over a long period of time and combine cognition and affect in intense and sometimes unpredictable ways. A good trainer must be well versed in the culture that she or he is attempting to open up to nonmembers so that she or he can use whatever material emerges in the context of the training experience.

The items presented in the training resources list included in this chapter are intended to be discussion provokers, to be primarily awareness raisers. They are not sufficient in themselves to produce any major, short-term shift in trainee consciousness. This chapter is about getting started with awareness training, and the materials reflect that purpose. Materials for facilitating communication across cultures are not discussed. However, as trainers become aware of trainees' readiness for further understanding, they will need to immerse themselves much more fully in the cultures that will be the focus for more in-depth programs.

As trainers fulfill the awareness-raising goals of provoking paradigm shifts and combining challenge and support in their programs, they must also keep in mind that messages about sensitivity often sink in only after they are repeated many times. Redundancy may be boring to the facilitator, but it is a critical element in stimulating awareness. The same audience that responds with hostility to a discussion in November may be open to the *same* discussion in January.

Working as pairs in conducting cultural awareness programs provides support, adds variety for both the instructor and the learner, and generally improves the effectiveness of program presentations.

Follow-up meetings with the same target audiences should be made by the same team of trainers if possible. Groups tend to respond quite favorably to familiar faces, particularly in the area of learning about awareness. The learner who is developing new awareness is changing in important ways and tends to want to share that process with people he or she knows and trusts.

At the beginning, rehearse new program presentations using the planning group as an audience. The rehearsal produces a critical sense of familiarity with the program on the part of the facilitator, a familiarity that is later reflected in a much more effective program presentation.

CONCLUSION

The purpose of this chapter is to provide concrete suggestions for planners who want to produce greater cultural awareness on their campuses, to provide enough suggestions for planners so that they will feel comfortable in getting the process started. In the discussions of process and content issues, the main messages are these:

1. Identify a small group of interested and able facilitators who can serve as planners, as facilitators, and as a support group for the effort.

2. Begin with what is already in place on campus and make it more visible.

3. Have a plan and a theoretical base before trying new programs.

4. Experiment with new programs on campus while developing a campus-wide plan.

5. Begin with low-budget plans.

6. Locate one or two people who will identify media sources and produce newspaper articles featuring cultural awareness efforts. Locate one or two more who will manage the reward and recognition plan.

7. Stick to a few target groups at first, including at least one "converted" group. This will be the group from whom new facilitators may be drawn.

8. Emphasize repeated programs. Carrying out a few programs well in many settings is better than trying many different programs simply for the sake of the variety.

9. Prepare for the conflict and disagreement that will ensue as awareness increases.

10. Stick to awareness programs for separate groups in the initial planning. Do not attempt a campus-wide program on intergroup communication skills until groups indicate readiness for learning these skills. Some may need to experience one or more failures to communicate before they are willing to learn new skills

11. Make heavy use of campus events as topics for discussion.

These suggestions are written with a variety of campus situations and settings in mind. Although readers may have already experienced failures after trying some of these suggestions, perhaps the suggestions were tried without the planning and systematic attention to specific campus needs discussed here. These approaches cannot guarantee success, but they can increase its likelihood. Finally, note that just a few ways of getting started with cultural awareness programming have been suggested. There are many more ways. However, the authors' experiences indicate that the ideas outlined here have a good chance of working in many settings.

TRAINING RESOURCE LIST

Simulation Games

1. *Bafa, Bafa* Delmar, CA: Simile. This is a 2-hour cross-cultural simulation that is based on the creation of two societies with different values and norms. Representatives of the societies must learn to understand and communicate with each other. *Bafa, Bafa* can be used in groups of 12 to 30. The instructions are somewhat complicated and must be studied by the facilitators well in advance. The simulation is effective because of the level of involvement that the participants usually achieve. Facilitators should be well versed in the typologies that are generally used to describe cultures and should be able to help participants translate their learning to real-life situations in which, for example, they may be involved with people from collectivist cultures as well as with people from individualist cultures. We highly recommend that facilitators conduct this simulation as a "trial run" before using it with targeted audiences. *Bafa, Bafa* is excellent for naive audiences because it is challenging, fun, and educational.

2. *Star Power*. Delmar, CA: Simile. This is a highly competitive trading game in which the outcome is predetermined because some of the players have more resources than others. It is helpful in explaining the structural disadvantages under which some cultures function in the United States and under which some countries operate in the world economy. Key concepts include the effects of power and powerlessness on individual behavior and the effect of one's position in the power hierarchy on one's understanding of fairness. The director's guide provides good advice for helping participants apply their learning to understanding the various "isms" that systematically disadvantage people in any society. To get maximum benefit from this game, the director must be well informed on power dynamics and the concepts of oppression.

3. *Bargaining, United Nations Style: Exploring the Impact of Cultural Values.* In J. W. Pfeiffer (Ed.), *1990 Annual Handbook for Group Facilitators.* San Diego, CA: University Associates. This simulation is comparable to but less complex than *Bafa, Bafa*. It contains four cultures that are easily comparable to nationalities and geographic areas, and it focuses not only on understanding and defining attributes of culture but also on finding ways to negotiate and create a climate of mutual understanding. It requires no equipment.

Films: General Approaches to Diversity and Prejudice

1. *Bill Cosby on Prejudice*. Santa Monica, CA: Pyramid Films. This is a film about stereotyping and its effects. Cosby uses his typical tongue-in-cheek

approach to criticize people from many groups—Asians, older people, Jews, African Americans, southerners, and women. He appears in a half-white face, which adds to the incongruity of his remarks. At the end of the film, he realizes that he has ultimately isolated himself from all other people and leaves the audience to discuss the issues he has raised as well as the consequences of stereotyping. The humor in this film lowers the threat level to participants in the discussion that follows the showing of the film.

2. *Valuing Diversity*. San Francisco, CA: Copeland Griggs Productions. This is a film/video series that recently has been updated and reissued. The series focuses on diversity in the workplace and includes discussion of ethnic, age, gender, ability, and sexual orientation differences. Topics include attitudes toward work, competition, authority, conflict, and other behavioral norms and values that differ by culture. The facilitator must be able to help the participants translate the meaning of events into their own contexts.

3. *Going International*. San Francisco, CA: Copeland Griggs Productions. This is a film series designed for visitors who are working in the United States and Americans who are working abroad. Transcripts are provided for people who are not sufficiently fluent in spoken English to understand the fast-paced dialogue. Producers explain that they maintained a fast pace in the film because Americans do not slow down for people from other cultures and do not understand that time is interpreted differently in different parts of the world.

4. *A Tale of O—On Being Different*. Boston, MA: Goodmeasure, Inc. A generic tale of the "outsider," this videographic presentation describes what happens when a person who is different according to any criterion attempts to enter a homogeneous group. The predictable reactions of the insiders to a new person are presented, including testing the person's competence, changing the language used, stereotyping, and exaggerating their own normal behavior to focus on the outsider's "otherness." Catchy music and clever puns make the video an enjoyable discussion starter. The difficulty in using this video comes from its generic nature. Participants occasionally cannot relate the abstract "X" and "O" paradigm to real treatment of individuals, but they can usually remember a time when they were an "O" and identify with the feelings of a new person or member of a minority group at some level. The facilitator must be able to help translate from a business context to an educational or a social setting.

5. *The Gods Must Be Crazy*. This is a popular film about the Bushmen of the Kalahari Desert and what happens to them when a pilot drops a soda (pop) bottle out of his plane while flying over their living area. The society begins to change as soon as this intrusion arrives from the technological world.

The film is the story of the group leader's attempt to return the bottle to his gods and his involvement with the English colonials who live along the way to the canyon where his gods reside. The contrast between the two cultures is excellent, as is the description of the problem of communication between two societies that describe reality differently. The film is available in commercial video stores.

6. *A Class Divided.* This is a Public Broadcasting System (PBS) video about an experiment in discrimination performed by an Iowa third-grade teacher to help her students learn about racism in the United States. It begins by showing how discrimination affects the attitudes of the children who are differentiated by the color of their eyes. Later segments show this teacher's work with adult populations in which she replicates the experiment with equally powerful results. The video is self-explanatory and easy to use.

About African Americans

1. *Black History: Lost, Stolen, or Strayed.* Bill Cosby conducts a tour of African American history in the United States, ending in the mid-1960s at a freedom school in Philadelphia. This film illustrates how the media and the arts have distorted or ignored the contributions of African Americans to American society and the negative effects this neglect has on the self-image of African American children. It is a useful review of history for students who do not know about or understand the civil rights movement and its antecedents. The film is available from Public Broadcasting System videos.

2. *Eyes on the Prize.* This is an extensive presentation of the civil rights movement in the 1960s and 1970s. The six-part award-winning series is available from PBS. "Eyes II" has been released, and information should now be available.

3. *Do the Right Thing.* This commercial film by Spike Lee shows racial tension building in a New York neighborhood on a hot day. It is useful in developing insight and generating intra- or interracial discussion. The film is available in commercial video stores.

About Asians

1. *The Sewing Woman.* Franklin Lakes, NJ: Deepfocus Productions. This is a story of a Chinese woman refugee and her life in the United States from her early immigration to relatively old age. This award-winning documentary focuses on how she makes meaning in her life and manages her sorrow, confusion, and conflicts with life in the new world.

2. *The Wash.* This is a story of a Japanese woman and her family living in San Francisco. The woman leaves her husband of many years because he is too

traditional, but she continues to do his wash every week. Her conflicts and desires to have more of an individual life are shown, as are discussions between her two daughters about the frustrations of biculturalism. Segments of the film show the woman's new male friend and their life, one daughter's marriage to an African American man, and the other daughter's conflicts about her life as a professional person as well as her parents' expectations for her in a traditional context. There are excellent conversations between the daughters and among the mother and daughters about change. The film is available in commercial video stores.

About Gay and Lesbian Persons

Pink Triangles. Cambridge, MA: Cambridge Documentaries. This classic film presents some of the recent history of abuse and discrimination experienced by lesbian and gay individuals. Homosexuals wore pink triangles in Hitler's concentration camps, which singled them out for specific types of abuse.

About Mexican Americans

Stand and Deliver. This is a popular film that depicts life among the Mexican American community of East Los Angeles. It shows an exceptionally dedicated math teacher working with students who accept their second-class status in American society and describes how he forces their aspirations to a higher level. The film also illustrates some of the severe value conflicts that develop when poor young people from a strongly family-oriented culture begin to aspire to achievement in the individualist, competitive Anglo culture. This film is available in commercial video stores.

About Jews

The Anti-Defamation League (ADL) of B'Nai B'Rith Hillel Foundation National Student Secretariat has excellent materials on coping with anti-Semitism on campus. Its national address is 823 United Nations Plaza, New York, NY 10017. ADL has regional offices, and campuses with local Hillel Foundations can contact the Student Secretariat directly. Other resources about Jews are listed in the Books section.

About Native Americans

Little Big Man. This is a commercial film starring Dustin Hoffman that shows some aspects of Native American culture. It presents the problem of a man who is kidnapped from his tribe at an early age as he attempts to move between cultures. Facilitators using the film as an educational tool must be knowledgeable about a broad range of Native American tribes.

Most nonnative people are unaware of the broad range of cultures and tribes that exist in North America.

About Women and About Men

The National Women's History Project has a wide range of films, books, and curricula about women and their contributions to American society. Such materials can be obtained by contacting the project at 7738 Bell Rd., Windsor, CA 95492.

1. *One Fine Day*. Windsor, CA: The National Women's History Project. This is a 5-minute film collage of women's achievements in the United States. It is an excellent discussion starter. The presenter must be familiar with the film as well as with women's history because the images move so quickly that they are easily missed.

2. *Killing Us Softly*. Cambridge, MA: Cambridge Documentaries. This is an educational film about representations of women in the media and the violent implications of some typical advertising cliches.

3. *Not a Love Story*. New York, NY: National Film Board of Canada. This is a powerful educational film about the pornography industry that describes the differences between eroticism and pornography. Its graphic portrayal of violence often causes conflict among observers and frequently provokes some members of the audience to leave the room. It should be shown only by a skilled facilitator who can help observers focus on their feelings and reactions and direct their anger in nondestructive ways.

4. *All of Me*. This is an entertaining commercial film by Steve Martin and Lily Tomlin about a woman who gets trapped in a man's body. It can be used to provoke a discussion of gender differences in world view, aspirations, and communication style if presented by a person who is knowledgeable in these areas. It is available in commercial video stores.

5. *The Pinks and the Blues*. This videotape is available from the Public Broadcasting System as part of the Nova series. It addresses the issue of sex-role stereotyping. There are interviews with knowledgeable researchers and video observations of boys and girls growing up in different settings. It is informative, interesting, and of low threat. It can be easily related to the life experiences of most middle-class college students.

6. *Bill Moyers Interviews Robert Bly on Masculinity*. This is an excellent 2-hour interview with Bly on his ideas of masculinity and why men seem to be having so much difficulty coping with life in the latter part of the 20th century. The film varies conversation and video observation of men's groups and direct recording of men's opinions about their own lives and their relationships with their fathers. It is available from the Public Broadcasting System.

Books and Other Resources

Banks, J. (1987). *Teaching Strategies for Ethnic Studies* (4th Ed.). Boston: Allyn Bacon, Inc. This is a compilation of approaches to teaching about ethnicity. The book contains good models for thinking about ethnicity, culture, and moving across cultures.

Beck, E. T. (Ed.). (1982). *Nice Jewish Girls.* Watertown, MA: Persephone Press. This is an anthology by lesbian Jewish women from both the Ashkenazi and Sephardic streams of the culture. The anthology describes difficulties in living in the Jewish world, which values marriage, family, and children, and the lesbian world, which defines family differently and does not emphasize children in the same way.

Bridges. This is a journal for Jewish feminists and friends. It contains fiction, poetry, political analysis, revision of ritual, and photography. It is available by subscription through P.O. Box 18437, Seattle, WA 98118.

Kolton, E. (Ed.). (1976). *The Jewish Woman.* New York: Schocken Press. This book describes the phases of a Jewish woman's life as defined and celebrated by ritual; the role of women in Jewish law; and Jewish women in the past, in modern society, and in literature.

Moraga, C., & Anzaldua, G. (Eds.). (1981). *This Bridge Called My Back.* Watertown, MA: Persephone Press. This anthology describes, from a personal point of view, the difficulties of challenging tradition and family norms in Hispanic and African American cultures. It contains personal essays and many poems.

Obear, K. (1985). *Opening Doors to Understanding and Acceptance: A Facilitator's Guide to Presenting Workshops on Lesbian and Gay Issues.* Amherst, MA: The Human Advantage. This is a manual that presents a variety of activities designed to help people challenge their homophobic attitudes and behaviors. It contains an extensive bibliography as well as articles designed to help facilitators become more informed on this topic. Activities range from low-threat information presentations to more demanding self-assessment and self-disclosure workshops.

The Anti-Defamation League (ADL) of B'Nai B'Rith Hillel Foundation National Student Secretariat has excellent materials on coping with anti-Semitism on campus. Its national address is 823 United Nations Plaza, New York, NY 10017. ADL has regional offices, and campuses with local Hillel Foundations can contact the Student Secretariat directly.

The National Women's History Project has a wide range of films, books, and curricula about women and their contributions to American society. Such materials can be obtained by contacting the project at 7738 Bell Rd., Windsor, CA 95492.

Finally, we invite trainers to collect and listen to ethnic music as well as the music from other underrepresented groups, and to play the music as part of training experiences. Trainers can discuss the emotional tone and, if they exist, the lyrics. Such music can often be found in the "other" bins of music stores, although women's music frequently has its own section.

REFERENCES

Downing, N. E., & Roush, K. L. (1985). From passive acceptance to active commitment: A model of feminist identity development for women. *The Counseling Psychologist, 13*(4), 695-709.

Helms, J. E. (1984). Toward a theoretical explanation of the effects of race on counseling: A Black and White model. *The Counseling Psychologist, 12* (4), 153-164.

Jackson, B. W., & Hardiman, R. (1983). Racial identity development: Implications for managing the multiracial work force. *The NTL Managers' Handbook*. Bethel, ME: National Training Laboratories.

CHAPTER 8

NCAA POLICIES AND THE AFRICAN AMERICAN STUDENT ATHLETE

Mitchell F. Rice

INTRODUCTION

A basketball coach's star center finished one semester with four Fs and a D. "Son," the coach remonstrated gently, "it looks to me like you're spending too much time on one subject." ("Best," 1989)

The recruitment, retention, and graduation of athletes have become major issues of concern and attention in the higher education arena. Colleges and universities have been extensively criticized for failing to establish and adhere to satisfactory academic standards for student athletes. The U.S. General Accounting Office, the investigative arm of Congress, found that over the 5-year period, from September 1982 to September 1987, about one-third of Division I football and basketball programs had graduation rates of 0% to 20%, and about one-third had graduation rates of 21% to 40% ("Many athlete," 1989). From another perspective, only 7 out of every 20 young men who accept football and basketball scholarships at major universities are expected to graduate (Barbash, 1990). Overall, the graduation rate of student athletes in all sports is 47% at Division I colleges and 41% in Division I-A colleges (LaPlante, 1990). For the student athletes who do graduate the value of their athletic scholarships has been placed at $40,000 (Barbash, 1990).

A large number of student athletes not graduating are African Americans. As of May 1986, the nationwide graduation rate for African American athletes was approximately 25% with some 75% of those who did graduate receiving degrees in physical education (Dixon, 1987). Yet, African American athletes comprise 38% and 58% of Division I football and basketball teams, respectively (Ashe, 1990). At these same institutions, African American students represent only some 5.5% of the total student body (Ashe, 1990).

Recently, there have been numerous accounts of African American student athletes who did not achieve academically. Deion Sanders (formerly of Florida State University and presently with the Atlanta Falcons) and Dexter Manley (formerly of Oklahoma State University and the Washington Redskins) are two examples. Sanders, when asked in his senior year if he wanted to be in college, replied "No, but I have to be" ("Myth," 1990). After he joined the Washington Redskins, Manley admitted that he was functionally illiterate (Barbash, 1990). Other African American student athletes who have been the subject of media attention for lack of academic prowess include Chris Washburn, formerly of North Carolina State University, and Kevin Ross, formerly of Creighton University ("When is," 1989).

Memphis State University over the 10-year period 1973-1983 graduated only 6 out of 58 basketball players. Most of the players not graduating were African American ("Myth," 1990). Sports sociologist Dr. Harry Edwards found that at the University of California during the period 1971 to 1978 some 70% to 80% of the African American athletes did not graduate (cited in Waicukauski, 1982). Recent figures place the graduation rate of African American student athletes at less than 30% (Moore, 1990; "Pitfalls," 1990). Edwards (1981) has labeled the dismal graduation rates of African American athletes as "exploitation" (see also Mulligan, 1986). Another observer has referred to college athletics as a "plantation system" for African American student athletes (Moore, 1990). Yet other observers argue that college and university sports programs should not be totally blamed for the exploitation of African American student athletes. Moore (1990) argues that the reasons have much to do with exploitation by college and university coaches, administrators, and boosters and naiveté on the part of African American youngsters and their families. African American youngsters and the African American community are more likely to view college and university sports as the main avenue to a lucrative professional sports career. Arthur Ashe, former tennis professional, notes that "Black families are eight times more likely to encourage their children to seek a pro career than White families" (cited in Moore, 1990). However, the odds for a professional career are extraordinarily low. Only 1 of 10,000 high school football and basketball players will reach the professional level. Further, there are only 1,316 positions in the National Football League and only 324 positions in the National Basketball Association (Moore, 1990).

The National Collegiate Athletic Association (NCAA), the sports-governing body for collegiate athletics, was formally organized in 1906 and consists of approximately 900 volunteer member institutions. Its fundamental policy is "to maintain intercollegiate athletics as an integral part of the educational program and the athlete as an integral part of the student body and, by doing so, retain a clear line of demarcation between college athletics and professional sports" (NCAA, 1985). Beginning in 1948 the NCAA adopted a code of conduct that has evolved into elaborate regulations designed largely to protect academic standards (Waicukauski, 1982).

The NCAA is a profit-making entity that has a multimillion dollar budget and negotiates and administers television contracts for itself and its members. The NCAA is engaged in a business venture of far greater magnitude than the vast majority of profit-making enterprises (Klein & Briggs, 1990). Simply put, the NCAA is big business—and recently a billion-dollar business. It signed a $1 billion, 7-year deal with CBS television to broadcast basketball games ("CBS lands," 1989). Further, it is not unusual for athletic department budgets at Division I institutions to exceed $10 or $20 million and for coaches to command salaries in the hundreds of thousands of dollars or even of $1 million (Klein & Briggs, 1990). Noteworthy is that the NCAA nevertheless views participation in collegiate sports as an avocation, motivated primarily by education and considers student athletes as amateurs. The NCAA's "Principle of Amateurism" (*NCAA Manual*, 1989-1990) reads:

> *Student athletes shall be amateurs in an intercollegiate sport and their participation should be motivated primarily by education and by the physical, mental, and social benefits to be derived. Student participation in intercollegiate athletics should be protected from exploitation by professional and commercial enterprise.*

At its national convention in January 1983, the NCAA promulgated rules that conditioned initial eligibility upon achievement of certain scores on college entrance examinations and upon the completion of a high school curriculum with certain specified courses and a minimum grade point average. The intended goal of the rules was to restore academic integrity to college athletics. These rules, known as Proposition 48, have generated much controversy and debate, particularly concerning the African American student athlete.

This chapter discusses the controversy. The first part of the chapter discusses the history and enactment of Proposition 48. The second part focuses on the controversy and debate that has ensued over Proposition 48 and the African American student athlete in the higher education community. The third part discusses the latest NCAA policies, Propositions 42 and 28. The conclusion argues that Propositions 48, 42, and 28, as the major thrust of the NCAA's movement toward academic reform for student athletes, represent the wrong approach, that the policies restrict educational access and do little to reduce the exploitation of student athletes by colleges and universities.

THE RISE OF PROPOSITION 48

When NCAA convened in San Diego in 1983, the delegates included nearly 100 university and college presidents from institutions with major sports programs. The focus was to be on issues relating to academic standards. At the time, NCAA Division I-A consisted of 277 institutions, of which 17 were historically Black institutions.

The American Council on Education (ACE)—with two of its committees, the President's Committee on College Athletics and the Ad Hoc Committee—had been strongly urging changes in student athletic admissions requirements. The Ad Hoc Committee was made up of 40 college presidents, the president and executive president of ACE, and a representative of the Association of American Universities. It was chaired by Derek Bok of Harvard University. The committee identified its purpose as being "to discuss ways in which chief executive officers can bring concerted leadership to bear on the way problems ... beset major athletic programs" (cited in Green, 1984).

Several weeks before the 1983 meeting, Chairman Bok and ACE President J. W. Petalson had written letters to college and university presidents describing two proposals that were to be introduced as motions to the convention. These came to be known as Proposition 48.

Proposition 48 proposed that freshman student athletes matriculating after August 1, 1986, must have achieved a minimum high school grade point average of 2.0 (on a 4.0 scale) in 11 core academic courses and have attained a combined verbal and mathematics score of 700 on the Scholastic Aptitude Test (SAT) or a 15 composite on the American College Test (ACT). For those students achieving more than the minimum requirement for either component, a sliding grade point average/test score scale was proposed. For example, an entering student athlete with a grade point average of 2.2 and above met eligibility requirements with a corresponding SAT score of 660 or ACT score of 13. Entering student athletes who attained an overall 2.0 grade point average but failed to meet the test score requirement were able to receive scholarship support but could not participate in games or practices during their freshman year. These students, who were to become known as partial qualifiers, could only participate in their sport for 3 years (sophomore, junior and senior) instead of 4. The intent behind the support of marginal academic athletes was to allow them to concentrate full time on academics during their freshmen year and make the adjustment to college life. Student athletes who met neither of the requirements were determined ineligible.

The debate on Proposition 48 at the convention was heated and the criticism vehement. Much of it focused on the potential exclusion of African American athletes from sports programs and on the lack of participation by historically Black institutions and African American representatives on the

Ad Hoc Committee that formulated the proposed eligibility requirements. The chief executive officers from historically Black colleges and universities, most notably Delaware State University, Grambling State University, North Carolina A&T University, Southern University, and Tennessee State University, spoke in opposition.

Jesse Stone, then president of the Southern University System (Louisiana), labeled the proposed standards as "patently racist." He saw the proposal as "...the desire to reduce the number of Black faces that we see dominating college athletics" (quoted in Jarrett, 1983).

President Joseph B. Johnson of Grambling State University noted that the Ad Hoc Committee of the American Council on Education, as the body proposing Proposition 48, had failed to conduct a study of the potential effects of the proposed changes on African American and other minority athletes:

> *The Committee's proposal, ladies and gentlemen, discriminates against student athletes from low-income and minority-group families by introducing arbitrary SAT or ACT cutoff scores as academic criteria for eligibility. The ACE's committee's proposal is based upon academic conjecture rather than empirical data. (NCAA, 1983, p. 103)*

President Johnson saw the ACE proposal as "victim blaming"—putting the blame on the student for total responsibility for academic success rather than on the institution (NCAA, 1983). He strongly criticized the ACE committee for failing to include African American presidents on the committee during its deliberative phases (Crowl, 1983).

Frederick S. Humphries, then president of Tennessee State University, questioned the inequity of rules among the three major NCAA divisions: Because all NCAA member schools were not treated alike by the NCAA because of different division status, why should a proposition be passed that would pertain only to Division I schools and not other divisions?

Luna I. Mishoe, president of Delaware State University, took strong exception to the SAT score as part of the eligibility requirements and argued that the SAT arbitrarily penalized a large number students on the basis of socioeconomic background. Mishoe made the following observation:

> *Students of low socioeconomic background score 100 points less than other students, and this has nothing to do with intellectual retention to do college work. It is based on external factors. We feel that those students, minorities and nonminorities, should not be penalized for those external reasons. (NCAA, 1983, p. 110)*

What these chief executive officers of historically Black institutions were protesting was that African Americans, who historically did not perform well on standardized tests, would be disproportionally affected by the test score requirements. The result would be lack of opportunity for African Americans to participate in athletic programs not only at White institutions but also at historically Black institutions. And the presidents of historically Black institutions felt most strongly that their students and their institutions would be those most harmed by the Proposition 48 criteria.

Joe Paterno, however, was a staunch proponent of the Proposition 48 proposal. Paterno, head football coach at Pennsylvania State University and reigning football champion at the time, declared:

> *It isn't fair for us to take unprepared students into our universities ... This isn't a race problem .... For the past 15 years we have had a race problem, however.... We've told [B]lack kids who bounce balls, run around tracks, and catch touchdown passes that that is an end unto itself. We've raped a whole generation of [B]lack students. We can't afford to do it again. (NCAA, 1983, p. 115)*

Further, the time was now or never, according to the head official from the University of Vermont:

> *If we fail to act on these issues today, we will state more profoundly than ever before to the public and to all who have an interest in intercollegiate athletics that we cannot and will not take a step to insist that athletes must be students before they can be intercollegiate athletes. (NCAA, 1983, p. 119)*

After a full day of debate, Proposition 48 was passed by the delegates, to become effective August 1, 1986.

Months following the adoption of the new rules of Proposition 48, the Educational Testing Service (ETS) released data showing that the SAT cutoff would disproportionately affect African American students (Vance, 1983a). ETS used the new SAT score of 700 with 1981 figures of college-bound students to show that 51% of African American men and 60% of African American women would have been eliminated (a grand total of 42,831 African American students). ETS further noted that although the White percentage would have been smaller, the absolute number (90,527) would have been more than double the number of African American students (Vance, 1983a, p. 18).

A Big Eight Conference study produced similar results: Some 60% to 80% of African American athletes at member institutions would have been ineligible under Proposition 48, whereas only some 10% to 27% of White athletes would have been affected (Vance, 1983b). Further, a study by the Center for the Study of Athletes (1989), commissioned by the President's Council of the NCAA, revealed that at Division I colleges 58% of African American basketball and football players, 35% of other African American student athletes, and 27% of African American extracurricular students scored in the lowest quartile on the SAT (752 or below).

THE EFFECT OF PROPOSITION 48 ON AFRICAN AMERICAN ATHLETES

In the 1986-1987 sport season 224 football and 121 basketball student athletes and 53 other athletes were declared ineligible under Proposition 48 (McKenna, 1987). Some 90% of these individuals were African Americans (Hoose, 1989). The Mid-Eastern Athletic Association Conference (MEAC), which is comprised of predominately Black institutions, lost 37 athletes in football and basketball (McKenna, 1987). When compared to other conferences of the same size, such as the Big Eight, Atlantic Coast, and Big Sky, the MEAC student athlete loss was most striking. Of the top 50 high school basketball recruits in 1986, which consisted of 9 Whites and 41 African Americans, 14 were partial qualifiers. Table 1 lists the top 50 high school basketball players in 1986 by race, college, and status (qualifier, nonqualifier). Of the nonqualifiers, 13, or 92.8%, were African American. However, although the percentage of nonqualifiers was tempered somewhat by the overall number of African American players who qualified, the percentage of African American qualifiers was still disproportionate to the number of White nonqualifiers. A closer examination of Table 1 shows that about one-third of the African American recruits did not qualify as compared to only 1% of the White recruits. By the 1989-1990 season African American athletes were still being disproportionately impacted by Proposition 48. In 1989-1990, 183 colleges and universities reported 584 partial qualifiers. Of this number nearly 67% were African American athletes. Some 16% of all freshmen partial qualifiers were African American as compared to 2.5% White (Lederman, 1990).

PROPOSITION 42 AND PROPOSITION 28

In January 1989, the NCAA convened in San Francisco. On the second ballot, by a vote of 163-154 the delegates passed Proposition 42. Supporters saw Proposition 42 as tightening academic standards and closing a loophole, thus ensuring that colleges and universities accept only the academically qualified. Any form of aid was denied to student athletes who did not meet basic test requirements, that is, coverage in 11 high school core subjects and a score of 700 on the SAT or 15 on the ACT ("When is," 1989). Beginning in August 1990, colleges and universities were to provide athletic scholarships only to incoming freshmen athletes who met all the requirements of Proposition 42. The partial qualifiers permitted under Proposition 48 were eliminated: They became instead nonqualifiers who had to finance their own tuition as freshmen or go to a junior college. Because many nonqualifiers are from low-income families, however, Proposition 42 served as a barrier to entering any college; and those aspiring athletes who chose to go to junior

Table 1
50 Top 1986 High School Basketball Recruits
(By Race, College, and Status)

	Name	Race	College	Status
1.	J. R. Reid	B	North Carolina	Qualifier
2.	Terry Mills	B	Michigan	Nonqualifier
3.	Rummeal Robinson	B	Michigan	Nonqualifier
4.	Rex Chapman	W	Kentucky	Qualifier
5.	Tony Pendleton	B	Iowa	Nonqualifier
6.	Dwayne Bryant	B	Georgetown	Qualifier
7.	Fess Irvin	B	LSU	Qualifier
8.	Scott Williams	B	North Carolina	Qualifier
9.	Larry Rembert	B	Alabama-Birmingham	Qualifier
10.	Sylvester Gray	B	Memphis State	Nonqualifier
11.	Derrick Coleman	B	Syracuse	Qualifier
12.	Nick Anderson	B	Illinois	Nonqualifier
13.	Ron Henry	B	Arkansas	Qualifier
14.	Keith Robinson	B	Notre Dame	Nonqualifier
15.	Earl Duncan	B	Syracuse	Nonqualifier
16.	Brian Oliver	B	Georgia Tech	Qualifier
17.	Stacy Augmon	B	UNLV	Nonqualifier
18.	Duane Schintzius	W	Florida	Qualifier
19.	Felton Spencer	B	Louisville	Qualifier
20.	Mark Randall	W	Kansas	Qualifier
21.	Chris Brooks	B	West Virginia	Nonqualifier
22.	Ricky Jones	B	Clemson	Qualifier
23.	Alsa Abdeinaby	B	Duke	Qualifier
24.	Anthony Allen	B	Georgetown	J C Transfer
25.	Steve Hood	B	Maryland	Qualifier
26.	Steve Thompson	B	Syracuse	Qualifier
27.	Marcus Broadnax	B	St. John's	Qualifier
28.	Mark Tillman	B	Georgetown	Qualifier
29.	Lionel Simmons	B	LaSalle	Qualifier
30.	Willie Burton	B	Minnesota	Nonqualifier
31.	Peter Chilcutt	W	North Carolina	Qualifier
32.	Lavertis Robinson	B	Cincinnati	Nonqualifier
33.	Keith Smith	W	California	Qualifier
34.	Derrick Miller	B	Kentucky	Qualifier
35.	Kevin Pritchard	W	Kansas	Qualifier
36.	Rodney Taylor	B	Villanova	Qualifier
37.	Karl James	B	UNLV	Qualifier
38.	Larry Smith	B	Illinois	Qualifier
39.	Chris Munk	B	Southern California	Qualifier
40.	Barry Bekkedam	W	Villanova	Qualifier
41.	Phil Hendeson	B	Duke	Qualifier
42.	Cheyenne Gibson	B	Memphis State	Nonqualifier
43.	Frantz Voloy	B	Seton Hall	Qualifier
44.	Elander Lewis	B	St. John's	Qualifier
45.	Louis Banks	B	Cincinnati	Nonqualifier
46.	David Minor	W	Indiana	Qualifier
47.	Kevin Walker	B	UCLA	Qualifier
48.	Greg Foster	B	UCLA	Qualifier
49.	Mike Christian	B	Georgia Tech	Qualifier
50.	Robert Coyne	W	Kansas	Nonqualifier

Source: Based on data derived by McKenna, 1987.

college were likely to find themselves with as few as 2 years of eligibility in Division I institutions.

The impetus for Proposition 42 had come from the scandal in the athletic department at the University of Georgia. The university was found guilty in 1986 of maintaining the eligibility of academically unqualified athletes ("When is," 1989). When the university's president ordered the athletic department to stop admitting partial qualifiers, the department became concerned that it was placing itself at a disadvantage to other athletic departments in the Southeastern Conference. The university successfully urged other conference institutions to follow its lead, and the conference passed its own legislation barring partial qualifiers from receiving financial aid beginning in 1993 (Reed, 1989). A domino effect followed: The conference felt that it would be at a disadvantage in other parts of the country and then led the charge to have the NCAA adopt the same rule ("When is," 1989).

Because standardized tests like the SAT and ACT are viewed as being biased against minorities ("Race becomes," 1989), Proposition 42 was labeled as unfair to low-income students, as "racist." Head basketball coaches John Thompson of Georgetown University and John Chaney of Temple University, themselves African Americans, vigorously opposed Proposition 42. Thompson viewed Proposition 42 as discrimination against athletes from low-income backgrounds ("Race becomes," 1989) and refused to participate in two basketball games in 1989 as a protest. Chaney saw Proposition 42 as "an insane, inhuman piece of legislation that will fill the streets with more of the disadvantaged" (cited in "When is," 1989). Chaney's further observations that "Proposition 42 will do one thing: Punish Blacks," that Proposition 42 was racist (Chaney, 1989), are noteworthy given two present societal conditions: (1) declining enrollment of African American men at colleges and universities and (2) retrenchment in federal financial aid for education (Reed, 1989).

Recent test data seem to support Thompson, Chaney, and other critics who state that the ACT or SAT score requirement puts African American athletes at a disadvantage. Whites overall score about 100 points higher than African Americans on the SAT and an average of 6 points higher on the ACT. African Americans average 353 verbal and 384 math on the SAT, whereas Whites average 445 verbal and 490 math. Even African Americans whose annual family incomes exceed $70,000 are outscored by their White counterparts by an average of 100 points on the SAT ("When is," 1989).

As a result of such criticism, delegates at the NCAA 1990 convention modified—but did not repeal—Proposition 42. This modification became Proposition 26, and took effect in August 1990. Proposition 26 allows athletes who do not meet the basic requirements of Proposition 48 to receive scholarships and other financial aid based on need. These students, however, are still barred from participation in athletics during their freshman year.

CONCLUSION

The NCAA's goal of promoting scholarship and academic achievement among student athletes is admirable. However, the promotion of this goal through the imposition of restrictions on would-be student athletes seems to constitute a negative action, particularly against minority athletes. The restrictions merely ensure a minimum measure of college preparedness and, as such, miss the point: the exploitation of the student athletes. *Exploitation* does not refer to the admission of unqualified African American student athletes but rather to the lack of a support system for providing ill-prepared athletes with a bona fide opportunity for academic success. Too often the African American student athlete receives little quality educational support from the university, and instead, the university seeks only to keep the African American student athlete eligible for the playing field.

Although graduation rates of African American student athletes are seen as a measure of academic success, and should be a focus of attention, graduation rates do not necessarily reflect a university's educational support system and commitment to student athlete. Graduation rates indicate only that a student athlete graduated. They do not indicate whether a student athlete performed to his or her capabilities in the classroom or had the full opportunity to compete academically to the best of his or her ability.

Some colleges have attempted to justify the low graduation rates of African American student athletes. For example, one member of the athletic council at a Division I athletic institution in the South remarked that even if an athlete never graduates, "He gets to see places he's never seen. He has some academic exposure. He improves his reading skills, his writing skills. He makes some lifelong contacts. He learns something" (LaPlante, 1990).

And when asked about the Dexter Manley situation, the president of Oklahoma State University pointedly said:

> *There would be those who would agree that Dexter Manley got exactly what he wanted at OSU. He was able to develop his athletic skills and ability, he was noticed by the pros, he got a pro contract. So maybe we did him a favor by letting him go through the program. (cited in Barbash, 1990, p. 40)*

These views, although expressly different, seem to suggest that even if an athlete does not graduate, the institution has done its job. They also suggest that the term *college education* can be simply defined as social and academic exposure and/or athletic preparation. Certainly such a definition would mean less debate concerning the graduation rate of African American student athletes.

A college or university's commitment to educational opportunity, however, means actively providing every possible support mechanism that will enable student athletes—and particularly African Americans who have been so negatively affected—to reach their academic potential. The NCAA should emphasize through its policies that colleges and universities must have in place a commitment to educational opportunity that includes strong academic support systems to provide poorly prepared athletes with a bona fide opportunity for academic success. Further, each institution's educational commitment must expand the role of counselors, administrators, and support personnel to serve as advocates for the academic and personal development of African-American, and indeed all, student athletes. A commitment to an educational philosophy that provides for fullest development of all people dictates nothing less.

REFERENCES

Ashe, A. (1990, January 20). NCAA propositions itself over Proposition 42. *Washington Post*, pp. D1, D5.

Barbash, L. (1990, July/August). Clean up or pay up. *The Washington Monthly*, pp. 38-41.

The best and the dullest. (1989, February 10). *National Review*, p. 18.

CBS lands sole rights to NCAA (1989, November 22). *Binghamton Press and Sun Bulletin*, Section C.

Center for the Study of Athletes (1989). *The experience of Black intercollegiate athletes at NCAA Division I institutions.* (Report No. 3). American Institutes for Research.

Chaney, J. (1989, January 23). A slap at Blacks. *Sports Illustrated*, pp. 18-19.

Crowl, M. (1983, January 19). NCAA votes stiffer academic requirements for participants in intercollegiate sports. *Chronicle of Higher Education*, pp. 1, 20.

Dixon, T. (1987). Achieving educational opportunity through freshman ineligibility and coaching selection: Key elements in the NCAA battle for academic integrity of intercollegiate athletics. *Journal of College and University Law, 14*, 383-398.

Edwards, H. (1981, November 15). *Exploitation and the NCAA.* Presentation at the Second Annual Conference of the North American Society for the Sociology of Sport, Chicago, IL.

Greene, L. S. (1984). The New NCAA rules of the game: Academic integrity or racism. *Saint Louis University Law Journal, 28*, 101-146.

Hoose, P. M. (1989). *Necessities: Racial barriers in American sports.* New York: Random House.

Jarrett, P. (1983, January 16). Why Blacks fought the NCAA. *Chicago Tribune*, Section 2, p. 7.

Klein, D. E & Briggs, W. B. (1990). Proposition 48 and the business of intercollegiate athletics: Potential antitrust ramifications under the Sherman Act. *Denver University Law Review, 67*, 301-340.

LaPlante, J. (1990, September 25). Athletes closely trail overall LSU graduation rate. *Morning Advocate* (Baton Rouge, LA), pp. 1, 5.

Lederman, D. (1990, February 28). Number of athletes failing to meet academic standards for freshmen up for second year in row, NCAA says. *Chronicle of Higher Education*, pp. A33-A34.

Many athlete graduation rates below 20%. (1989, September 10). *New York Times*, p. 1.

McKenna, K. M. (1987). A proposition with a powerful punch: The legality and constitutionality of NCAA Proposition 48. *Duquesne Law Review, 26,* 43-77.

Moore, T. (1990, April 23). Despite grim statistics, Blacks continue to enter plantation system. *Atlanta Journal and Constitution,* p. F-3.

Mulligan, E. (1986, August 12). Sudden impact, grades in on Proposition 48, 397 athletes affected so far. *Philadelphia Daily News,* p. 77.

National Collegiate Athletic Association. (1983). *Proceedings of the annual convention of the National Collegiate Athletic Association.* San Diego: NCAA.

National Collegiate Athletic Association. (1985). *1985-1986 Manual of the National Collegiate Athletic Association.* Kansas City: NCAA.

Pitfalls of pro sports block Black athletes. (1990, September 28). *USA Today.* p. 2-C.

Race becomes the game. (1989, January 30). *Newsweek,* pp. 56-59.

Reed, W. F. (1989, January 23). A new proposition. *Sports Illustrated,* pp. 16-19.

The myth of the student-athlete. (1990, January 8). *U.S. News and World Report,* pp. 50-52.

This case was one for the books. (1986, February 24). *Sports Illustrated,* pp. 34-37.

Vance, L. (1983a, February 16). Testing service head hits NCAA's academic rules. *Chronicle of Higher Education,* p. 18.

Vance, L. (1983b, February 16). Academic rules would affect Blacks far more than Whites, study finds. *Chronicle of Higher Education,* p. 17.

Waicukauski, R. (1982). The regulation of academic standards in intercollegiate athletics. *Arizona State Law Review,* 79-108.

When is the playing field too level? (1989, January 30). *U.S. News and World Report,* pp. 68-69.

CHAPTER 9

RACIAL VIOLENCE ON CAMPUS

Camille A. Clay and Jan-Mitchell Sherrill

INTRODUCTION

At the University of Massachusetts at Amherst, a group of 20 African American students were allegedly attacked by over 3,000 White students after the 1986 World Series. At Yale, the Afro-American center and the holocaust memorial were damaged. A poster in the African American theme house at Stanford University was defaced, and the skinheads, an emerging hate group, have been actively recruiting members on the campus. An African American fraternity house on the grounds of the University of Mississippi was burned down. At Oberlin College posters with the caption "White supremacy lives! Kill all niggers!" were displayed.

Episodes of growing racial intolerance and violence are occurring not only in geographically or socially isolated pockets such as urban centers or rural areas but also nationwide at public and private, 2- and 4-year institutions. Is any college or university immune? If the higher education community intends to lead the nation in addressing this problem, will it do so by example?

At least two organizations have collected data in an effort to describe statistically the magnitude of the problem. The Campus Violence Prevention Center (CVPC) at Towson State University distributed its National Campus Violence Survey to 1,100 colleges and universities. Student affairs, police/security, and residence hall personnel were asked to supply the requested information from their 1987-1988 records. Of the 3,300 questionnaires distributed, over 1,000 were returned, representing more than 330 higher education settings. The results (CVPC, 1988) showed that 174 incidents of racial violence were reported at 95 institutions. One college reported as many as 10 incidents during the year, 5 schools reported at least 6, and 24 schools reported between 2 and 5 situations. Less than 7% (6.8%) of the institutions surveyed perceived racial violence to be a problem on their campuses. It is interesting to note that 6.8% of respondents also reported a perception that they had experienced an increase in racially violent incidents during the 1987-1988 school year.

The National Institute Against Prejudice and Violence (NIAPV), a Baltimore-based organization, studies, monitors, and develops strategies to address bias and its attendant aggression. NIAPV (1987) catalogued more than 160 episodes of campus racial violence reported by the media in the past year. The Institute has coined the term *ethnoviolence* to encompass those acts motivated by prejudice and performed with the intent of causing physical or psychological damage. From its 1987 research, the Institute has found that 20% of all minority or culturally different students in traditionally White institutions have been subjected to acts of ethnoviolence. At least one-fourth of those have reported experiencing more than one assault. These ethnoviolent acts range from subtle classroom and dormitory harassment, name-calling, and insults to blatant physical attacks and property damage. Also called *hate crimes* by the National Gay and Lesbian Task Force, most of these assaults are not reported. This phenomenon accounts for the low number of institutions that recognized racial violence as a problem in the CVPC survey. The NIAPV also found the majority of ethnoviolent acts committed on campuses to be psychologically rather than physically violent and harmful.

On many campuses these acts of violence, harassment, or insensitivity are often perceived by minority students as a series of unchallenged indignities. Then, after a "last straw," victimized students mount a protest to demand such changes in the racial environment as hiring African American faculty, increasing the minority enrollment, and transforming or reforming curricular offerings. For example, at Towson State University, following a judicial decision that students felt was unfair to the student involved, African American students staged a demonstration and made several demands. These included an investigation of the campus police; a review of judicial policy; increased hiring of African American faculty, administrators, and coaching staff; introduction of more courses that include the scholarship and contributions of people of African descent; and the formation of an oversight committee to handle complaints of racial injustice on campus. Similar demands were made by students at Stanford University, University of California at Los Angeles, University of Massachusetts at Amherst, University of Wisconsin, Pennsylvania State University, and the University of Maryland, Baltimore County.

FACTORS RELATED TO CAMPUS ETHNOVIOLENCE

Useful insights into the many complex sociopolitical and psychological factors that undergird this revival of overt racist acts on campus have been offered by several authors. Shelby Steele (1989), for example, viewed these racial conflicts as growing out of equality rather than inequality because African American students have equality under the law and therefore cannot be denied access to classes and extracurricular activities. Steele wrote that "campus racism is born of the rub between racial difference and a setting...devoted to interaction and equality" (p. 50). He felt that incidents arise as students protect themselves from racial anxiety—manifested as guilt in White students and feelings of inferiority in African American students. From another perspective, Manning Marable (1988b) has blamed the Reagan administration for its agenda that symbolized a "shattering assault against the economic, social, and political status of the African American community" (p. 53). His other explanations for campus ethnoviolence included (a) the conservative political atmosphere, which according to Marable (1988a) has fostered a reactionary mentality among many White students; (b) the fact that the majority of college students today were born after the major thrust of the civil rights movement, and thus many students, both African American and White, enter college believing racism no longer exists; and (c) the pervasive perception of limited resources and the belief that minorities are getting more than their share or that they will be competitors for jobs, affordable housing, and the few resources that exist.

Educators are left to face the fact that racism is alive and well on our campuses. Howard Erlich (1988), from NIAPV, has termed campus racial violence *the new racism*. The new racism is more subtle, rejects old stereotypes, denies the existence of racism, uses new code words and phrases such as *equality* and *reverse discrimination,* and is hidden in policies and rules. Today's racism, it seems, remains a belief in White superiority combined with the power to exercise and retain that belief to the social, political, economic, and psychological advantage of White people. Racism is a phenomenon that many academicians prefer to ignore, but as psychologist Kenneth Bancroft Clark (1965) suggested years ago, racism is intricately interwoven into the fabric of American society. Racism is an integral part of American culture. As racism is manifested institutionally, culturally, and individually in the greater society, so it is also expressed in colleges and universities—particularly when there are no countervailing messages provided in the academic environment. Currently, the practices and policies of higher education institutions only reflect and reinforce—rather than correct—the national sentiment that covert racism is acceptable. For minority students, the perception that college administrations countenance this kind of racism leads to greater and greater frustration; it is a palpable presence in their collegiate lives. We should expect, therefore, even more racial contention on our campuses.

IMPLICATIONS

Racial tension on campus is an ominous trend, one that, if not addressed appropriately, will have unfortunate consequences for all parties involved: ethnic minority students, White students, and society at large. The harmful effects of physical ethnoviolent acts on victims are apparent. However, the psychological damage inflicted by individuals, groups, and institutions may be far more dangerous. Many institutions are funneling significant resources into minority retention efforts, but unless the campus racial atmosphere is taken into account, colleges and universities will lose a sizeable proportion of minority students. These students, who experience the environment as unreceptive, feel only a fragmented sense of belonging to or connection with the institution.

Currently, minority students complete undergraduate degrees at rates much lower than their majority counterparts. American Council on Education demographer and senior fellow Harold Hodgkinson (1980) has made it abundantly clear that by the year 2000 one-third of the nation will be minority, and that minority workers will comprise one-third of the net additions to the United States labor force. Should one-third of the labor force be educationally disenfranchised?

Many minority students do persist—and suffer the effects of being educated in an isolating or hostile environment. As a colleague at a prestigious private university has said, "Eighty percent of the African American students graduate, but you wouldn't believe the shape they are in when they do." At the Massachusetts Institute of Technology (MIT) the results of a quality-of-life survey and a African American alumni survey were combined to provide a picture of African American lives at the university.

The MIT study (MIT Minority Student Issues Group, 1986) reported that African American students experienced (a) feelings of isolation; (b) insecurity about their admission because others believed there were lower standards for minority admission; (c) anxiety about their families' abilities to provide the financial assistance necessary; (d) feelings of nonacceptance, if not contempt, from nonminority students, faculty, administrators, and staff; (e) little or no support, negative expectation, and, at times, discriminatory behavior from White faculty; and (f) a generally nonsupportive environment in which minorities must constantly prove they are intellectually and socially equal.

In spite of functioning in this setting, most students are able to perform satisfactorily, and many form trusting relationships. Many are able to maintain their racial identity; some are obliged to compromise their cultural values in order to fit in. Negative perceptions and expectations by White faculty may be internalized by minority students resulting in limited aspirations and diminished self-confidence. In other words, the study demonstrated that a significant proportion of MIT's African American students and graduates felt the institution provided an environment for which they had to make exceptional adjustments in order to succeed.

The typical adjustment problems felt by most college students—pace, workload, pressure, and preparation—are exacerbated by the factor of race. For example, while becoming acclimated to academic pressures and expectations, African American students must also determine whether it is better to separate or assimilate in order to survive in the campus environment. Finally, the study indicated that the majority of African American students at MIT do succeed, nevertheless, by using a combination of resources and strategies including personal ability and determination, institutional support services, concerned faculty, and African American residential and social arrangements.

Our society needs a fully educated, mentally healthy populace. Fundamental to mental health is a realistic sense of worth and identity. Minority students in predominantly White institutions today are constantly bombarded with messages that impugn their competence, cultural values, intrinsic worth, and rightful place at the institution. The long-term effects that may be associated with these psychological assaults to the mental health of African American students in these settings are unknown.

Less evident than the physical or psychological damage done to minority students when racism is allowed to flourish in institutions of higher learning is the disservice imposed upon White students. Institutions that do not make concerted efforts to hire minority faculty and administrators, to infuse the scholarly contributions and concerns of African Americans and other minorities across the curriculum, to handle judiciously alleged incidents of discrimination and ethnoviolence, and to provide opportunities for racially and/or culturally different students to interact and learn from and about each other have not adequately prepared students to be productive citizens of a pluralistic society. Psychologically, the self-esteem, identity, and sense of self of White students is also at risk if, even in part, these factors are based on the myth of White superiority. Again, society needs to reap the benefits of a fully educated, mentally healthy populace.

The American Council on Education (1975) stated emphatically the threat posed by the lack of minority participation in education and American life: "Left uncorrected, the current trend signals continuing social tension and is an omen of future national decline" (p. 16).

RESPONSES

Most institutions are sent in search of solutions to racial problems on campuses when the first bias-related incident is brought to public attention. Of course, it is necessary to handle the emergency; but after the emergency, long-term strategies must be formulated. Long-term response strategies may be viewed in three stages: assessment, reaction, and proaction. By gaining an understanding of the racial climate, the assessment stage informs and directs corrective intervention. The institutions reaction to an ethnoviolent act communicates its posture on intolerance to the community. Proactive measures are designed to prevent future ethnoviolence.

Assessment Strategies

The assessment enables the selection of corrective or preventive measures, appropriate for the level of racism determined. James Jones (1972) defined three levels or types of racism: institutional, cultural, and individual. The first of these, institutional racism, may be the conscious manipulation of institutions to achieve racist objectives or, more likely, the unintended but real byproduct of certain institutional practices that operate to restrict, on a racial basis, the choices, rights, ability and access of groups and individuals. For example, a policy establishing SAT entrance cutoffs well above minority averages—a policy, in effect, denying access to minority applicants—is an institutionally racist act.

Cultural racism in a university setting may be manifested by a curriculum that does not include the contributions of African American and other minority scholars. A combination of institutional and individual racism, cultural racism is a belief in the superiority of the Eurocentric cultural heritage.

Individual racism is most akin to prejudice: Irrational attitudes held by a member of one racial/ethnic group toward a member of another group and the behavior that results from that attitude. Derogatory posters, offensive statements, and racial brawls are manifestations of individual racism.

The first step to assessment must be to undertake a comprehensive evaluation of the racial climate. The Office of Minority Affairs of the American Council on Education (1975) has published an excellent guide for conducting such an inquiry. Questions that need to be explored include:

1. Has the leadership asserted the university position against bias and discrimination?

2. Is that stated position evident in minority faculty and staff hiring promotion as well as in minority student enrollment and retention rates?

3. Is the curriculum relevant and reflective of the cultural heritage, scholarship, and contributions of African Americans and other minorities?

4. Is there a clear, well-publicized policy and procedure for swift and equitable handling of bias-related complaints?

5. Is there a high-level administrator with responsibility for minority affairs?

6. Has there been a body charged, preferably by the president, to monitor the campus racial climate?

7. In what ways does the environment foster a positive sense of self for all students?

Answers to these and related or similar questions facilitate an analysis of the level of institutional and cultural racism that may be operating and suggests corrective steps to be implemented. To appraise faculty and student opinions and attitudes, formal and informal survey methods can be employed (NIAPV, 1987). Questions similar to the following should be asked:

1. Is there evidence of racism or racial insensitivity on the campus?

2. Have you been a victim of or witness to an ethnoviolent act?

3. What do you think is the percentage of African American students on campus?

4. Are there too many special programs for minorities?

The answers may yield important feedback. When a racial environment survey was conducted on one college campus, fewer than 50% of the White students and over 80% of the African American students felt there was evidence of racial insensitivity. Almost 50% of the White students did not know that African American students were not at least 40% of the campus population. In actuality, African American enrollment at that institution was less than 10%. Over 60% of the White students felt there were or may be too many special programs for African American students. Less than 20% of the African American students agreed. Forty-five percent of the White students felt their ethnic/cultural heritage was adequately reflected academically and socially; only 11% of the African American students felt their heritage was reflected. Fewer than one-fourth of the African American students felt constantly aware of their race; only 20% of the White students felt that way. One 21-year-old African American student explained that in matters of race she felt "alone" and "as if my other classmates really can't understand me." An 18-year-old White male asserted, "I'm tired of hearing African American this and African American that. With all the crying and complaining going on in the African American community, the White race has become a minority." Responses such as these indicate the disparity between White and African American student perspectives of the campus racial environment. These divergent views may be evidence of underlying racial tension that may be expressed through ethnoviolent acts or in the formation of reactionary White students' leagues such as a group at Temple University (Clay, 1986).

Reactive Strategies

When a racially violent act occurs on campus, it is important that the institution's response not escalate the problem. Each complaint should be taken seriously and the investigative mechanism should be initiative-activated.

The needs of the victim must be ascertained and addressed, and medical and mental health personnel should be utilized appropriately. It may be useful to provide support groups for victims. The appropriate responses such as mediation, disciplinary action, or criminal charges should be determined and carried out judiciously and swiftly. All reports of racial discrimination and violence should be recorded and shared among the offices that received such complaints (e.g., campus police, affirmative action officer, student affairs representatives), and the minority affairs officer and central administration should be represented in and informed of deliberations. The response needs to be educational. It is particularly important that bias-related violence be made known, at least generically, to the entire campus community and not allowed to be "owned" by a particular population. A racial incident does not belong to African American students but to the entire community. A campus's racism must be seen as an equally troubling problem for White and African American students, for all faculty and administrators.

It is imperative that the campus perceive a response to bias-related violence. Intolerance of ethnoviolence must be well known, documented, and demonstrated. Intolerance of ethnoviolence must be developed among those who both practice as well as endure ethnoviolence. Students, faculty, and staff—all, in fact, who inhabit and enrich a campus—claim the fundamental right to conduct their studies and their occupations with dignity, safety, and freedom from any form of abuse. One constituency, even the majority, has no more of a right to unimpeded study than does another. What constitutes an impediment to an institution's educational goals has recently been opened to legal interpretation; the expectation itself has never been questioned.

Because a community dictates the tone of its own commerce, person to person and group to group, it also, therefore, is the arbiter for the quality of life within that community. It follows that a campus, just as any other U.S. community, determines how a member of that community experiences life there. A campus controls the quality of the education it offers by what it tolerates. No one who is scrutinized, doubted, or dismissed because of the color of his or her skin can fully partake of the education that may be available. To paraphrase T.S. Eliot, there is no difference between *what* someone says and *how* someone says it. Neither minority nor majority students are, therefore, distilling the educational content from the sometimes racist packaging or subtle affront in the delivery of that education.

Institutions must begin to direct their energies to attacking vigorously the situations that foster the perception of institutional racism. Awareness of racism is not enough to combat it, no more than is awareness of structural flaws in a building sufficient to keep that building standing.

Proactive/Preventive Strategies

Approaches selected for assessing racism and ethnoviolence should be appropriate to the character of the institution. However, it is most important that an intervention not be chosen only to avoid confronting a more serious problem. All members of the university community contribute to the racial climate, and therefore, all constituencies should be involved at whatever level is practical in efforts to improve it.

As with any extremely complex problem, racism on campus calls for a diverse approach to its resolution. Change at the institutional level requires commitment from the leadership to put into place structures that, at a minimum, will increase the likelihood that policy-making bodies will take into consideration the full range of needs and concerns of minorities. The leadership may need to serve as role model in some cases, to use incentives in others, and, in still others, to be punitive. For example, in the issue of hiring minorities, the president and other top administrators should have representative minority staff. Or the chief executive officer may offer a financial bonus to the department that best meets the university affirmative action hiring goals. But the president of the institution may have to censure publicly or withhold funds from a department that continually refuses to act in good faith or does not attempt to meet established affirmative action guidelines. Of course, students, faculty, or staff who harass or commit other acts of ethnoviolence must be dealt with quickly, fairly, consistently, and, when necessary or appropriate, severely.

To address culturally biased academic programs, mechanisms for curricular change should be explored, selected and implemented. The appreciation—and, ideally, the celebration—of diversity should be apparent in academic, social, and cultural programs. When students, faculty, administrators, and other university personnel begin to examine their own racial attitudes, beliefs, and behaviors and begin to understand how they diminish themselves by maintaining these patterns of thought and action, they will begin to change the environment. Ideas such as those described attack the problem at an individual level; but in the same way that acts of individual, cultural, and institutional racism are interrelated, so must be the strategies employed to address them. Individual interventions must be complemented by ongoing examination and, as necessary, by alteration of the institutional culture and structure in ways that benefit minority as well as majority students.

SUMMARY

From all indications, the increasing racial tension on campuses is not an aberration but rather a condition of U.S. society. Colleges and universities, which have often reacted defensively and, too frequently, angrily when a smug, "don't preach to the converted" attitude is challenged, should feel the most threatened by these increasing racial tensions. These tensions will periodically erupt in one form or another until institutional racism is confronted and eradicated and cultural differences are truly accepted and valued. It is the role and the responsibility of the higher education community to lead by example in this ongoing pursuit.

Ethnoviolence, more than any other form of violence, presents the challenge. Education is antithetical to racism in any guise. These facts must be taught over and over, embodied again and again.

REFERENCES

American Council on Education. (1975). *Framework for evaluating institutional commitment to minorities*. Washington, DC: Author.

American Council on Education & Education Commission of the States. (1988). *One-third of a nation: A report of the Commission on Minority Participation in Education and American Life*. Washington, DC: Authors.

Campus Violence Prevention Center. (1988). *National campus violence survey*. Towson, MD: Towson State University.

Clark, K.B. (1965). *Dark ghetto*. New York: Harper & Row.

Clay, C.A. (1986). *Towson State University Racial Environment Survey*. Available from Towson State University, Towson, MD 21204-7097.

Ehrlich, H. (1988). *Racial violence on campus*. Presentation to the 2nd National Conference on Campus Violence. Towson, MD: Towson State University.

Hodgkinson, H. (1980, January). *Teaching for the 90s: Who are our students?* Address to the Faculty Development Association of Towson State University, Towson, MD.

Jones, J.M. (1972). *Prejudice and racism*. Reading, MA: Addison-Wesley.

Marable, M. (1988a) Race and the demise of liberalism: The 1988 presidential campaign reconsidered. *Black Issues in Higher Education, 5*, 76.

Marable, M. (1988b). The beast is back. *Black Collegiate, 19*(4), 52-54.

MIT Minority Student Issues Group. (1986). *The racial climate on the MIT campus, a report*. Cambridge, MA: Massachusetts Institute of Technology, Office of the Dean for Student Affairs.

National Institute Against Prejudice and Violence. (1987). *Ethnoviolence on campus: The UMBC study* (Institute Report No. 2). Baltimore, MD: Authors.

Steele, S. (1989, February). The recoloring of campus life. *Harpers Magazine*, pp. 47-55.

Washington, J.L. (1988). Black students, White campuses, the plight, the promises. *Black Collegiate, 19*(1), 48-50.

Wilson, R., & Justis, M.J. (1988). Minorities in higher education: Confronting a time bomb. *Educational Record, 4*,(1), 8-14.

PART III
FUNDING AND EVALUATING
CULTURAL PLURALISM
PROGRAMMING

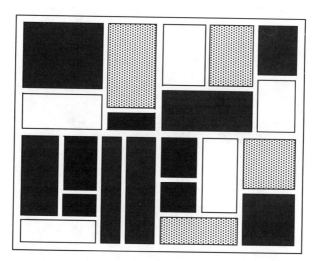

CHAPTER 10

PLANNING FOR CULTURAL DIVERSITY: A CASE STUDY

James B. Stewart

INTRODUCTION

This analysis presents a case study examining efforts at a large, eastern, public university (LEU) to institutionalize programs designed to address underrepresentation and promote diversity. The purpose of the case study of this institution, which is also a multicampus research university, is to illustrate that the design and implementation of diversity planning are most effectively undertaken as an integral part of overall institutional planning rather than as independent processes. The case study also demonstrates that success in integrating diversity planning and institutional planning is significantly affected by an institution's level of understanding of the relationship between initiatives to enhance diversity and its traditional mission.

A model developed by Foster, Jackson, Cross, Jackson, and Hardiman (1988) is adapted here to identify the developmental stages of the LEU related to cultural diversity planning. In the model of Foster et al., there are three stages of awareness: the monocultural stage, the nondiscriminatory stage, and the multicultural stage. In the monocultural stage, no inclusion of so-called minority groups exists, and critical actors exhibit no social conscience and are resistant to change. Policies and intergroup relations in the nondiscriminatory stage involve some inclusion of excluded groups, but power distinctions between majority groups and minority groups persist. In addition, interaction among members of different groups is limited. In the multicultural stage, equality and shared power are achieved, frequent multicultural group interaction occurs, and previously excluded groups are included in all aspects of the institution's activities. The multicultural stage requires a broader consensus among constituencies than in the other two stages, contributing to the difficulty of fully operationalizing this stage. The usefulness of such a model is supported by the work of Richardson (1989), who uses a similar model to examine the relationship between institutional climate and the academic achievement of students of color.

The case study covers the period 1983-1990, during which the institution underwent a transformation of its awareness of the ramifications of cultural diversity for its mission. In particular, during the period 1983-1987 the institution was required by court order to implement a desegregation plan. This period is characterized by the institution's commitment to nondiscrimination, as in the model of Foster et al. After 1987, however, internal dynamics induced a transformation toward *multiculturalism*, that is, toward an institutional commitment to achieving equity as part of the institutional mission.

The manner and extent to which issues related to cultural diversity are incorporated into overall planning processes vary substantially among institutions. This range is compounded by the variety of planning approaches available to colleges and universities. Strategic planning has become increasingly popular in higher education circles. This approach is designed to increase the capability to anticipate and respond to new challenges. In the case of colleges and universities, two critical challenges of concern to diversity advocates are forecasted demographic trends and changes in society's educational expectations as global interdependency increases (National Commission on Excellence in Education, 1983; De Vita, 1989).

The LEU instituted a strategic planning process in 1983, the same year that it was required by court order to implement a desegregation plan. Although strategic planning and desegregation processes were initiated at about the same time, the two planning efforts were operated as independent entities throughout most of the period covered by the case study. Problems related to the transformation toward multiculturalism created by the incomplete integration of the two planning processes are examined in detail in this chapter. The role of institutional planning in facilitating transformation from the nondiscriminatory to the multicultural stage is also featured.

General organizational and programmatic characteristics of diversity initiatives associated with the different stages of institutional commitment to cultural diversity are suggested and used to interpret the LEU's efforts. The general measures of institutionalization used here are the extent to which the enhancement of diversity is (a) systematically addressed in institutional planning, (b) managed through effective and efficient structures and processes, and (c) supported with adequate fiscal and human resources. Specific indicators used to distinguish between the stages of the LEU's commitment to diversity include (1) specification of institutional mission; (2) priority assigned to cultural diversity initiatives in planning; (3) structure, organization, and participation in cultural diversity planning; (4) areas in which diversity initiatives are accepted as appropriate and necessary; (5) budgetary allocations to implement diversity-enhancing initiatives; (6) target groups to be incorporated in diversity planning efforts; and (7) target groups served by diversity-enhancing programs.

The background to the LEU's desegregation efforts and the desegregation process are examined in the next section. The institution's strategic planning process is described in the third section, and comparisons to the desegregation planning process are presented. The fourth and fifth sections examine the post-1987 efforts to integrate strategic planning and diversity planning as well as the changing environmental context in which this attempt at synergy is proceeding. The final section summarizes the implications of the case study for diversity planning efforts at other institutions. Some general propositions to guide these efforts are suggested. These propositions are designed to be useful to both private and public institutions without regard to the institutional planning process currently in place. The propositions are sensitive to the fact that institutions are at many different positions along the continuum of stages of development related to the commitment to, and understanding of, enhanced diversity. Table 1 contains descriptions of organizations and abbreviations referenced in the case study.

PLANNING FOR DESEGREGATION

The LEU's formal desegregation process was initiated as part of a settlement in the *Adams v. Richardson* class action litigation filed by the NAACP Legal Defense Fund in 1970 against the U.S. Department of Health, Education, and Welfare. The suit charged the agency with nonenforcement of certain provisions of Title VI of the Civil Rights Act of 1964. The litigation led to several federal court orders requiring the government to secure desegregation plans or terminate funding for states found in violation of Title VI (Loomis, 1990).

The status of the LEU in the litigation was ambiguous because unlike the group of state-owned institutions, the LEU and several other public institutions are not controlled by the state. The LEU receives substantial state funding but is privately governed. Initially, the state developed a desegregation plan that included only state-owned institutions. Belatedly, the state agreed in 1983 to submit a plan that included quasi-public institutions, including the LEU, and community colleges in addition to state-owned universities.

This complicated configuration of institutions resulted in a delay in formal desegregation planning in the LEU's state in comparison to the "first tier" *Adams* states (i.e., those which submitted acceptable desegregation plans in response to the initial court order). This delay created the theoretical possibility that the design of desegregation plans might proceed from a detailed review of the record in other states. There is, however, no evidence that any effort was made to use the experiences of other states as a guide.

Lack of systematic preplanning resulted in the need for hasty completion of the state's plan, of which the LEU's plan was one component. Haste

Table 1

Glossary of Organizational Abbreviations and Descriptions

Desig.	Title	Description/Function	Membership	Leader	Budget
AAAS	Activist African American Students	Informal group organized to demand changes is institutional policies affecting African Americans	Voluntary	None	Independent
AAFSA	African American Faculty Staff Association	Informal body organized to represent the interests of members to the administration	Voluntary/dues paid by interested individuals and to facilitate networking	Elected by membership	Independent
AST	Administrative Swat Team	Formal body established to monitor and improve the campus climate as it relates to potential and actual acts of racial, ethnic, religious, and gender intolerance and to oversee the institutional response to such acts	Administrators of critical areas including Safety Campus Life, Affirmative Action, Public Information, and the Office of the President	None	No
AUEC	All University Equity Commission	Formal body established to recommend policies to the president to promote equity for people of color	Administrators, faculty, staff, students (appointed by the president and supported by staff of the LEU planning office; membership based on the principal of equal representation of all groups)	Elected by membership	Yes (operating only)
CRC	Concerned Rainbow Coalition	Informal body organized to advocate on behalf of underrepresented racial/ethnic groups	Voluntary	Elected by membership	Independent

LEU	Large Eastern University	Multicampus research university that is the subject of the case study	Not applicable		
SEPAC	Senior Officer for Pan-African Concerns	Position proposed by the AAAS group to coordinate all activities targeted at African Americans	Not applicable		
UDC	University Desegregation Committee	Originally established to oversee desegregation efforts targeted exclusively at African Americans and to fund projects in support of the desegregation process; charge was later expanded to include responsibility for other underrepresented groups	Administrators, faculty, students (appointed by the president and supported by staff of the LEU planning office; membership based on the principle of cooperative decision making by representatives of critical units)	Appointed by the president	Yes
UWEP	University Women's Equity Project	Formal body established to advocate for women's equity and recommend programs in support of this objective to the president	Administrators, faculty staff, students (appointed by the president and supported by staff of the LEU planning office)	Elected by membership	No
UWPC	University-Wide Planning Committee	Formal body established as the first stage of the strategic planning process	Administrators, faculty, staff, students (appointed by the president and supported by staff of the LEU planning office)	Appointed by the president	No
VPFUG	Vice President for Underrepresented Groups	Position established to coordinate institutional activities related to racial/ethnic/gender diversity	Not applicable		

drastically curtailed exploration of opportunities for interinstitutional collaboration. One manifestation of the lack of collaboration and coordination was intense competition among institutions for a limited and declining pool of college-bound African Americans. The long-term effect of this competition was to cause both the state and the individual institutions to forego development of linkages with elementary and intermediate schools, a strategy that might have addressed projected shortages in the numbers of qualified potential entrants in the latter years of the plan. The federal officials with whom the LEU negotiated did not, however, consider such an approach to be appropriate, even though the aggregate goals for all institutions in the latter years of the plan exceeded the expected pool of African American high school graduates. Coordinated action among the institutions might have enabled more effective negotiation with federal officials about enrollment goals and pre-high-school initiatives.

To meet the strict time constraint on the submission of the state's desegregation plan to the federal court, the LEU relied solely on its planning office to generate the LEU's plan. The staff of the planning office solicited various units for suggestions for programs. These suggested programs were incorporated into the plan without detailed review of overall feasibility, monitoring procedures, possibilities for interunit coordination, and management oversight. Overall fiscal implications of the programs were included in the plan, but specific funding mechanisms were not delineated. The planning process thus was fragmented at the outset, and few individuals other than planning specialists participated in the design of the plan.

Following submission of the plan, the University Desegregation Committee UDC (see Table 1) was established to oversee and monitor progress in each of the areas of activity specified in the LEU's desegregation plan, characterized as a "plan for equal opportunity." The term *equal opportunity* was specifically chosen to avoid anticipated adverse reaction to the connotations of the term *desegregation*. In the perception of LEU administrators, use of the term *desegregation* seemed to be an implicit admission that the LEU had been guilty of segregation. The use of the term *equal opportunity* invoked no such imagery; rather, it was used to convey the sense that the institution was simply reaffirming existing commitments. Although this strategy was successful in part, there were at least two negative outcomes. First, uncoupling the process from the descriptor *desegregation* made it necessary to rationalize continually why such a major effort was being undertaken. Second, because Title VI protects groups other than African Americans, use of this referent created expectations among other groups that they could benefit directly from the various initiatives. When other ethnic minority group members found that this was not the case, resentment grew, contributing to the emergence of new interest groups advocating for changes after the court order was vacated. These events underscore how the language choice of institutions reflects its stage of awareness and affects the contours of the pursuit of diversity as suggested by Foster et al. (1988).

The areas of activity identified in the equal opportunity plan included undergraduate recruitment, undergraduate retention, graduate student recruitment and retention, faculty and staff recruitment and retention, and collaborative programs with the state's historically Black institutions. Concurrent with the appointment of the UDC, a task force was established to develop guidelines regarding programmatic design for each activity area. These guidelines were to be used in making decisions regarding the funding of proposed projects. The key ingredient in the process was the provision of a large pool of funds to support worthy projects. This fund was controlled solely by the UDC, which maintained direct responsibility for project oversight. This funding base enabled the LEU to initiate activity more quickly than could most of the other institutions in the state, especially in the area of recruitment.

Several aspects of the desegregation implementation process should be emphasized. One is that there was no obligatory connection between the programmatic recommendations of the task forces and the commitments made in the desegregation plan. Recommendations for programs were generally developed by identifying successful programs at other colleges and universities rather than by using commitments contained in the desegregation plan as a point of departure. Each of the task forces was provided with the portion of the plan related to its particular charge, but none had access to the entire plan. In addition, the task forces generally avoided the issue of program evaluation (see chapter 11 by Harris in this volume).

Other noteworthy aspects of the desegregation implementation process are that initiation of programs and projects by offices was largely voluntary rather than mandated, and that the UDC managed the funding base in a manner equivalent to a foundation that solicits proposals and selectively funds projects on a competitive basis. No sanctions were imposed upon units for nonparticipation in the process. The competitive aspect of the process fueled a lack of enthusiasm on the part of those units that prepared proposals but received no awards. The philosophy guiding allocation decisions emphasized the role of the UDC in funding pilot projects. It was expected that the projects eventually would become absorbed into the ongoing operations of the office, that any necessary increment in permanent funding would then be provided through regular budget channels. To induce movement in this direction, units submitting program proposals were increasingly required to demonstrate a matching contribution to project costs. This requirement had the potential to reward relatively well-endowed units and punish units with little budget flexibility.

The UDC allocation process also created the possibility of uneven development among the various programmatic areas, depending upon entrepreneurial orientations within each unit. Despite these problems, well in excess of 100 proposals were submitted each year beginning in 1984. That volume of proposals created significant management problems for the UDC, leading to continuing efforts to streamline the process. The volume also hampered the UDC's efforts to institute viable evaluation mechanisms to assess program effectiveness. That thrust also was absent from the original planning effort.

One of the strategies used by the UDC to ensure that at least a minimum level of activity was underway in each college was advocacy for creation of an office with responsibilities for providing special support services for target group students in each unit. Another strategy, enacted later, required administrative heads to document their personal involvement in activities. In addition, support was provided to create a unit with responsibility for facilitating success of target group faculty members in achieving tenure and promotion. Although this initiative reflected recognition of the critical role of faculty in achieving desegregation, the overall structure of the process enabled nonminority faculty not only to avoid involvement but also to manifest indifference to and ignorance of the fact that a desegregation (equal opportunity) process was underway. The faculty inadvertently became a principal barrier to structural change in the postdesegregation compliance environment because they had not participated in many of the socializing activities, such as task forces, program design, and submission of project proposals to the UDC. Throughout the desegregation implementation process a large number of traditional human relations training workshops were offered. However, attendance was usually voluntary, and faculty typically were not participants.

The faculty also emerged as a barrier because the campus desegregation efforts largely ignored the critical area of curriculum. This exclusion was possible because federal mandates did not focus on this important issue. The LEU's efforts in the previous decade to increase representation of African Americans through programs that identified students as disadvantaged had left a legacy of structured remedial courses designed to serve as a bridge to the general curriculum. This legacy fueled a general perception among faculty that efforts to increase enrollment of "disadvantaged" students necessitated a reduced emphasis on the core academic functions. As a consequence, when the question of cultural diversity in the curriculum was raised in the postdesegregation compliance order environment, many faculty couched the issue in terms of a trade-off between excellence and diversity. This perspective contrasted with an emergent understanding on the part of some other segments of the institution that in a truly multicultural institution there is synergy between the attainment of institutional excellence and enhanced diversity. This evolving multicultural perspective saw the path to excellence as requiring the institution to tap the resources and the internal cultural understandings of its diverse faculty, staff, and student constituencies. In short, using the language of Foster et al.(1988), a segment of the institution was moving toward the multicultural stage of awareness while another remained ensconced in the ideology of nondiscrimination.

As the desegregation process proceeded, the tenuous status of the UDC became increasingly apparent. Established as an ad hoc committee, as opposed to a permanent unit with line authority over critical functional offices, the UDC had limited capacity to shape the course of events. In addition to the funding incentives described earlier, the only mechanism available to the UDC to generate appropriate responses on the part of administrative units was the status and influence of UDC's chair, then a senior administrator. Evaluation of the comparative importance of the position of chair and the line responsibilities as a senior university official in inducing cooperation is neither feasible nor necessary. The critical point is that the confluence of the two effects served to create flawed assessments of the sources of successful achievements. In particular, changes were often incorrectly attributed to the rationality of the UDC processes rather than to the power and prestige of the central administrative role per se (see chapter 11 by Harris in this volume regarding program evaluation).

In addition to the significance of the status of the chair, the early gains by the UDC were also catalyzed by the newness of the LEU's central administration. Creation of the UDC was acceptable as part of the normal process of institutional reorganization that occurs when administrations change. A major reorganization followed on the heels of the establishment of the UDC in November 1983. The administrative units most affected by the reorganization included the offices of admissions and student services along with the academic support units providing tutorial and counseling services to disadvantaged students. The most noteworthy dimension of the institutional reorganization was the virtual absence of explicit concern for improving the efficacy of the desegregation process. This resulted in part from the inaccurate assessment of the reasons for the perceived successes of the UDC and the pervasive notion among LEU faculty and staff that the desegregation initiatives were temporary.

It is significant to note that an organization representing the interests of African American faculty and staff, the African American Faculty Staff Association (AAFSA), had been consulted regarding the reorganization (see Table 1). Concerns voiced at a meeting in November 1983 between the head of the planning unit and representatives of the AAFSA led to the inclusion of the UDC in the new institutional organizational chart even though the UDC was not a permanent office. The AAFSA also had recommended appointment of a senior administrator to oversee the desegregation process. That recommendation was rejected. In theory the AAFSA constituted a potential resource to strengthen desegregation efforts because of its formalized and historical contributions on campus. However, this potential could not be easily tapped by the institution because, historically, consultation with the group occurred only during periods of crisis induced by lack of attentiveness to student and minority community concerns. The LEU's administration apparently assumed that, since desegregation was in the interest of all minorities, the African American faculty and staff would actively support desegregation efforts without the LEU creating specific structures to reward those faculty and staff involved in such efforts.

Concurrent with the institutional reorganization noted previously, two new permanent university-wide committees were created, one focusing on recruitment and the other retention. In the latter case, the committee's charge involved oversight of the development of plans to improve retention of all undergraduate students. These new structures created further confusion regarding the new committees' relationships to the UDC. In fact, the two committees cultivated cooperation from units by emphasizing that the programs targeted at African American students were pilot projects which, if successful, would eventually be extended to all students.

Several of the weaknesses in the LEU's desegregation planning and implementation process are obvious. The planning process itself was largely unstructured and allowed only limited participation of individuals who were not planning specialists. The implementation process was fragmented and coordinated through a temporary structure with no line responsibility. The implementation design encouraged uneven participation across the institution, and critical areas of activity (e.g., curriculum) were largely ignored. There was limited attention paid to the importance of evaluation of program outcomes. The potential to foster bona fide institutional transformation was hampered by the failure to couple the initial funding process to a process for transferring fiscal responsibility to permanent budgets. Finally, the desegregation process was seen as temporary and peripheral, with no organic relationship to the institutional mission. At the same time, however, the high volume of activity undertaken under the auspices of the UDC prepared the LEU to begin the transformation toward multiculturalism. The design and implementation of the institution's strategic planning process, discussed in the next section, avoided many of the pitfalls of the desegregation planning process.

STRATEGIC PLANNING:
IT'S A DIFFERENT WORLD

Two of the most widely used volumes describing strategic planning are Keller (1983) and Bryson (1989). Bryson's work has been used to guide the LEU's current planning efforts, and Keller's work shaped the LEU's first planning cycle (1983-1989).

Bryson drew four distinctions between strategic planning and traditional approaches to long-range planning. He noted that strategic planning (1) focuses on issues rather than on goals and objectives reflected in current budgets and work programs, (2) focuses on the assessment of the internal and external environment, (3) has a greater capacity to generate an ideal vision of the organization, and (4) provides a stronger action orientation. Bryson also argued that "[s]trategic plans...even though they rarely have a legal status, can often provide a bridge from legally required and relatively rigid policy statements to actual decisions and operations" (p. 9).

By Bryson's definitions the LEU's original desegregation planning process qualified neither as traditional long-term planning nor as strategic planning. However, two features of the desegregation process did fit into the conceptualization of long-range plans: (1) there were specified goals and objectives associated with the desegregation process, and (2) desegregation planners assumed that critical trends (e.g., rates of growth of high school graduates) would continue without having conducted an assessment of external factors. However, unlike realistic long-term planning, there was no functional mechanism whereby goals and objectives were translated into current budgets and work programs.

The overall structure of the desegregation planning process bore little, if any, resemblance to a strategic planning process, although it could be argued that the funding process established by the UDC did increase the flexibility of the organization to respond to changing circumstances.

The preceding discussion is helpful in understanding the character of the desegregation planning process; but the fundamental issue is that two separate planning processes were initiated concurrently at the LEU. Strategic planning is designed to encompass *all* aspects of the institution. At the same time, desegregation planning was also a university-wide initiative, although the range of issues considered was arguably of more limited scope. The existence of a separate desegregation planning process led to limited focus on addressing underrepresentation of certain groups and the enhancement of diversity in the strategic planning process per se. As a consequence, the strategic planning process did not "provide a bridge from legally required and relatively rigid policy statements to actual decisions and operations" (Bryson, 1989, p. 9).

One of the logistical reasons for this lack of integration is that the implementation of a strategic planning process cannot be accomplished effectively unless that implementation is undertaken in a manner consistent with the philosophy of strategic planning. This means that an assessment of the internal climate is a prerequisite for deciding how best to implement the strategic planning process and in particular to engender the active participation on the part of faculty and staff.

The LEU addressed these issues with a two-pronged strategy. The first strategy was to begin the process of linking future budget allocations to the content and quality of units' strategic plans. Implementation of this strategy was constrained by the existing budgetary allocation processes and the time required to prepare strategic plans.

The second strategy flowed directly from the philosophy of strategic planning, that is, the creation of structures that allowed broad-based participation. The University-Wide Planning Committee (UWPC) was established by the president (see Table 1). Interestingly, the overall structure of the UWPC and how it pursued its role bore remarkable similarities to the desegregation planning process previously described. As an example, the analog to the task forces developed as part of the desegregation process was a set of subcommittees that included both members of the UWPC and representatives of other units. In fact, some of the subcommittees were further divided into task forces to focus on specific issues. The subcommittees associated with the strategic planning effort were (1) the Subcommittee on Mission and Goals Statement, (2) the Subcommittee on the Identification of Strategic Planning Units, (3) the Subcommittee on External Environmental Assessment, (4) the Subcommittee on the Assessment of Internal Strengths and Weaknesses, and (5) the Subcommittee on Planning Unit Data Needs.

Although the task force structures associated with desegregation and strategic planning bore similarities, the underlying linkages to the LEU's organization were vastly different. Unlike the desegregation planning and implementation process, *all* units were *required* to participate actively in the strategic planning process. Direct connection to the budgetary allocation process was the strategy used to ensure active participation. In addition, a special incentive to produce a quality plan was introduced in the form of a commitment to provide substantial increments in funding to enhance specific units. The units selected for special funding were to be chosen on the basis of opportunities to improve the LEU's national ranking among universities. A second difference between the two processes was the use of external consultants and a series of workshops to aid units in undertaking the process. This established credibility for the strategic planning process. The only equivalent effort associated with the desegregation process was an annual workshop sponsored by the UDC that reviewed efforts of various offices. Attendance at these workshops was limited essentially to senior administrators.

Another indicator of disjunction between the two processes is the lack of involvement of non-Whites in the early phases of the strategic planning process. Of the total UWPC membership of 14, only one individual was a member of a historically underrepresented group, and the role of that person was largely peripheral. (The individual was an Asian American research assistant.) Of the non-UWPC members participating on the various task forces, 3 of 46 were members of historically underrepresented groups (one African American, one Hispanic American, and one Asian American).

The second phase of the strategic planning process was initiated by the distribution of a strategic planning guide to all strategic planning units. There were few references to the issues of concern to desegregation planners. In the discussion of population trends, it was noted that the African American population in the state was declining. Interestingly, this situation was characterized not only as a constraint but also as an opportunity to refine retention programs for both minority and nonminority students.

In the area of federal regulation, no mention was made of federal monitoring of desegregation and affirmative action. In the discussion of societal, technological, and scientific trends, brief mention was made of trends to integrate minority groups and women. One of the more cogent considerations of relevant issues was found in the discussion of support functions under the general topic of graduate and professional education. Here the absence of a strongly supported institutional climate, including sufficient numbers of minority faculty and staff, was noted as well as the absence of intercultural awareness, understanding, and appreciation.

The preceding constituted the information base available to strategic planning units in initiating planning efforts related to underrepresented groups. It is significant to note that there was no mention of the UDC in the strategic planning guide. In addition, the UDC was not officially represented in the deliberations of the UWPC. Finally, it is critical to note that UDC was not designated as a planning unit. The invisibility of the UDC in the early stages of the strategic planning process limited the extent to which cultural diversity initiatives could be proposed, defended, and endorsed. The only vehicle for the advocacy of diversity-enhancing initiatives was the strategic plans of those offices with ongoing responsibility for serving underrepresented groups.

The restricted opportunities for introducing cultural diversity into strategic planning discussions led to the expectation that limited mention of the relevant issues would be included in the official strategic plan. Although this was the case, at the same time portions of the strategic plan signaled an institutional shift toward the multicultural stage of institutional awareness. In many respects, the institution was undergoing a collective identity crisis because implementation of the desegregation process was ongoing under the auspices of the original charge to operationalize nondiscrimination.

The mission statement that was developed for the institution articulated the LEU's responsibility to address unmet needs of women and minorities through coherent program design. One of the 15 strategic goals addressed the need to promote a culturally, ethnically, and intellectually rich academic community. Some support for this strategic goal was offered in the discussion of the key elements of the university and the discussion of external factors affecting the LEU's efforts to achieve greater national and international prominence. Mention was made of the value of having an ethnically and economically diverse student body. The discussion of external factors noted the potentially disruptive effect of regulations related to affirmative action, including hidden costs associated with compliance.

The action plan associated with the cultural diversity strategic goal was essentially devoid of specifics, although it referenced a major study underway examining the status of women that would serve as a model for addressing underrepresentation of minorities. As noted previously, highlighting this constituency constituted a signal that the transition from the emphasis on African Americans mandated by the desegregation process was implicit in the strategic planning process.

Another signal of the transition from the nondiscriminatory stage of awareness to the multicultural stage was found in language used to support the goal to promote growth in international programs and services. In particular, the objective was enunciated to incorporate an international component in the university's general education requirements. Thus, although the discussion of domestic pluralism was largely restricted to considerations of remediation and disadvantage, concerns related to internationalism and women's equity were treated more comprehensively. Discussions of domestic ethnic and racial minorities were restricted to discussions about students, with no acknowledgement of the need to recruit and retain a relevant complement of faculty and staff who are also members of these ethnic and racial groups.

The foregoing constituted the broad direction of the LEU's strategic planning efforts both during and immediately after the vacating of the desegregation order. The strategic planning process was kept on track through the preparation of annual updates by each administrative unit. There was sufficient flexibility in the strategic planning process for individual administrative units to reorder priorities, but the process was not fluid enough to enable readjustment of the official statement of the LEU's strategic goals. This type of planned flexibility did not exist under the desegregation initiatives.

As external and internal conditions changed, many units were forced to adjust their short-term operational-diversity-related activities to respond to new challenges. These unplanned commitments, however, were made outside of the strategic planning process per se. The need for such adjustments stemmed in part from the initial lack of integration between the strategic and desegregation planning processes.

At the most fundamental level, the lack of integration of the desegregation and strategic planning processes reflected the lack of a clear understanding of how increased diversity could complement other aspects of the institution's mission. As a consequence, although lip service was given to the importance of diversity, these issues were relegated to the periphery. Demands by new constituencies in the period after the revocation of the court order came to underscore the inadequacy of both the desegregation and the strategic planning processes for meeting new challenges.

NEW CONSTITUENCIES AND THE TRANSITION FROM DESEGREGATION TO MULTICULTURALISM

The vacation of the court order driving the LEU's desegregation effort in 1987 helped to catalyze two major developments among various segments of the population of underrepresented groups. The first was the crystallization among African American students of a "power" movement modeled after the Black power movement of the 1960s. The current movement fed on the concern that the court's vacating of the desegregation order could lead to retrenchment of many programs. It also fed on the growing Black nationalist sentiment across the U.S. that was partially the product of the national government's retreat from substantive commitment to equality.

Also producing renewed nationalist consciousness was a dramatic increase in the number of incidents of racial violence across the country and, most significantly, on college campuses. These students were empowered by the recent successes of another group of student activists, largely nonminorities, who had challenged the LEU on its policies regarding investments in corporations with operations in South Africa. The interplay of these processes on the LEU campus was critical in shaping the broad outlines of the institution's cultural diversity agenda.

The second postcompliance development of significance was the transformation of other groups' resentment and sense of exclusion from organizational initiatives. These initiatives were critical in altering the rhetoric used to describe programmatic thrusts beyond "desegregation" and "equal opportunity" toward "cultural diversity." The empowerment of other groups was covertly catalyzed by the affirmative action office, which increasingly introduced the term *people of color* into discussions regarding diversity and equity. Throughout the desegregation period, this office also increasingly interjected itself into programming areas largely unrelated to traditional enforcement and compliance activities. This phenomenon contributed to a lessening of the direct influence of the UDC.

Both the increasing use of the term *cultural diversity* and the proliferation of new formal and informal structures confused those elements of the institution that had had only limited involvement in the earlier efforts. As an example, in the area of curriculum change, individuals and departments were faced with calls for appropriate inclusion of materials related to various groups in courses. The faculty's prior distance from the institution's diversity efforts created the need for substantial external guidance in identifying resources and making optimal decisions among strategies involving (a) courses focusing on a specific group, (b) courses designed to compare the experiences of various groups, and (c) efforts to integrate materials related to one or more groups into existing courses.

CHANGES IN THE LEU'S ORGANIZATION AND PLANNING PROCEDURES

Given the focus of this investigation on planning processes, a special concern is how the various developments described in the preceding section have affected and are affecting a new strategic planning process at the LEU. The critical issues are (a) whether the outcomes of the previous strategic planning and desegregation planning processes have adequately prepared the institution to address the new realities and (b) to what extent the new strategic planning process is likely to avoid the pitfalls inherent in the previous strategic planning process. Increasing complexities in the post-court-order environment are making the process of planning more difficult.

Immediately after the desegregation order was vacated, the LEU declared its commitment to continue its desegregation efforts. At the same time, however, a reorganization of the UDC was undertaken. The reorganization served two purposes. The first was to reduce the size of the body and produce more homogeneity in terms of level of responsibility within the organization. Membership of the reconstituted body was to consist of administrators charged with responsibility for critical program areas. The second purpose of the reorganization was to expand the charge of the committee from the previous, almost exclusive, focus on African Americans. The committee was now charged to address underrepresentation of Hispanic Americans, Native Americans, and Asian Americans as well as to participate in ongoing efforts to promote equity for women.

As a result of time and lobbying from the Concerned Rainbow Coalition (CRC), a group representing the new constituencies, the membership of the UDC was expanded to include individuals designated to represent the interests of the other racial/ethnic target groups, i.e., Hispanic Americans, Native Americans, and Asian Americans (see Table 1). The logic of this membership augmentation was curious because there was no equivalent designated representative for African Americans within this body.

The emphasis on women's equity issues was equally problematic for the inclusion of ethnic group representatives. The existence of other officially sanctioned bodies with responsibility for addressing women's concerns created potential confusion. One group in particular, the University Women's Equity Project (UWEP), was designated by the university president to recommend programs and policies in this area and reported directly to the Office of the President (see Table 1). Unlike the UDC, however, this body had no budget from which to fund programs. As a result, charging the UDC with responsibilities in this area provided a mechanism for connecting recommendations of the UWEP to funding sources.

The UWEP served as the model for the All University Equity Commission (AUEC) (see Table 1), a formal group proposed by the CRC. During the same period, AAAS—the group of African American students espousing a Black nationalist ideology—demanded the establishment of a senior administrative position, the senior officer for pan-African concerns (SEPAC), to coordinate all activities targeted at African Americans.

The LEU's response to the advocacy of these two groups was to create the commission requested by the CRC and to create a facsimile of the position demanded by the students, the vice president for underrepresented groups (VPFUG), to coordinate institutional activities related to racial, ethnic, and gender diversity. As noted previously, a position very similar to the one actually designed by the administration had been proposed several years before by the AAFSA and rejected by the LEU's administration in favor of the UDC structure.

Although the VPFUG position has the potential to provide the centralized leadership required to spearhead the diversity effort, this has not yet been achieved at the LEU. Although the position has now been filled, the length of the search process led to further fragmentation of responsibilities among other administrators and an interim appointment of a person to take on some of the responsibilities without the requisite authority to provide leadership.

These various developments have further confused the perceptions of location of authority for oversight and planning related to the LEU's new emphasis on cultural diversity. The LEU's response to racially related acts of intolerance on campus has further blurred lines of responsibilty. After failure to issue a timely formal denouncement of some highly publicized acts of intolerance, the president created the Administrative Swat Team (AST) to monitor the campus climate and assume responsibility for responding to such acts (see Table 1).

In addition, the issue of curricular reform has moved to center stage. The AAAS demanded that all students be required to take an African American studies course. Other advocates of curriculum reform proposed various forms of a cultural diversity requirement.

To the credit of the faculty and administration, the University Faculty Senate overwhelmingly passed a cultural diversity requirement in 1990 for implementation in 1991. A substantial amount of hard work remains to implement this requirement. This process, however, may well become the vehicle through which the LEU fully enters the multicultural stage of institutional awareness.

The LEU has realized that success in achieving its long-range goals of increasing enrollment of students from underrepresented groups can be fostered through establishing educational partnerships with elementary and secondary schools. To the extent that these initiatives bear fruit, the pool of future students to diversify the undergraduate population will be increased. Just as importantly, involved faculty will develop a better sense of the characteristics of their future students. This will enable instructors to engage in the necessary self-education to meet the needs of new student populations.

Table 2

Institutional Awareness and Cultural Diversity Planning/Implementation Indicators

Institutionalization Indicators	Stages of Awareness/Development*		
	Monocultural	Nondiscrimination	Multicultural
1. Relationship to other missions	No recognition of other than traditional missions; denial of need to augment mission	Perceived trade-off between "excellence" and diversity initiatives; diversity initiatives are optional	Diversity and excellence are complements; diversity initiatives required of all units
2. Planning process	None; denial of need to reflect presence of subpopulations in plans	Top-down; temporary structures (e.g., committees)	Multimodal; clearly delineated responsibilities for plan review
3. Constituencies served	Serving special constituencies perceived as "reverse" discrimination	Limited; remediation thrust; attempts to force different interest groups to merge into artificial umbrella groups	Old and new constituencies served equitably via an empowerment thrust
4. Staffing	Existing staff assumed to have the capabilities to serve all subpopulations	Representation of target groups in staff positions serving special populations only; one-shot human relations workshops for staff in selected areas	Involvement of members of various target groups throughout organization; coherent staff development program
5. Conflict resolution	Crisis determined	Reactive; process oriented	Proactive; outcome oriented
6. Evaluation procedures	None	Ad hoc	Systematic
7. Budgetary support	Ad hoc, no special funds available	Exclusive use of special funds; limited commitment of resources obtained through normal budget channels	Planned funding strategy involving combination of reallocation; special funds and external resources
8. Programming	Monocultural	Special events/public figure lectures, orientation, (e.g., Black History month, MLK celebration)	Comprehensive innovations reflecting a synergism of curricular and co-curricular activities
9. Management	None	Diffuse; lack of centralized authority	Central coordination; clearly defined communication and decision-making channels

*Stages of Awareness/Development adapted from Foster et al. (1988). Work force diversity and business. *Training and Development Journal, 42*(4), 38-41.

The new cycle of strategic planning includes several modifications designed to integrate cultural diversity planning. All strategic units will be required to focus on a set of fixed strategic issues in planning activities. The issue of cultural diversity is one of the mandated strategic issues. In addition, an informal group has been established to review formally the components of the first drafts of the new strategic plans focusing on cultural diversity. The effectiveness of these modifications, however, will depend on the extent to which budgetary allocations based on strategic plans actually reflect due consideration of units' commitments to cultural diversity as an integral part of their missions. That dependence is the type of budgetary linkage implied in the discussion of indicators of institutionalization in the first section of this chapter.

More generally, differences in the treatment of cultural diversity issues between the period in which the desegregation order was in effect and the postorder period can be summarized by referring to Table 2. Table 2 contains general operational characteristics indicating the extent of institutionalization of diversity initiatives by stage of awareness/development. The second and third columns, which focus on the nondiscriminatory and multicultural stages respectively, are those directly relevant to this discussion.

In the post-1987 period, the LEU clearly began to articulate a complementarity between diversity and excellence; the new strategic planning process required that all units address this mission. The number and type of groups targeted by initiatives were expanded, movement toward centralized coordination is occurring, and there is a greater emphasis on program evaluation. The incompleteness of the transformation can be seen in the continuing ad hoc character of the review process for assessing how administrative units have addressed diversity in their strategic plans. There is still an absence of channels for nonadministrative units to affect the content of strategic plans. Finally, the development of an effective central coordination mechanism is incomplete. Despite these shortcomings, it is clear that the LEU's transformation to a multicultural institution is proceeding apace. The LEU's record of grappling with critical issues provides useful guideposts for other institutions.

CONCLUSION

The experience of LEU presented in the case study suggests five general propositions that may be useful for institutions attempting to move toward multiculturalism.

1. There should be a centralized locus of responsibility for planning and implementation of diversity initiatives. As Bryson (1989) has noted, "[t]here is no substitute for leadership...[y]ou need a process champion" (p. 227). The criticality of a high-level administrator as an advocate for the

diversity agenda derives from the fact that "[t]he big innovation in strategic planning is having key decision makers talk with one another about what is truly important for the organization or community as a whole" (p. 227).

2. The institution must develop and articulate a clear understanding of the complementarity among cultural diversity initiatives and other aspects of its mission. Perceived ambiguities in commitment, as, for example, in positing a trade-off between enhancing diversity and institutional quality, will be seized upon by critics of diversity efforts. Cultural diversity initiatives must be treated as a priority area in institutional planning.

3. Involvement in planning diversity initiatives should not be restricted to those with administrative responsibility for planning. Involvement of students, faculty, and staff can both enhance the quality of plan components and reduce suspicion about the sincerity of the institution's efforts. One strategy to accomplish this is to develop an ongoing dialogue between formal planning bodies and informal organizations representing the various constituencies targeted by diversity initiatives. Such a process can help ensure that planning and implementation processes accommodate the goals and objectives of both "older" and "newer" constituencies. The process that generates organizational initiatives may produce groupings similar to many of those that emerged at the LEU and that are delineated in the glossary.

4. Budgetary commitments to diversity initiatives should not be transitory. Special resources must be made available to support pilot projects, but there should be a requirement that administrative units cost share and eventually assume full fiscal responsibility. Two particularly critical budgetary initiatives are incentives to hire faculty and staff who are members of target constituencies and scholarship funds to facilitate diversification of the student body.

5. A comprehensive strategy to educate the institution's various constituencies should be incorporated in diversity planning. Distinct programs for faculty, staff, and students should be developed that reflect the particular role of each constituency in promoting diversity. These programs should take into account the initial stage of understanding of each constituency regarding the extent to which cultural diversity is an important ingredient of the institutional mission. Special attention should be focused on professional development of the various target constituencies as a strategy to increase the pool of faculty, staff, and administrators. A comprehensive development strategy can facilitate the emergence of a broad-based communication network capable of harnessing the untapped wisdom embedded in diverse understandings and experiences. These, in turn, can be sources of new and creative ways to address contemporary and future problems and possibilities.

The transformation toward multiculturalism is not easy. Systematic planning can, however, ameliorate many of the problems that are likely to be encountered and prepare institutions of higher education to meet the many challenges of the 21st century.

REFERENCES

Bryson, J. M. (1989). *Strategic planning for public and nonprofit organizations*. San Francisco: Jossey-Bass.

De Vita, C. J. (1989). *America in the 21st century, a demographic overview*. Washington, DC: Population Reference Bureau.

Foster, B., Jackson, G., Cross, W. E., Jackson, B., & Hardiman , R. (1988). Workforce diversity and business. *Training and Development Journal, 42*(4), 38-41.

Keller, G. (1983). *Academic strategy: The management strategy in American higher education*. Baltimore, MD: Johns Hopkins University Press.

Loomis, F. (1990). *Desegregation in higher education: A brief history*. University Park: Pennsylvania State University, Office of Planning and Analysis.

National Commission on Excellence in Education. (1983). *A nation at risk, the imperative for educational reform: A report to the nation and the Secretary of Education* (Doc USEO 1.2N21). Washington, DC: Author.

Richardson, R. C. (1989). *Institutional climate and minority achievement*. Denver, CO: Education Commission of the States.

CHAPTER 11

EVALUATING UNIVERSITY PROGRAMMING FOR ETHNIC MINORITY STUDENTS*

Shanette M. Harris

Theoretical and practical considerations suggest that minority students in predominantly White university settings experience difficulties that contribute to dissatisfaction and high attrition rates (Fleming, 1981; Loo & Rolison, 1986; Miller, 1981; Nettles, Thoeny, & Gosman, 1986; Suen, 1983). To assist minority youth, particularly African American and Hispanic American students, in completing college, programs have been designed to combat the negative experiences of ethnic minorities enrolled in predominantly White institutions. Support services such as study skills, mentor programs, peer counseling, academic advising, and cultural centers have been implemented to address the problems of student alienation, cultural isolation, and overall minority student dissatisfaction that are associated with poor academic performance and attrition (Garcia & Presley, 1981; Lee, 1982; Pantages & Creedon, 1978). Despite increased emphasis on developing and implementing assistance programs for minority students, little evaluative data exist to distinguish effective approaches from ineffective ones. Rather, evaluation of minority student programming is often perceived as tangential to the main function of providing services to this population. Yet this perspective increasingly is under attack by the federal government, private sponsors, and participants who have come to expect an accounting of program achievements. From an ethical standpoint as well as from a fiscal responsibility perspective, program managers must account for the success or failure of minority student programs.

---

*This chapter is based on the author's unpublished doctoral dissertation.

A general goal or benefit of program evaluation is to provide information that can be utilized to increase the effectiveness of existing programs and to assist with the appropriate planning, design, and development of new programs. Specific advantages include (a) providing information about the services offered and the approaches employed by the director and staff, (b) offering a sound rationale for a program to be continued in the future, (c) assisting program managers in selecting among alternative programs, and (d) providing justification for the introduction of a program to a university system. Evaluation also can be useful in determining the fit between a program and the culture of an institution; each program must reflect the unique institutional signature (Cheatham, 1989).

This chapter provides a perspective for applying generic program evaluation procedures to the assessment of assistance programs for minority youth on White campuses in order to identify the unique factors affecting their success. What follows is a framework based upon principles associated with evaluative research that serves as a model for conducting evaluations of ethnic minority student programs and a description of an evaluation of a multidimensional program. The recommendations and results of the evaluation are discussed in terms of contextual variables on other university campuses.

A MODEL FOR EVALUATING MINORITY STUDENT PROGRAMS

Several factors are involved in plans to evaluate services for minorities. The most important variable to useful evaluation is a program designed and implemented on the basis of evaluative principles. The evaluative process can be effectively undertaken by following four major steps. The first step (to be taken during the developmental stages) should include the following tasks: (a) specifying the rationale for services offered, (b) classifying theories and assumptions that support the intervention methods, (c) defining program components and associated activities operationally, (d) identifying staff and their responsibilities, (e) defining intermediate and long-term objectives operationally, and (f) estimating costs. The second evaluative step involves determining how the program actually operates; the third involves selecting a method to answer questions about the program. The fourth and final step in the evaluative process is to interpret the data and disseminate the findings to relevant university officials.

The First Step

Specifying the Rationale

The decison to deliver services to students must be based upon sound rationale that connects the institution, the program, and the participants served. For example, a university needs assessment may contribute information concerning the type of services to be developed for African American students. Specifying a rationale is important because services designed for one group of students (e.g., Asian Americans) may or may not meet the needs of students from another minority group (e.g., Hispanic Americans). The rationale for program development might also include an academic profile of students who enter the university and the number of students that could potentially benefit from the services.

Classifying Theories and Assumptions

Various theories can be used to select program components and services for students. A behavioral approach might lead to the development of a summer program designed to orient entering students to the college environment. Such a program assumes that summer attendance can be generalized to the regular academic year. Peer advising/counseling programs are based upon the assumption that peers are better able to assist students than regular university employees. However, these and similar assumptions should be assessed experimentally or through previous research before being used as the foundation of a program. The assumptions selected should also be testable and serve to relate program services offered to students to the short-term goals and long-term objectives of the program.

Defining Program Components

The activities selected to meet student needs should be specified in detail in order for evaluation to be conducted. Unclear and vague programs do not facilitate replication by other university officials, make it difficult to attribute effects to the program, and cannot be linked to the stated goals and objectives of the program. Programs vary in the number and types of activities offered to students. For example, a summer transition program on Campus A might involve attending required courses, attending psychosocial workshops, and attending a series of lectures. On Campus B, a summer transition program might include attending required courses and a series of lectures. Further, on Campus C a summer transition program might only include attending required courses. As a result, the activities of each program component and the interrelationship among program components should be specified in order for the evaluator(s) to develop an understanding of the dynamics of the program to be evaluated. Precise specification of the activities also assists in determining ways to measure effects attributable to each activity.

Identifying Staff and Responsibilities

Staff and their associated responsibilities are integral to any program. In some instances certain types of programs may be effective or ineffective due to characteristics of individuals selected to deliver student services. For example, a counseling program designed for African American students that does not employ staff with experience related to this population or provide systematic training to staff members who lack prior experience may not accomplish its objectives. Similarly, a peer counseling program that fails to monitor the academic performance of the students selected to counsel and advise program participants may be unable to account for the program's lack of success.

Defining Objectives

Operational definitions of intermediate goals and long-term objectives are prerequisites to usable evaluation. Ambiguous objectives do not provide a connection between the program activities and expected effects. Definitions of intermediate and long-term objectives should entail the type of change expected to be produced by the program (e.g., long term vs. short term), the particular domain to be targeted for change (e.g., cognitive, behavioral, affective), the degree to which the program will be considered as having met a goal (e.g., 50% decrease in attrition), and the durability of the change (e.g., from freshman to senior year).

Program objectives need to be specified in measurable terms for other reasons as well. First, a program may produce changes in domains that were not specified in the objectives. These unintentional effects need to be differentiated from expected effects. For example, a retention program may not lead to a decrease in attrition as expected by program developers but may evidence a significant increase in grade point average for program participants who remain at the university. Likewise, unexpected effects may be produced by a program. Programs designed to assist students in adjusting to a university could result in higher attrition rates because counseling students indirectly influences their decisions to transfer to other universities (Giddan, et al., 1987). Such a result may be positive in many ways for the students but present unexplainable issues for those seeking to connect the program to specific outcomes.

Second, university officals and administrators often vary in their perceptions of the importance of program objectives. Although significant reductions in yearly attrition rates might be a worthwhile objective to one administrator, student perceptions of a hospitable university atmosphere may be the primary objective of another. As a result, it may be beneficial to arrange objectives in a hierarchical fashion according to the importance attached to each. Finally, operational statements minimize confusion that may result from redundant or overlapping objectives.

Estimating Costs

Both program effects and costs must be evaluated to make appropriate institutional decisions. If the dollar amount is the deciding factor as to whether a program is continued at a university, cost analyses can justify the continuation of an existing program or the introduction of a program to a university system. When performing cost analyses for minority student programs, the primary goal is to obtain an idea of the actual expenditures. Cost analyses are one way of representing these differences to administrators and understanding how the costs of programs and the effects are related. However, the concern is with finding major dollar differences among programs rather than nonsignficant financial gains and/or losses. Additionally, a cost-effective program is of no use if it is not acceptable to staff, students, parents, administrators, and others affected by the program. Four cost-analysis approaches, including cost effectiveness, cost benefit, cost utility, and cost feasibility, are clearly articulated in Levin (1983).

The Second Step: Determining How the Program Operates

The second evaluative step to be taken involves specification and assessment of the program. This stage of the evaluation process seeks to determine exactly how the program operates, and it is essential to understanding the dynamics of the program process. The components of the program and associated services are identified and assessed to determine their role in the functioning of the program. This assessment should determine if the elements are functioning in a way that maximizes the possibility of attaining expected outcomes. The evaluator(s) can use several strategies to evaluate program inputs, including structured or open-ended interviews with staff, directors or managers, program participants, and other individuals familiar with the services; questionnaires designed to assess inputs; analysis of records and documents used by staff; and direct observation of the program process. The evaluator(s) might also choose to assess less obvious aspects of program inputs specific to all program components, such as the general atmosphere of the program, training and qualifications of staff, attitudes and morale of the staff, and the styles of communicating used by staff to interact with participants. A microlevel assessment of specific components may also provide valuable feedback to the program directors. For example, evaluators assessing a program that includes a component employing any form of skills training may focus upon characteristics specific to this area, such as the teaching style of the instructor(s) and materials used by the instructor. In most instances the evaluator(s) will be unable to employ previously validated measures for these purposes and will need to design instruments specific to the program being evaluated.

Table 1

Evaluation Model for Minority Student Programs

STEP 1

1. Population
2. Program rationale
3. Program assumptions
4. Program components and activities
   a. Assessment instruments
   b. Record keeping system
5. Staff/responsibilities
6. Objectives
   a. Short term
   b. Long term
7. Estimating program costs
   A. Cost effectiveness
   B. Cost benefit
   C. Cost utility
   D. Cost feasibility

STEP 2

Specification of program components
   A. Strategies
      1. Structured and/or open-ended interview
         a. Staff
         b. Managers/university officials
         c. Participants
      2. Questionnaires
      3. Records and documents
   B. Characteristics of each component
   C. Relationship between components
   D. Objectives/goals of each component

STEP 3

Method
   A. State questions/hypotheses
   B. Select design (Campbell & Stanley, 1963) and identify possible control groups
   C. Analyze data

STEP 4

1. Interpret data
2. Write report/recommendations
   A. Strengths
   B. Weaknesses

The Third Step: Selecting a Method to Answer Questions

The third evaluative step pertains to the method that will be used to answer questions about the program. A program or set of services must be connected with observed changes in participants before concluding that the program is responsible for the changes. Thus evaluators need to be aware of factors that diminish the usefulness of evaluation results. Some of these factors termed "extraneous" have been identified by Campbell and Stanley (1963) and are the standards by which a quasi-experimental design is judged. The fewer the sources of extraneous variation, the more confidently the evaluator can say that the observed results are due to the program. These factors include history, maturation, testing, instrumentation, regression to the mean, selection of subjects, attrition, and reliability of measures.

These concerns can be addressed in a number of ways specific to each of the nine potential problems as well as with more general techniques. The best way to decrease the influence of extraneous variables is to employ a similar group of participants to serve as a comparison group. That is, students who participate in a program (experimental group) can be compared to students who do not participate in the program (control group). Members of the control or comparison group should be as similar to those who participate in the program as possible. This comparison group can be selected from the same university as the participant group or from a similar university. If the comparison group is selected from a university different from the university attended by participants, consideration should be given to selecting those that are similar in student composition, academic requirements, location, and mission. Relevant student variables to be considered include age, gender, academic classification, academic major, college entrance examination scores, high school grade point average, size of high school, socioeconomic status, high school, and extracurricular activities.

If the results of the evaluation study can be attributed to the program and its components, then questions are usually asked regarding generalizability of the findings to other similar programs, universities, student participants, and points in time. Problems similar to those discussed in attributing the results of an evaluation to the program rather than extraneous factors are also involved with generalizing the findings of an evaluation on one campus to other settings, persons, and times. Campbell (1969) cited six factors that could potentially limit generalizability. The results can only be generalized to those settings, persons, and times that are represented in the evaluation being conducted. Thus the degree to which the results of an evaluation study can be generalized is dependent upon the amount of similarity among the programs, universities, students, and times in which the evaluation is conducted. The more similar the programs and universities, the more likely that the findings of one evaluation will be similar for other programs. For a further discussion of this issue the reader is referred to Campbell and Stanley (1963).

The Fourth Step: Interpreting the Data and Disseminating Findings

Once the data have been analyzed, the fourth evaluative step that is undertaken focuses upon interpretations made by the evaluator(s). These interpretations should consider the validity of the methods used. That is, the weaknessess of the data collection procedure, reliability and validity of the measures used, factors specific to the design chosen, and the analyses should be discussed in conjunction with the effects of the program. Institutional staff affiliated with computing services and knowledgeable of statistical procedures should be able to offer assistance with data analysis. These individuals should be consulted before program implementation, during the program's operation, and after the summative evaluation procedure. In most instances, it may also be beneficial to select a person with expertise in statistics and research design to serve as a member of the program staff. Table 1 summarizes the four steps involved with the evaluation of minority student programs.

EVALUATING A RETENTION PROGRAM

The previous section considered the problems specific to conducting research in natural settings. Given these inherent difficulties, is it possible to conduct evaluations in a way that will provide information beneficial to decision making? A description of an evaluation of the Virginia Tech Academic Success Program (V-TASP) may provide a better understanding of the relationship between these methodological principles and minority student programming. Undoubtedly certain aspects of program evaluation will be different for other program types and for other universities; however, the overall process is probably typical for evaluation research on most college or university campuses.

Program Description

The Virginia Tech Academic Success Program was instituted in 1984 at Virginia Polytechnic Institute and State University (VPI&SU), a selective 4-year land-grant university located in the mountains of southwest Virginia. V-TASP was originally designed for African American freshmen at the university because, compared to national data, the attrition rate and graduation rate of all Virginia Tech students were well above national figures and did not relect the experiences of Virginia Tech minority students, who had a much higher attrition rate. For example, a 1986 study of university graduation rates for African American and for majority students showed that of the 4,028 freshmen who entered during fall of 1980, 65.5% of majority students graduated within 5 years but that only 42.9% of African American students graduated in the same time period (J. Williams-Greene, personal communication, May 20, 1989).

V-TASP was developed to increase the recruitment and retention rate of African American students by providing coordinated systematic student course placement, enhancing problem solving and study skills, intensifying academic advising, and enhancing counselors' and administrators' awareness of academic support programs. The objectives of V-TASP are based upon the achievement variables described by Noel, Levitz, and Salurie (1985). These achievement factors include diagnostic testing of student skills, offering courses and curricula consistent with students' diagnosed skills, and comprehensive educational planning and academic advising. Specifically, the objectives of this program are to (a) assess the academic skills level of students; (b) help students develop appropriate study skills; (c) prevent the placement of students in courses that are beyond their skills level; (d) provide personal and academic counseling; (e) enhance reasoning and learning skills needed for academic progress; (f) train academic special advisers, graduate students, and peer advisers to advise students; and (g) monitor students' academic performance throughout each academic term.

Staff and Tasks

V-TASP personnel include the assistant provost; a full professor in the College of Education; associate or assistant deans from seven colleges; a counselor; nine graduate assistants; and student peer tutors. The assistant provost is responsible for directing the program. This responsibility includes such duties as interviewing and hiring potential staff, meeting with staff to discuss program issues, and delegating responsibilities. The associate or assistant deans are responsible for supervising the work of the graduate advisers assigned to their respective departments. This supervision includes making certain that the graduate advisers contact all V-TASP students in their respective colleges and providing the correct information about courses and grades. The faculty members also advise target students when the graduate adviser is unable to answer a question and contact students when their grades drop below the minimum required grade point average. The counselor is responsible for assisting the students with enrolling in tutorial sessions and study skills classes and for assisting with personal concerns. The counselor also supervises peer advisers' contact with the target students.

The graduate assistants are responsible for maintaining a close relationship with their advisees to ensure that students are aware of the college course requirements, financial aid services, drop/add schedule, registration process, summer school options, and related issues. The graduate assistants maintain records on each student and monitor the information provided to students.

Finally, the peer advisers are responsible for visiting the students and providing information about campus living and similar courses they have taken. Peer advisers also respond to personal concerns target students might feel comfortable discussing.

Program Components

The Virginia Tech Academic Success Program is comprised of four primary components: preassessment testing, a three-tier advising system, study skills and counseling services, and the Advanced Study Skills and Reasoning course. Preassessment testing is carried out during the fall before students actually begin classes.

The three-tier advising system is mandatory and involves volunteer faculty advisers, graduate student advisers, and peer student advisers. One graduate adviser and two peer advisers are assigned to the faculty advisers in each college. The responsibilities of the staff affiliated with the three-tier advising system were discussed earlier.

The Advanced Study Skills and Reasoning class is divided into two components. The first component involves students' participation 2 days per week in intensive training and practice of study and thinking skills. The second component involves students' work on competency enhancement 1 day per week using individualized learning systems (microcomputer courseware programs organized for each student). Problem-solving and reasoning skills are also addressed by means of training and practice in word processing and computer programming skills.

The Evaluation

V-TASP was evaluated according to a framework proposed by Suchman (1976). The framework is comprised of five criteria: (a) effort (What was done and how well was it done?), (b) performance (Did any change occur? Was the change the one intended?), (c) adequacy of performance, (d) efficiency (Is there any better way to attain the results, e.g., cost analysis?), and (e) process (How and why did the program work or not work?). The program was evaluated according to each of these criteria.

The *effort* criterion that answers the question What was done? was assessed through interviewing staff, administrators, and program participants. The goal of this assessment was to determine if the operation of the program was consistent with the program's description. As a result, all individuals involved with V-TASP were interviewed, and specific questions were asked about each program component (e.g., study skills class, counseling). The results of the interviews confirmed that V-TASP staff provided services to African American freshmen and sophomores aimed at increasing retention and graduation rates.

The remaining four criteria—performance, adequacy of performance, process, and efficiency—were used to evaluate the *effort* of staff and administrators. These four criteria were assessed by using data specific to Virginia Polytechnic Institute (within-university comparisons) and data from two similar land-grant institutions (between-university comparisons).

Following the definitions offered by Suchman (1976) for each of the four criteria, the following hypotheses were tested by making *within-university comparisons*:

Process

1. The alienation, meaninglessness, and powerlessness experienced by V-TASP participants is less than that experienced by students who were asked to participate but refused the offer (nonparticipants).

2. V-TASP participants will perceive greater behavioral and cognitive changes than nonparticipants.

3. Seniors who participated in V-TASP will report greater long-term social and academic changes than seniors who did not participate in V-TASP.

Process

4. V-TASP participants are satisfied with the services of the total program and the individual program components.

Performance

5. There is a difference in student grades and the number of students retained at VPI&SU after the implementation of V-TASP as compared to previous years.

The within-university evaluations allowed for the investigation of different outcome questions, such as the effects of the total program, analysis of the various components of the program, and the impact of the program upon students. The program was evaluated according to process and performance criteria, which were defined earlier. The within-university comparisons focused only upon the academic success program. *Process* was assessed in hypotheses 1,2, and 3 by comparing program participants (experimental group) and nonparticipants (control group) to determine how and why the program works (i.e., meets stated objectives) or does not work by examining possible differential effects of the program for student participants. *Process* was also assessed in hypothesis 4 which examined program participants' degree of satisfaction with the total program and each of the components. *Performance* was assessed through hypothesis 5 by comparing African American students enrolled at the university in their second year before V-TASP was instituted (1978-1983) with African American students enrolled in their second year after the program was instituted (1984-1988).

For purposes of assessment, three instruments were developed: the Student Satisfaction Questionnaire (SSQ), Perceived Changes Checklist (PCC), and Program Effectiveness Questionnaire (PEQ) (Harris, 1989). Reliability coefficients were computed using the Cronbach's alpha formula for the current sample to gain an index of the internal consistency for the three inventories after removing all open-ended questions. Also used for assessment was the University Alienation Scale (Burbach, 1972).

Program participants to be assessed were selected by obtaining a list of students participating in the program for each cohort year since the program was implemented in the fall of 1984. The specific cohorts included first-time (i.e., freshmen) participants for 4 consecutive years (i.e., 1984-1985, 1985-1986, 1986-1987, and 1987-1988). All students on this list and enrolled at the university were contacted by telephone to request their participation in the evaluation. A sample of nonparticipants to be assessed was obtained by systematically sampling the undergraduate African American student population enrolled at the university minus program participants. These students were also contacted by telephone to request their participation in the study. Both student groups were informed that their responses were confidential and would be used to provide feedback to the administrators of a retention program on campus. All students were informed of the date, time, and location to complete the assessment materials.

Two 2-hour meetings were held for students to complete the assessment packet with its several paper-and-pencil measures. The packets also contained an informed consent form. Freshmen, sophomores, and juniors attending either meeting were asked to complete the SSQ, PCC, and PEQ. Seniors were asked to complete an additional questionnaire, the University Alienation Scale. To ensure confidentiality and candid responses, participants were asked not to write their names on the questionnaires. Assessment packets were collected after the instruments were completed.

The *between-university comparisons* were made to provide answers to questions that the within-university comparisons could not easily address, such as how successfully the academic success program accomplishes its goals as compared to other programs designed to retain and graduate African American students. The academic success program (experimental group) was compared to retention programs implemented at two similar universities (control groups).

The sample of minority student programs was obtained by contacting program directors of regional institutions (of similar type, student population, academic requirements, and university mission) by telephone and letter to determine if they had a specific retention service for enrolled African American students. If a verifiable set of services or one major service existed on the campus with a goal of retaining and graduating students, each director was asked to provide 4 years of retention and graduation data for participants.

Three of Suchman's evaluative criteria were investigated: performance, efficiency, and adequacy of performance. The following questions were examined by making between-university comparisons:

Performance

1. Do V-TASP participants have a higher year-to-year return rate and graduation rate than participants of comparison programs?

Efficiency

2. Is the academic success program as cost effective or more cost effective than retention programs at similar universities?

Adequacy of Performance

3. Are the effects of V-TASP more adequate to meet the total amount of program participants' need than are the effects of comparison programs?

For question 1, *performance* was defined as year-to-year retention and graduation within a 4-year period. The retention and graduation rates of each cohort for the two comparison programs were compared to the retention and graduation rates of the academic success program cohorts. For question 2, *efficiency* was defined as the total costs per student for participating in the program for the length of time specified in the proposal. Cost per student was determined by comparing the costs of the alternatives with the costs of the academic success program. Indirect program costs vary greatly and thus were omitted. Finally, for question 3, *adequacy of performance* referred to the programs' capacity to meet the total amount of university need (i.e., retaining African American students).

Results

Within-University Comparisons

Hypothesis 1—that V-TASP participants experience less alienation, meaninglessness, and powerlessness than nonparticipants—was partially supported. Student participants reported fewer feelings of meaninglessness and powerlessness than students who did not participate in the program.

An analysis of the relationship between program components and feelings of alienation, meaninglessness, and powerlessness appears to suggest that students visiting the graduate advisers report fewer feelings of meaninglessness than students who do not use this service. Students who attended the study skills course reported fewer feelings of powerlessness than students who did not attend the course. Students who attended the course also reported less alienation than students who did not attend the course. However, using the services offered by the counseling center did not seem to influence significantly students' feelings of meaninglessness, powerlessness, or alienation. The total program did not significantly impact upon participants' feelings of alienation, meaninglessness, and powerlessness.

Hypothesis 2—that participants would percieve greater behavioral and cognitive changes than nonparticipants—was partially supported. Students who attended the study skills course and those who visited the advisers reported more changes on these dimensions than students who did not use V-TASP services. The data gathered on attending the counseling center did not differentiate between students who participated in the program and those who did not participate. However, if students used all program services, the differences between students who participated in the program and those who did not participate approached statistical significance.

Hypothesis 3—that seniors who participated in V-TASP would percieve greater long-term social and academic changes than seniors who did not participate in the program—was supported. The findings indicated that participants who attended the counseling center, used the advising component, and participated in the total program reported more social and academic changes than students who did not participate in the program. However, there were no differences between the groups on the study skills course component.

The results of the hypothesis 4 study suggested that participants were satisfied with V-TASP and the individual program components. However, the advising and advanced study skills course components, in contrast to the counseling services component, received some ratings indicating dissatisfaction. Four percent of the respondents were dissatisfied with the study skills course component. The total program and the three components also received combined ratings of 12% indicating high satisfaction. A few specific items were, however, demonstrated as high or low on satisfaction. The respondents seemed most satisfied with the services offered by the advisers and felt comfortable using them. However, participants felt unable to discuss social and interpersonal concerns with the advisers. The respondents did not feel comfortable at the counseling center and did not feel they were able to apply information learned in the advanced study skills course to other classes. Yet the majority of the respondents rated 22 of the 25 items within a range of "moderately satisfied" to "somewhat satisfied."

Finally, hypothesis 5—that students attending the university before V-TASP (1978-1983) would have lower enrollment figures and grade point averages than those enrolled after the implementation of V-TASP (1984-1987)—was supported. The data indicated that before V-TASP was implemented on the campus, an average of 78.4% of students were enrolled in their second year as compared to an average of 76.9% after V-TASP. In addition, although small, there was some increase in the mean overall grade point average of students after the implementation of the program as compared to earlier years.

The main conclusions derived from the within-university analyses were that (a) the program components seemed to decrease students' feelings of alienation, meaninglessness, and powerlessness; (b) the individual program components had different influences upon meaninglessness, powerlessness, and alienation; (c) participants reported more changes in behaviors and thoughts associated with college; (d) seniors who participated in the program as freshmen and sophomores reported more changes in behavior than students who did not participate in the program; and (e) the impact of counseling differed for upperclass and underclass students. The finding that attending the counseling center did not have an impact upon alienation, meaninglessness, powerlessness, and perceptions of cognitive and behavioral change is consistent with previous researchers who generally found that the provision of counseling services may not be an effective strategy for some college students (Garni, 1980; Herr, 1985). In addition, Cheatham, Shelton, and Ray (1987) reported that among African American students most help seeking is for academic counseling. This finding is also consistent with research indicating that counseling services may interact with student academic level and result in different outcomes (Giddan, et al., 1987). These findings support the data that students who use services designed to improve adjustment to predominantly White campuses may benefit in emotional and behavioral ways. The findings also suggest that the effects of retention programs may be mediated by various program characteristics (e.g., type of services offered) and student characteristics (e.g., academic level).

Between-University Comparisons

The *performance* hypothesis (question 1)—that V-TASP participants would have a higher year-to-year retention rate and graduation rate than participants of comparison universities—was partially supported. The results indicated higher 4-year graduation rates for V-TASP. However, the year-to-year retention rates were lower for V-TASP cohorts 1, 2, and 3 than rates of the two comparison programs. For cohort 4, a higher percentage of V-TASP participants returned for the second year (98%) than did participants of the Peer Counseling Program (PCP). The results also revealed an increase in the number of students returning for V-TASP cohorts from 1984 to 1987. The year-to-year retention rate appears to have started to increase with cohort 3.

The *efficiency* hypothesis (question 2)—that V-TASP is as cost effective or more cost effective than retention programs at comparable universities—did not appear to be supported by the results of cohort 1 (1984-1985), cohort 2 (1985-1986), and cohort 3 (1986-1987). However cost per student for cohort 4 was lower for V-TASP than cost per student for the University Transition Program (UTP), although higher for the PCP. The total cost for V-TASP was lower than the total cost for the UTP and higher than the total cost for the PCP. This study was unable to include indepth cost analyses, but these areas of evaluation are important to consider when making decisions about modification of the total program, individual components, or alternate methods of retention and graduation.

The *adequacy of performance* hypothesis (question 3)—that the effects of V-TASP are more adequate to meet the total amount of participant need than the effects of comparison programs—was not supported by Suchman's (1976) "total amount of need" definition, although supported by the "impact of participants served" definition of adequate performance. The results indicated that V-TASP was less adequate to meet the needs of all participants of cohort 1, cohort 2, and cohort 3 as compared to the UTP and the PCP when those needs were defined as year-to-year retention. The findings also suggested that V-TASP has become more effective in retaining students from year to year.

Based upon the between-university analyses, it appears that V-TASP has continued to change since 1984 in terms of cost per student, increases in year-to year-retention, and adequacy of performance. The program also seems to have a greater impact upon some participants than others across time as evidenced by the higher short-term graduation rates (4 year) for program participants as compared to the graduation rates of comparable programs within the same time span.

The results of this evaluation appear to offer several areas for interpretation. However, the findings must be carefully tempered in terms of psychometric considerations, research design, contextual variables, and generalizability. The inability to assign subjects randomly to participant and nonparticipant status does not allow any definitive statements to be made about the data. It is possible that the results stem from factors specific to the students (e.g., motivation) rather than the program.

Variables specific to the universities such as admissions criteria, academic drop policies and procedures, and the required minimum grade point average may have contributed to the findings that revealed that V-TASP had lower year-to-year retention rates and slightly higher costs per student than comparison programs. Thus the results of this evaluation should be interpreted within the context of the possible sociopolitical, student, and university influences that could not be manipulated.

In addition, the findings of this evaluation can only be generalized to those students who were included in the sample. Further research is needed to generalize beyond these cohorts.

Summary

Considering the limitations, the results of the evaluation suggest that V-TASP has some positive practical effects for participants. The data and analyses indicated that the implementation of V-TASP in 1984 may have had a positive impact upon students' grades and enrollment percentages for the sophomore year. The data also seem to suggest that the program components may have an effect upon students other than those effects directly related to grades, retention, and graduation. Participants appear to benefit from the program in socioemotional ways as well, which may indirectly influence retention and graduation rates. The indication that students perceive themselves as less aimless and as having control over their environments because of participation in the program deserves futher study. The finding that V-TASP decreased participants' feelings of alienation, meaninglessness, and powerlessness is important, given the fact that the attrition rate of minority students is not due solely to academic performance (Astin, 1977). Programs that focus on academic performance at the expense of social factors may ignore the intricate relationship between academic performance and life events and encounters.

The results suggested that V-TASP has positive effects for program participants. However, student data before participation were unavailable to compare to the data obtained after participation. Assessing student behavior prior to program participation is important to interpreting the impact of the services at a later point in time. If preprogram behaviors are unavailable to compare to student behaviors during and after program participation, it is difficult to attribute student performance to the program components. Preassessment data also provide information that can be used to develop a student profile to predict for whom the program is likely to be most beneficial and under what conditions.

However, assessment should be made not only of pre- and postprogram behavior. Student behaviors should be monitored throughout the program. Data resulting from these interviews can be used to modify or remove components that might be less effective. Sharing such information may also provide students with an increased feeling of being intricately involved with the program's operation, thus increasing their feelings of belonging and power over themselves.

The present evaluation indicated that the counseling services component did not contribute significantly to the performance and well-being of the participants. However, the results varied as a function of students' academic level. Due to the costs of the total program, this component might require more attention to meet students' needs before it is cost effective. A marketing campaign designed to enhance the attractiveness of this service and to decrease the negative stereotypes of those who utilize counseling services might provide an opportunity to increase the effectiveness of this component. However, if such a campaign does not lead to more positive feelings, it might be cost beneficial to expand a component that is effective (e.g., three-tier advising system) and to remove the counseling services component.

The results also indicated that, on the whole, students were highly satisfied with the advanced study skills course but encountered difficulties applying the skills taught in the course to regular classroom work. This finding suggests that the component has positive effects in some meaningful ways but does not meet the objective of assisting students with other courses. Strategies that can increase the similarities between the study course and class requirements could address this conflict. Obtaining information about the exact nature of students' problems might assist with the development of techniques that promote a better transition between the study skills course and the application of these skills. Factors involved in this process, such as the types of courses in which students have the most problems generalizing, might also aid in shaping the direction of the course.

Student participants were quite satisfied with the advising system. However, they also reported that the advisers only dealt with academic concerns. Such a focus satisfies the programs' objectives for this component, but many African American students on predominantly White college campuses experience difficulties that are only indirectly related to academic performance. Factors such as perceived institutional racism, identity issues, relationship concerns, financial pressures, and family stressors also impact upon students. Advisers might be more helpful to students if they investigated the significance of socioemotional concerns upon students' academic performance. In instances that performance is determined to be related to one of these issues, encouragement to visit the counseling service component could be beneficial. This encouragement should include what the student can expect from his or her first visit and answers to any questions the student might have. Training in the referral process and in the assessment of socioemotional issues should increase their effectiveness.

Finally, it seems clear that the program and each component should be evaluated on an ongoing basis. Continuous assessment and monitoring at micro- and macrolevels is important to accomplishing the program's objectives. Small-scale evaluations that involve experimental and quasi-experimental designs could be used to obtain information about the program's daily operations, short-term effects, and overall impact upon students.

RECOMMENDATIONS

Based upon the results of the evaluation, the following recommendations were disseminated to the program director: (a) assess entering students before program participation, (b) periodically interview participants to obtain their feedback, (c) modify or remove the counseling services component, (d) increase the generalizability of study skills course material, (e) train advisers to attend to student concerns indirectly related to academic issues, and (f) conduct other evaluations in order to assess each program component thoroughly.

CONCLUSION

As the competition for funding university services increases, evaluation of minority student programs that often are perceived as duplications of existing services will increasingly dominate funding considerations. It is necessary to establish the value of programs designed to provide ethnic minority students with a quality education equal to that provided to majority students. The growing number of ethnic minorities and the economic plight many experience are the primary reasons to employ experimental evaluation. Minority groups now account for a large percentage of the United States population, and it is estimated that soon after the year 2000 minority-group members will become the majority of citizens in some parts of the country and a majority of the total population soon after (Fields, 1987). Yet a great number of minorities enroll in 4-year colleges and universities and never receive a college degree. Clowes, Hinkle, and Smart (1986) evaluated enrollment patterns in postsecondary education between 1961 and 1982 to address whether postsecondary education was peforming an egalitarian function. Based upon their findings they concluded "This is evidence of a solid egalitarian function provided by postsecondary education" (p. 128). However, institutions must become more successful in retaining and graduating ethnic minority students as they strive to create an egalitarian educational system. There is convincing evidence that through education the cycle of poverty can be broken. Evaluation of the worth of services assisting in this struggle is essential to the development and implementation of programs that effectively retain and graduate students.

The simple declaration that these programs work is no longer acceptable. In general, the evaluation of programs developed for minorities is likely to be beneficial to administrators and participants. The implications of an educational system that fails to educate its members are reflected in social problems such as unemployment, illiteracy, and criminal activities. It has been asserted that the costs in social service assistance and incarcerations may be much higher than the cost of promoting equity in educational institutions. If minority students are to be effective in their quest for higher education, administrators and students must be involved with programs of documented efficacy and excellence. Program evaluation can maximize the probability of ethnic minority students' survival and success on predominantly White university campuses and thereby assist those institutions in fulfilling their stated commitments to equity, equality, and justice for all students.

REFERENCES

Astin, A.W. (1977). *Preventing students from dropping out*. San Francisco: Jossey-Bass.

Burbach, H.J. (1972). The development of a contextual measure of alienation. *Pacific Sociological Review, 15*, 225-234.

Campbell, D.T. (1969). Reforms as experiments. *American Psychologist, 24*, 409-429.

Campbell, D.T., & Stanley, J.C. (1963). *Experimental and quasi-experimental designs for research*. Boston: Houghton Mifflin.

Cheatham, H. E. (1989). Reversing the decline of African American enrollment in U.S. higher education. *Southeastern Association of Educational Opportunity Program Personnel Journal, 8*, 14-22.

Cheatham, H.E., Shelton, T.O., & Ray, W.J. (1987). Race, sex, causal attribution, and help-seeking behavior. *Journal of College Student Personnel, 27,* 559-568.

Clowes, D.A., Hinkle, D.E., & Smart, J.C. (1986). Enrollment patterns in postsecondary education: 1961-1982. *Journal of Higher Education, 57,* 121-133.

Fields, C.M. (1987, September 23). Southwestern states urged to step up their minority education efforts. *Chronicle of Higher Education,* p. 32.

Fleming, J. (1981). Stress and satisfaction in college years of Black students. *Journal of Negro Education, 50,* 307-318.

Garcia, S.A., & Presley, K. (1981). An assessment and evaluation program for Black university students in academic jeopardy: A descriptive analysis. *Journal of Community Psychology, 9,* 67-77.

Garni, K.F. (1980). Counseling centers and student retention: Why the failures? Where the successes? *Journal of College Student Personnel, 21,* 223-228.

Giddan, N.S., Levy, D.M., Estroff, R.M., Cline, J.C., Altman, E.B., Isham, K.A., & Weiss, S.J. (1987). College counseling and student retention: Data and speculations. *Journal of College Student Psychotherapy, 1,* 5-28.

Harris, S.M. (1989). *An evaluation of a university minority student retention program.* Unpublished doctoral dissertation. Virginia Polytechnic Institute & State University, Blacksburg, VA.

Herr, E.L. (1985). *Why Counseling?* Alexandria, VA: American Association for Counseling and Development.

Lee, C.C. (1982). Black support group: Outreach to the alienated Black college student. *Journal of College Student Personnel, 23,* 271-273.

Levin, H.M. (1983). *Cost-effectiveness: A primer, new perspectives in evaluation.* Beverly Hills, CA: Sage.

Loo, C.M., & Rolison, G. (1986). Alienation of ethnic minority students at a predominantly White university. *Journal of Higher Education, 57,* 58-77.

Miller, C.L. (1981). Higher education for Black Americans: Problems and issues. *Journal of Negro Education, 50,* 208-223.

Nettles, M.T., Thoeny, R.A., & Gosman, E.J. (1986). Comparative and predictive analysis of Black and White students' college achievement and experiences. *Journal of Higher Education, 57,* 289-318.

Noel, L., Levitz, R., & Salurie, D. (1985). *Increasing student retention.* San Francisco: Jossey-Bass.

Pantages, T., & Creedon, C. (1978). Studies of college attrition: 1950-1975. *Review of Educational Research, 48,* 49-101.

Suchman, E.A. (1976). *Evaluative research: Principles and practice in public service and social action programs.* New York: Russell Sage Foundation.

Suen, H.K. (1983). Alienation and attrition of Black college students on a predominantly White campus. *Journal of College Student Personnel, 24,* 117-121.

EPILOGUE

Harold E. Cheatham

A companion theme for *Cultural Pluralism on Campus* is the role of U.S. colleges and universities in educating ethnic minority students. The contemporaneous mission or goal statements of many institutions include commitments to cultural diversity and cultural pluralism. The contention in this volume is that despite enunciated commitments to provide diversity it already exists: Various cultural and ethnic minorities populate most of the the nation's campuses. What is needed, rather, are institutional commitments to ensure cultural pluralism, that is, a state of society in which members of diverse ethnic, racial, religious, or social groups maintain an autonomous participation and development of their traditional culture or special interest within the confines of a common civilization. That means mutual participation in the life of the nation with no single model defining all of life.

Despite enlightened movement in some areas, strong currents prevail for homogenizing diverse cultural experiences as opposed to ensuring cultural pluralism. Too many educators and educational institutions still are engaged in the misguided goal of socializing rather than educating ethnic minorities. A recent example is a newspaper account boasting of a certain school district's success with children whose second language is English: "They come from around the globe...drawn to [a university community] where their parents are graduate students... with a cornucopia of languages, 24 in all," the announcement stated. However, "The good news for the board of education was that the diverse babble won't last too long. It takes about 6 months to turn a foreign-speaking kindergartener [sic] into an English-speaking child, officials say" (Jordan, 1990). In a pluralistic society, that boast—the antithesis to *Cultural Pluralism on Campus*—ought to be of the school district's success in teaching children love and preservation of their mother tongues. Teaching that stigmatizes and separates people from their cultures and languages continues a misguided philosophy of education. To erase such perspectives U.S. higher education must move to fulfill its role to provide multicultural education, to train teachers and administrators who value diverse cultures.

Throughout its history, U.S. higher education has been called upon to reform and restructure in the service of certain societal goals. Probably no clearer or more eloquent entreaty and comprehensive prescription exists than that from the Truman Commission (President's Commission on Higher Education, 1947). That document's call for education that ensures equal liberty and equal opportunity and that liberates and perfects the intrinsic powers of every citizen is an old idea that has taken on new political and practical dimensions. The future of this society depends as never before on higher education addressing and reversing the cumulative effects of the unequal schooling opportunity historically experienced by certain groups' members. Many social and economic barriers to educational opportunity have receded, largely in response to the 1960s civil rights movement and to the legislation that culminated that era. Yet cursory observation reveals continuing underrepresentation of ethnic minorities attending and graduating from the nation's colleges and universities.

Ethnic minorities and particularly African Americans have too often and for too long been perceived and treated by some collegiate personnel as an academically deficient monolith and as doomed casualties of the academic experience. Considerable effort exists on U.S campuses to provide for academic development of these students. A considerable literature also provides an attest that where resources and conspicuous programmatic efforts and hospitable environs exist ethnic minority students register impressive personal and intellectual gains. Much has been accomplished—and much more must be done to ensure the academic and personal growth of ethnic minority students, who will predominate in collegiate enrollments in the next century.

This volume addresses specific aspects of the cocurriculum—the part of the educational experience for which counselors, student development specialists, and other student personnel professionals are uniquely prepared. The authors collectively advance the proposition that the effective educational institution discovers and incorporates the truths and values of its consumers into the curriculum and cocurriculum. Thoughtful generosity is needed to dismantle calcified views and institutional conventions that ignore and repress citizens and the dynamics of U.S. history. The authors call upon collegiate personnel to challenge Western cultural authority courageously, to lead the way in developing collegiate environs that reflect the society's diverse cultures, and to contribute to developing a collegiate community that sustains and authenticates all people. To enunciate cultural pluralism as an institutional goal is a first step. A next crucial step is establishing programs and strategies that instate pluralism. Part of each institution's task is to confirm minority students' place on campus by removing remaining barriers between ethnic minority and all other students. Developing programs that reflect diverse groups' cultural history provides eloquent testimony to their worth and dignity while delivering on the institution's commitment to concepts of educational equity. Ideally the chapters in this volume will greatly assist practitioners charged to assist in fulfilling institutional commitments to cultural pluralism.

Cultural Pluralism on Campus is about a fresh, compelling vision of U.S. higher education. It is about a vision of movement within this critical segment of society into active, committed leadership for resolving what otherwise looms as a social crisis. It is about a vision of leadership that acknowledges the differences between what is and what must be. And it is about a vision of commitment to mobilize societal resources to deliver finally on the distinct and distant ideal of equality in U.S. society. This volume is offered as one step in the direction of reform that benefits the whole society.

REFERENCES

Jordan, B. (1990, November 13). From Telugu to English in 6 months. *Willamantic Chronicle*, p. 3.

President's Commission on Higher Education for American Democracy. (1947). *A report of the President's Commission on Higher Education: Vol. 1. Establishing the goals*. Washington, DC.

Notes

Notes

Notes

Notes